FRENCH MANAGEMENT: ELITISM IN ACTION

French Management:
Elitism in Action

Jean-Louis Barsoux and
Peter Lawrence

CASSELL

Cassell
Wellington House
125 Strand
London WC2R 0BB

PO Box 605
Herndon
VA 20172

First published 1997

British Library Cataloguing-in-Publication Data
A catalogue record for this book is available from the British Library.

ISBN 0-304-70237-4 (hardback)
    0-304-70238-2 (paperback)

Typeset by Kenneth Burnley at Irby, Wirral, Cheshire.
Printed and bound in Great Britain by Redwood Books, Trowbridge, Wiltshire.

Contents

Acknowledgements

BOTH AUTHORS would like to thank their many French subjects – managers, business journalists, academics, and consultants – whose co-operation made this book possible. All the French managers who allowed themselves to be interviewed, and in some cases to be observed at work, are owed a particular debt of gratitude.

In addition Jean-Louis Barsoux would like to thank colleagues at INSEAD and CEDEP, in particular Jean-François Manzoni and Mark Lehrer, for their support and encouragement. And Peter Lawrence would like to thank his friends Roland Calori at ESC Lyon, and Joseph Szarka at the University of Bath, for ideas and suggestions.

Peter Lawrence would also like to thank Freda Clarke, his secretary at Loughborough University Business School, for help in preparing the manuscript.

JEAN-LOUIS BARSOUX AND PETER LAWRENCE

To Astrid and to Pat

Preface

THIS BOOK attempts a broad brush stroke characterization of French management. It tries to give some idea of what French management is like, of how it compares with management in Britain and in the USA, and of its strengths and weaknesses.

At the same time there are many points at which the discussion goes beyond the broad-brush portrait, many issues which are explored rather in fine detail. This would be so of our consideration of the educational background of French managers and of the dynamics of selection and advancement, of the nature of elite composition and interaction, of interpersonal relations and ritual in the management setting, and of the operation of authority.

We have also endeavoured to explore some of the relevant linkages, macro and micro. In a broad sense we have considered the relationship between French management on the one hand and French society and its values on the other. We have also sought to trace the linkages between education, elitism, authority, and career.

This offering is not entirely original. The present authors did research on French management in the late 1980s and wrote a book on the basis of this work entitled *Management in France*. This was published in 1990 with a paperback edition a year or so later.

The present book is, however, significantly different from its predecessor, and this difference goes beyond the conventional up-dating measures of changing tenses, getting rid of incriminating references, and removing dated material. In the seven years since the appearance of *Management in France* the authors themselves have had what might be called 'developing experiences', having variously worked on a major two-country comparison, taken part in several multi-country studies of business strategy among European companies including French companies, worked on other single-country studies of management in and outside Europe, and lived in France for several years with the enhanced sensitization to nuance and change which that implies. We like to think that these experiences have had a positive effect.

Reading through the completed manuscript before taking it to the publisher we are conscious of two broad changes. The earlier work was more exclusively sociological in its approach, whereas the present book is more concerned to situate French management in a business context. And the second difference is that we have been more critical in the present book, though it is not easy to say how this has come about! Most probably in our earlier endeavour we were more impressed with the fit between society, values, and management style and practice, which is admittedly very striking in the French case, whereas in the present book we have been more concerned with viewing France against an implicit back-drop of management universals.

Looking back over our now ten-year familiarity with business and management in France, our strongest impression is something of a paradox. This is that French management has seemed to us to have been remarkably stable – same background, same recruitment, same perceptions and values – while on the other hand the business context has been subject to dynamic change. The key question for the future is whether business change will affect the French management establishment and the French understanding of elitism.

JEAN-LOUIS BARSOUX AND PETER LAWRENCE

Abbreviations and acronyms

The following list gives some of the most common abbreviations and acronyms relating to French management.

APEC	Association Pour l'Emploi des Cadres
Bac	Baccalauréat (equivalent of 'A' levels/high school certificate)
BTS	Brevet de Technicien Supérieur
CCI	Chambre de Commerce et d'Industrie
CCIP	Chambre de Commerce et d'Industrie de Paris
CEDEP	Centre Européen d'Education Permanente
CEGOS	Commission Générale d'Organisation Scientifique
Centrale	L'Ecole Centrale (private engineering grande école)
CEREQ	Centre d'Etude et de Recherche sur les Qualifications
CFDT	Confédération Française Démocratique du Travail
CGC	Confédération Générale des Cadres
CGT	Confederation Générale du Travail
CNOF	Comité Nationale de l'Organisation Française
CNPF	Conseil National du Patronat Français
CPA	Centre de Perfectionnement aux Affaires
CRC	Centre de Recherches et d'Etudes des Chefs d'Entreprises
Dauphine	Management University, Paris-IX
DEA	Diplôme d'Etudes Approfondies
DESS	Diplôme d'Etudes Supérieures Spécialisées
DEUG	Diplôme d'Etudes Universitaires Générales
DUT	Diplôme Universitaire de Technologie (awarded by IUT)
ENA	Ecole Nationale d'Aministration
ENE	Ecole Nationale d'Exportation
ESCAE	Ecole(s) Supérieure(s) de Commerce et d'Administration des Entreprises also called Sups de Co)
ESCP	Ecole Supérieure de Commerce de Paris
ESSEC	Ecole Supérieure des Sciences Economiques et Commerciales
ESTP	Ecole Spéciale des Travaux Publiques
lNEGE	Fondation Nationale pour l'Enseignement de la Gestion des Entreprises

FO	Force Ouvrière
Gadzarts	Alumni of l'Ecole des Arts et Métiers
GARF	Groupement des Agents Responsables de la Formation
HEC	Ecole des Hautes Etudes Commerciales
INSEAD	Institut Européen d'Administration des Affaires
SEE	Institut National des Statistiques et des Etudes Economiques
ISA	Institut Supérieur des Affaires
ISSEC	Institut Supérieur de Sciences Economiques et Commerciales
IUT	Institut(s) Universitaire(s) de Technologie
LEST	Laboratoire d'Economie et de Sociologie du Travail
MIAGE	Maîtrise de méthodes informatique appliqueés à la gestion
MSG	Maîtrise de Sciences de Gestion
MSTCF	Maîtrise de Sciences et Techniques Comptables et Financières
PCF	Parti Communiste Français
PDG	Président Directeur Générale (equivalent CEO or MD)
PME	Petites et Moyennes Entreprises (equivalent of SME)
Prepa	Post-baccalauréat preparatory school and feeder to *grandes écoles*
Sciences-Po	Institut d'Etudes Politiques (Paris)
X	L'Ecole Polytechnique

1 Déja vu et jamais vu

FRANCE IS BOTH DIFFERENT AND DIFFICULT for outsiders to apprehend. But the quality of the difference should inspire the effort. France with its style and élan, its economic achievements and inflexibilities, its paradox of equality and elitism, and of individualism and insecurity, is the best 'society-mystery' on offer in Europe.

France of course has a strong image in the wider world. It is not one of those wishy-washy countries about which people can think of nothing meaningful to say. It is the most visited country in the world. France is not bland, it is not colourless; it evokes reactions, foreigners have views about it (often strong views) and people often have strong visual images of France as well.

Yet this image enjoyed by France in the wider world also lacks balance. It has more to do with history than geography, more to do with politics than economics, and has more to do with traditional luxury goods than with the technologies of the later twentieth century.

The image also tends to be a little dated. There is a touch of the First World War about it, of ugly subsidized apartment housing, and dubious public urinals. The gaunt impersonality of the state predominates while in this image the cosiness and comfort of northern Europe seems to be lacking.

Yet this mild tendency of foreigners to fix France in the past involves another misapprehension, an inclination to under-estimate. The plight of France for the first half or more of the twentieth century is less than fully recognized abroad, as indeed are the recovery, growth, and achievements of France in the second half of the century.

First the plight. Industrialization in France during the nineteenth century was less far reaching than in say Britain, Germany, or the USA, and France entered the twentieth century with a more traditional occupational structure and less manufacturing capacity than these countries. France had already been defeated once by Germany (Prussia) in the Franco-Prussian War of 1870–71, and the only achievement this experience afforded France was that of paying off its reparations to Prussia in three years rather than the scheduled five, and thereby securing the withdrawal of the Prussian army of occupation in double-quick time.

Again while France was on 'the winning side' in the First World War (1914–18), rather like its neighbour and ally Italy, it emerged from the war looking more like a defeated nation than a victor. French loss of life had been considerable, the north of France had been endlessly fought over and mostly occupied by the Germans for four years, and the French came to the Versailles Peace Conference of 1918–19 in a mood that combined resignation and desperation as they struggled to establish safeguards and guarantees against future German aggression.

They failed. In the spring of 1940 the Germans did in six weeks what they had failed to do in four years in the First World War – they conquered the whole of France. Another four years of German occupation followed compounded by the indignity of submitting to the rule of the Vichy government – a right-wing, socially retrograde, collaborationist regime supported by the Germans at war while it suited them.

The euphoria of the Liberation in the summer of 1944 was intense, reaching its high point in the liberation of Paris on 20 August 1944. With the benefit of hindsight we can see that the German threat to France had been ended for all time, but that was not immediately obvious at the end of the War.

What was obvious was the depletion of France's national resources, looted by the Germans or destroyed in the fighting, the dislocation that went with the overthrow of the Vichy regime, and the need for help that eventuated in France being a massive beneficiary under the European Recovery Programme, more popularly known as Marshall Aid, and instituted in June 1948.

But even in the early years of peace, new problems arose. General de Gaulle's provisional government, set up at the time of the Liberation, gave way to the Fourth French Republic (1946–58) that both presided over the early stages of economic recovery and introduced some progressive social legislation. Yet this regime was unstable, a bewildering succession of prime-ministers, elections, crises, and ministerial reshuffles. And the Fourth French Republic was dogged by colonial problems.

The French Colony of Indo-China had been occupied by the Japanese during the Second World War. After the war the French tried to re-assert their control over it, and failed. The rising tide of local nationalism and independence movements proved too strong for the French in Indo-China as they were for the British in India and the Dutch in Indonesia. Indeed the French were routed in a conventional battle, Dien Bien Phu in 1954, rather than undermined by guerrilla warfare, the stock-in-trade of anti-colonial insurgents. This débàcle was not the end. The same year saw the start of the Algerian uprising which proved more protracted, nearer to home, and more damaging politically and morally.

Again with the benefit of hindsight 1958 rather than 1944 is probably the turning point for France, the date after which good news predominated bad news, the end of its twentieth-century woes.

In 1958 the Fifth Republic was inaugurated, with de Gaulle as President. The political instabilities of the former Fourth Republic seemed to be banished for all time. Indo-China was repackaged as Vietnam, and the problem passed to the Americans. The Algerian problem was solved within five years, admittedly by simply 'giving it away' (granting independence) but this was the only viable solution and could be implemented by a leader of de Gaulle's stature whose patriotic devotion was beyond doubt.

De Gaulle also worked for the *rapprochement* with Germany building a strong relationship with West Germany's first (post-war) chancellor, Konrad Adenauer. Later generations have come to take peace in at least Western Europe for granted, but there was nothing taken for granted about it in the time of de Gaulle and Adenauer.

Meanwhile economic recovery and indeed growth had begun, and there are a number of factors involved. First of all the post-war government inaugurated a succession of five-year plans, that designated particular industries, such as cement and transportation, as national priorities because of their importance for reconstruction. Later on, these five-year plans became more a matter of political window-dressing than of economic substance, but in the early days of the Fourth Republic they were real and had the merit of designating priorities and of focusing national endeavour. These five-year plans also had the secondary advantage of bringing together politicians and civil servants on the one hand and industrialists on the other, and of achieving a loose consensus of views and objectives. This state-industrialist-manager consensus is a *leitmotiv* of the present book, but it is important to add that it had a certain novelty in the early years after the Second World War, a time in which many industrialists had discredited themselves and their class by collaborating with Nazi Germany via the Vichy regime.

Second, in the early post-war years France benefited from Marshall Aid, and received more under this scheme, the European Recovery Programme, than any other European country except Britain. It is a relatively minor theme, but in the same period France also benefited from the administration of their occupation zone in Germany after the war. Here they repossessed the fruits of earlier German looting, taking back for example railway rolling stock. They looted on their own account. And they fixed the terms of trade between France and the French Occupation Zone of Germany, forcing the Germans to export from the Zone to France at fixed (low) prices, and to import from France at fixed (high) prices.

Third, France benefited from the post-war growth in world trade and from the unprecedented economic growth in the industrialized world during the period after the Second World War. This growth occurred throughout the Western World, and is independent of the policies of particular regimes and their five-year plans. In France this period is dubbed *les trentes glorieuses*, the 30 glorious years of economic growth and the enhancement of real incomes, a period that seemed to come to an end with the first oil shock of 1973–74 and its attendant inflation.

Fourth, but rather more difficult to pin down, there is probably in the post-war period a collective resolution in France to advance and succeed economically. This resolution was a long time 'in the making', and owes much to the adversarial relationship between France and Germany over the previous hundred or so years, where it was assumed that part of the German (military) success stemmed from industrial superiority. This new resolution in France was also a reaction to the country's recent economic history. As noted earlier French industrialization in the nineteenth century was far from complete; the First World War strained and drained the nation, and the inter-war period (1918–39) was marked by economic stagnation. The resolution to succeed economically is in the spirit of 'Goodbye to all that'.

The magic year of 1958 had a further significance. Not only did it inaugurate a generation of Gaullism, end the instabilities of the Fourth French Republic, presage the solution of the Algerian problem, and consolidate the Franco-German *rapprochement;* 1958 also saw the inception of the European Economic Community (EEC), or Common Market in popular parlance, with France as a founder member alongside Germany. In the contemporary debate it is clear that founding the EEC was seen as a critical event in France, as a *rendez-vous avec l'histoire*. At the time setting up the EEC was a decisive event, a real challenge that would expose France to the rigours of European competition, i.e. to German competition; and on the whole, this was a challenge to which French industry rose.

Another feature of the post-war period was the emergence in France of various high-tech industry and product success stories, in a country famous primarily for various luxury goods – the *grands vins*, champagne, cognac, *haute couture*, and so on. It is probably fair to say that these have now become familiar stories – the TGV high-speed train, success in civil and military aviation, in helicopters, in high-tech armaments, in telecommunications, in rocket launching, nuclear power, and so on – but they do represent a new development in the second half of the century and when aggregated they impact substantially and favourably on the image and reputation of France.

As the twentieth century draws to a close, France is a member of the G7

Group of major industrial countries, has a GNP per capita substantially higher than that of Britain, and is the world's fourth largest exporter after the USA, Japan, and Germany. Moreover, the country is secure, has no major foreign enemy, no fear of Germany, and is free to opt in and out of NATO at will! All this would have seemed very unlikely when the century began.

Power, orders, and ambiguity

So far we have suggested that France is peculiarly susceptible to misapprehension; that it is easy, for instance, to underestimate both the woes of France in the first half of the twentieth century and its triumphs thereafter, and thereby to have too little sense of the change that France has undergone.

The problems are not entirely in the eye of the (foreign) beholder. The inclination to misapprehension is in part attributable to certain paradoxes in French society, to certain inconsistencies of volition among French people. Consider in this connection – and it is very relevant to an understanding of behaviour in business organizations – the French response to authority.

A German writer, basing his views on the findings of Germany's famous public opinion survey firm, the Allensbach Institut, has produced the following comparisons (Ackermann, 1988):

Proportion of employees in each country who accept the proposition: 'Basically, I will carry out instructions from my superior':

Country	%
Denmark	57
England	49
Ireland	45
Holland	39
Belgium	33
Spain	29
Germany	28
France	25
Italy	24

Here, one may feel, is the stroppy individualist Frenchman we all know: folk wisdom verified by social science! The next line in Ackermann's table seems to support this view:

Proportion of employees in each country who accept the proposition: 'I only follow the instructions of superiors when my reason is convinced':

Country	%
France	57
Germany	51
Spain	41
Italy	39
England	34
Holland	33
Ireland	26
Denmark	21

A nice consistent picture: France is nearly bottom of the first list and on top of the second, probing the same phenomenon from opposite directions.

Now let us juxtapose another finding from a different source. The Dutch psychologist Geert Hofstede surveyed and tested employees of the same American multinational company in some 50 countries. His broad finding is that there are substantial differences in work-related attitudes and values from country to country, revealed by his extensive and unique sample (Hofstede, 1980). But he further systematizes his findings by ranking the respondent countries on four dimensions, two of which are germane to the French authority paradox.

The first of these is the dimension of power distance, or the willingness of people in different cultures to accept differences in the power possessed by individuals; and remember that in industrial societies power distance refers primarily to differences of power enjoyed by people at different levels in formal organizations. Here are the French, in comparison with a few other countries (Hofstede, 1980, 315):

Country	Power distance
France	68
Italy	50
USA	40
Germany	35
Great Britain	35
Mean for 40 countries	52

Note that the higher the number, the *greater* the tolerance for *inequalities of power*. Is it not intriguing that the French, who are less willing to take orders, are more willing to accept that some people have much more power than others?

There is another bit of this jigsaw in the form of Hofstede's second principal dimension. This is uncertainty avoidance, or the desire to eliminate ambiguity and doubt, to know where you stand, to leave little to chance. This uncertainty avoidance is not constant throughout the world, but again varies from country to country, and France is distinctive (Hofstede, 1980, 315):

Country	Uncertainty avoidance
France	86
Italy	75
Germany	65
USA	46
Great Britain	35
Mean for 40 countries	64

As with the previous table on power distance, the higher the figure in the uncertainty avoidance column the stronger the desire to avoid uncertainty. This finding is again intriguing, since a standard remedy for reducing uncertainty is to accept orders – but the French are reluctant to do this. So we have an apparent contradiction between French attitudes to orders (negative) and to power differences (positive), and between desire to avoid uncertainty (positive) and uncritical acceptance of orders as the means to this end (negative).

We have demonstrated these contradictions not in order to give a full and lucid explanation at this stage – though they are explained in the body of the book – but to signal the subtlety and complexity of the issue. Where the French are concerned, stereotypes will get us to the starting line but not to the finishing post.

The idea can be expressed differently. Some societies are seamless garments, so that management and behaviour in work organizations are not compartmentalized. In the USA for example, management style is like everyday life; it has the same features, expresses the same convictions. But not in France, where behaviours are more compartmentalized. One can deduce little about management style or organizational behaviour in France from everyday life. One can go to France a hundred times as a tourist and know relatively less than one would about Canada or the Netherlands, Germany or Israel. And one has to recognize that compartmentalization is in the eye of the perpetrator.

Paradoxes

This France, with its Minitel and its Exocet missiles, its nuclear power and its TGV, is not a 'modern society' in every way. In its attachment to values and tradition it has more in common with Britain than with America. There is a remarkable continuity in the expression of their values. The state building and centralization of the seventeenth century is re-enacted in the later twentieth century – de Gaulle's conception of the glory of France is not too removed from that of Louis XIV. And there are interesting transmogrifications: from Colbert's fortifications in the reign of Louis XIV, to the Maginot Line of First World War fame, from leadership in style to leadership in space, from the cult of nobility to the noble product.

There is also a tension in France between nationalism and internationalism. The best of the French past seems to transcend national frontiers. Cartesianism is a logical system on offer to the world, not just to France. The Rights of Man, formulated in the early stages of the French Revolution, are a charter for humanity, not special pleading for the French. The metric system has conquered most of the world, as has the Napoleonic Code, in the form of codified law rather than case law.

At the same time, post-war France has given national self-interest a clear focus not witnessed since the days of Palmerston in Victorian Britain. France's aid to the Third World is mostly tied aid – the beneficiaries buy French goods with it. Within the EU the common agricultural policy has bolstered French farmers. Oil crises come and go, yet France always knows how to *soigner les relations* with the Middle Eastern states that matter.

French industry too is torn between a backwards and a forwards orientation. In the previous pages we have emphasized the forwards: the successes, noble products, triumphs of state initiative crossed with technological virtuosity. But there is also an old-fashioned side. A grudging, incremental acceptance of industrial democracy (surpassed only by Britain), the low profile of firms such as Michelin, corporate paternalism, workplace discipline and the traditional rewarding of seniority.

One might indeed encapsulate some of these tensions by postulating a 'diabolic hexagon'. *L'Hexagone* is a popular term for France, whose geographical shape is roughly hexagonal. Were we to ascribe values to the six sides constituting the hexagon, then the upper lines must bear witness to the classic values of the French Revolution that still adorn every town hall. Yet these need to be counterbalanced by other predilections that illuminate French behaviour in organizations. So our hexagon might look something like Figure 1.1.

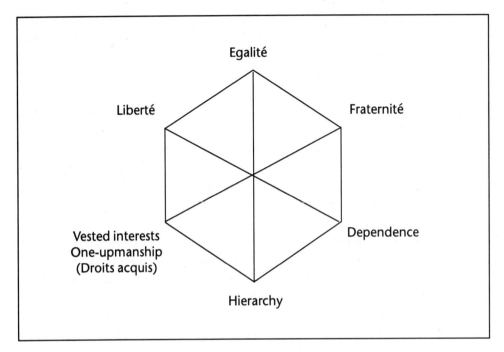

Figure 1.1: Schematic diagram of the 'hexagon' that constitutes France

Much of that which follows in subsequent chapters will constitute an unpacking of these tensions. Meanwhile there is a need to 'unpack' the paradoxes of French capitalism.

The French economy

The French economy has some unusual features. Central to its distinctness is the considerable role of the state in the post-war reconstruction period. As one authority (Gordon, 1996:1) puts it: 'More than any other OECD country, the state has played a crucial and all-pervasive role in France in determining the major directions in which business activities have moved.'

There are a number of dimensions to this state involvement in the business life of France. The first of these is the series of five-year plans already referred to. Second, and at a later stage (1960s to early 1980s) the French authorities devised industrial policies that would develop national champions in a variety of industries, big companies that could hold their own with their corporate opposite numbers in other countries. Examples would include Rhône-Poulenc, Péchiney, Saint-Gobain, and SNIAS (Aérospatiale). This was achieved by state-managed mergers and take-overs, and in the facilitation of long-term credits from state-controlled financial institutions. Third, this was facilitated by a remarkable degree of political continuity. From the inception of the Fifth Republic in 1958 when de Gaulle assumed the presidency until the election of a socialist president in the person of François Mitterand in 1981, France was ruled by one party, the Gaullists.

But to take for the moment the even longer-term view of state involvement in the business life of the country, France has been unusual in that the state has owned more of the economy than has been the case in most western countries. This really is a long-standing tradition, where some industries, for example, tobacco, have always been state monopolies. Colin Gordon (1992) whom we quoted earlier, describes France as *interventionniste, dirigiste*, and *colbertiste* (where Colbert was a minister of Louis XIV in the seventeenth century much given to state-initiated public works).

If one asks what proportion of the economy is in the state funds then the answer varies depending on *when* the question is posed. Against this background of an interventionist state the immediate post-war period saw a number of companies being nationalized, of which the most famous was Renault, typically to punish industrialists for collaboration during the Vichy regime/Nazi occupation. State–industry links were then intensified as a result of the plans and policies noted in the previous paragraph.

When Mitterand and the socialists came to power in 1981 they embarked upon what Joseph Szarka has called 'massive and flamboyant nationalization' (Szarka, 1996). As a result of this systematic increase in the number of state-owned enterprises Colin Gordon (1996) estimated that by 1984 at its height, the public sector represented 16 per cent of the working population, 28 per cent of turnover, 36 per cent of investments, and 91 per cent of bank deposits. This orgy of nationalization, however, gave way to an episode of privatization and deregulation in 1986–88, and more privatization was to follow in the 1990s, of which more later.

Capital and ownership in France

Once upon a time there was a tendency to assume that capitalism was a monolithic system, much the same everywhere, and strongly counterposed of course to communism. With the demise of European communism in the 1989–91 period there arose a heightened awareness of possible permutations and variations among capitalist systems, with key discussions by, for example, Michel Albert (1991) and later Lester Thurow (1992).

In attempting to sketch the distinctive French form of capitalism it may be helpful, as Joseph Szarka suggests, to start by saying what it is not. First of all, shareholding by British-style financial institutions such as unit trusts and pension funds are quite unimportant in France; shareholdings of this kind stood at only 7 per cent of all quoted shares, this proportion having been stable from the 1970s to the 1990s (Szarka, 1996). Second, the proportion of shares held by householders has actually fallen, from 41 per cent in 1977 to only 34 per cent in 1992 (in spite of an initial rise in share purchase by the general public during the privatizations of the 1986–87 period). Third, most (80 per cent) French shares are not even publicly quoted (Babeau, 1994).

So what we have instead is what Joseph Szarka calls 'a distinctively French model of large-scale capitalism' with financial empires structured around banks and leading companies. The institutional components of those empires are not fixed, and there was some realignment in the mid-1990s as a result of the losses of Crédit Lyonnais, but according to one authority (Morin, 1994) there are now (late 1990s) two of these empires, viz: Paribas, AGF, Société-Générale, Alcatel-Alsthom; and Suez, BNP, UAP

In addition there are a lot of small firms that are in family ownership, something that is well known and has always been a distinctive feature of the French manufacturing scene. Rather less well known is the fact that many large and well-known companies are also privately owned. Indeed one study (Morin, 1988) found that 71 out of the largest 200 firms had as majority shareholders a single individual or family.

All this is a far cry from what Thurow (1992) has dubbed 'Anglo-Saxon capitalism'!

Personal ties between state and industry

A theme developed in this book is that France is a society characterized by a unitary elite. What unifies this elite is a common educational experience at the *grandes écoles*, the top tier of the higher education system, of which more in subsequent chapters. Sufficient to say for the present, that civil servants and corporate executives are both overwhelmingly drawn from these *grandes écoles* and have been shaped by the predominant values of these institutions as well as by the competition to gain admission to them.

Against this background of a common origin and congruence as between business and administrative/civil service elites there are some more particular ties, relevant to one of the themes being developed in this introductory chapter. In the case of the remaining nationalized industries, it is the state, of course, that appoints the chief executive officer (CEO). And this will normally be someone whose experience, or most of it, has been in state service rather than in private sector industry. What is more, when a company is privatized, again it is the state who will appoint the CEO, and on the same criteria. Indeed when privatization occurs the incoming, state-chosen CEO may well be able to choose who will be the company's principal shareholders, given the role of government influence and the narrow distribution of company shares outlined in the previous section. These pathways are recognized by aspirants to senior executive posts such that the best graduates from the very top *grandes écoles* systematically opt for initial employment in what are called the *grands corps,* the most prestigious departments of the French civil service, rather than for management posts in companies. The bridgeways from state to industry are well trodden.

Management style versus business change

There is a further paradox in French business life. This is that French management is for the most part stable – in character, origins, and in its blend of considerable strengths and patterned weaknesses – while business, the corporate scene, and even patterns of employment are experiencing a variety of changes. A characterization of French management style and behaviour is the main concern of this book, but it may be helpful to indicate some of these changes of business context.

Privatization

The first of these developments is of course privatization itself. The most critical period is that of 1986–87 when Jacques Chirac came to power as right-wing head of a right-wing government, albeit 'serving' under socialist President Mitterand. Of this period Colin Gordon writes:

> Privatization of not only the newly nationalized companies but also of those which had been in the state sector since immediately before or after the war, became a burning issue, with the CGE (later to change its name to Alcatel-Alstholm) and Saint-Gobain (glass) in the industrial sector, Société Générale and Paribas in banking, Agence Havas (advertising) and the television channel TFI reverting to private hands before the October crash in 1987. (Gordon, 1996:5)

This privatization initiative continued, intermittently into the 1990s. Joseph Szarka comments: 'By 1995, Balladur and Chirac, the architects of privatization, had almost completely dismantled the Socialist "mixed economy"' (Szarka, 1996, 9).

As we have now seen, this privatization is not as meaningful as 1980s-style privatization of nationalized industries under Margaret Thatcher's administration in Britain, given the continuity of chief executives, or at least of their prominence, together with the relative absence of a market-sensitive distribution of shareholdings. Nonetheless this privatization does have some importance, it is not merely the expression of an ideological mood. Its importance is that it is consistent with certain other developments, for which liberalization might serve as an umbrella term.

Liberalization

This liberalization allowed what Colin Gordon has termed 'a dismantling of supply-side rigidities' (Gordon, 1996) – companies experienced tax reductions, more freedom in price-setting, and were allowed to hire labour without seeking state permission. There was a corresponding freeing up of the interface between France and the external world economy, an interface that traditionally the French state had policed in a rather protectionist and irridentist fashion, so that some very traditional French firms in, for example, the food industry, were allowed to pass into foreign ownership, and foreign direct investment was permitted in areas that were highly visible, for instance the establishment of the Daewoo car plant in Lorraine. Or again French companies were allowed to make international moves that would redound to the disadvantage of a narrow French constituency; Michelin of Clermont Ferrand, for example, was allowed to acquire Uniroyal in the USA although it led to unemployment at Michelin's home base. The 1990s also saw a high-profile cross-border strategic alliance between Renault of France and Volvo of Sweden, albeit one that was dissolved without achieving its objectives.

De-merger is also a part of this move to liberalize. The background to discussing any new de-merger initiatives is the widespread practice in France of cross-shareholding, with companies taking a stake in each other's capital and seats on each other's boards – a situation that is not conducive to critical appraisal or to change. Furthermore, the French tax authorities have treated demerger as tantamount to liquidation, and levied up to 60 per cent tax on such moves.

Against this background came the announcement in March 1996 that the French media and textiles group Chargeurs planned to split into two separate quoted companies, representing the two arms of its business. The announcement is significant in that Chargeurs is in a way 'very French'. The company consists of a highly personal collection of assets built up by the Chairman, Jerome Geydoux, who holds a 29 per cent share.

Focusing on core business has not traditionally been a French strategy, but there have been intimations thereof in the 1990s with Péchiney selling off non-aluminium operations, the troubled Crédit Lyonnais removing non-core assets from its balance sheet, and Indosuez (banking arm of the Suez group) withdrawing from property lending.

Or again the 1990s have seen examples of a new, for France, enthusiasm for take-over, driven by individual entrepreneurs. One case in point in the Spring of 1995 was Jean-Luc Lagardère's attempt to buy the military side of Thompson, Thompson CSF, and to beat off the rival bid by Alcatel. The show started when Lagardère burst into a press conference and interrupted his own finance director to announce his interest in Thompson CSF in declaratory style. This sort of thing has not been typical of French business in the past!

Internationalization

As we have seen with reference to cross-border acquisitions and inward investment, there is a certain internationalism, a development in the last two decades of the twentieth century. Taking FDI (foreign direct investment) as the touchstone, the changes have been dramatic. Joseph Szarka, commenting on economic developments during François Mitterand's fourteen-year presidency (1981–95) observes:

> Moreover inward direct investment increased almost five-fold during 1981–92 as compared to 1973–80 (from 15.7 to 70.8 billion dollars), whilst investment by French firms abroad increased nearly ten-fold (from 13 to 124 billion dollars). Although comparable increases were witnessed in the UK, Japan, and other OECD countries. (Szarka, 1996, 4)

In a way this internationalization is not new. For half a century France has been 'a good European'. Not only was France a founder member of what is now the EU (European Union) in 1958, but contemporary sources make it clear that France saw the inception of the trading block as a key development. The same awareness on the French part was re-enacted in the late 1980s in the run-up to the inauguration of the Single European Market (1992) where the French arguably took the developments more seriously than the British and the Germans. And again since 1992 France has been positive on further European integration.

Yet there is a new edge to the internationalism of the 1990s. Part of it is a willingness, in some cases an eagerness, to focus on regions outside Europe (indeed much of French outward FDI has been in the USA). And another aspect has been a new willingness to accept elements of international business that would previously have been thought inimitable to French National interests. Szarka's judgement is that: '. . . France's business classes increasingly favoured the outward-looking strategies of liberalization, Europeanization, and internationalization' (Szarka, 1996, 16).

Flexibility

There have been changes, arguably related to the privatization-liberalization-internationalization syndrome explored in the previous pages, in the direction of workforce flexibility.

The starting point is that the social costs of employment are high in France: a little higher according to Gordon (1996) than those of Germany, Holland, and Sweden, and much higher that those of Britain, the USA, and Japan. And one may add to this comparative handicap the fact that French public sector pensions are a growing burden to the state, and are not like British pensions typically funded, in a sense privately, by unit trust-style investment in the shares of quoted companies.

The next piece of the jigsaw is to note that trade union membership is low, less than 10 per cent of the workforce, and it has been at this level since the late 1980s. While trade union membership rates have been declining generally, the rate of decline has been more dramatic in France, and the rate as of the mid-1990s is the lowest among the EU countries. And in spite of export growth and a favourable trade balance in the years from 1992, France has a high rate of unemployment, amounting to 12.6 per cent of the workforce at the end of 1996.

All these considerations will typically lead to pressure on employment, on a move away from jobs that are full time, permanent and pensionable, and towards more flexible forms of employment. There have been evidences of this in other countries, and by the mid-1990s these trends are perceptible in France as well.

Out of a workforce of over 25 million at the start of the 1990s there are in the mid-decade some six million who are in less than full employment. That is to say there are nearly three million on part-time contracts, and smaller groups of temporary workers and workers on fixed-term contracts. Indeed by 1996 fixed-term contracts represented three quarters of 'new hires' in companies employing more than 50 people. There has been growth only in part-time employment, particularly marked among female employees, many of them being in the service sector.

While similar developments are common in other western countries such developments represent more of a break with the past in France. France has been the country that rewarded seniority (long service to a single employing organization) in which people enjoyed *droits acquis* (rights built up over time). In the French past, mobility between companies has been the exception rather than the rule for both workers and managers.

Ethics are good for us

A final development that seems to have begun in the 1990s is the imposition of ethical standards on companies and business leaders. This has been in the form of arrests, investigations, prosecutions of business leaders thought to have done wrong, and the decade has also seen some attempts at corporate self-reform.

A pre-eminent example of the last of these concerns the utilities company Lyonnaise des Eaux. Early in 1996 Lyonnaise des Eaux unveiled a package of measures to put standards in place and to improve its public image – producing ethics codes for various component organizations, appointing a director with primary responsibilities for ethical issues, appointing foreign (non-French) directors (some assurance to the employees of acquired companies abroad and their customers), together with top-level pronouncements about environmental responsibility and dealings with municipal authorities.

In part, of course, this is a response to past wrongdoing. The company's relations with politicians, especially in the 1994–95 period, have been called into question, and these corporate-politician links were highlighted during the company's (initially) hostile bid for the British utility, Northumbrian Water, in 1995. But the *cause célèbre* was the trial in Lyon in November 1995 of Alain Carignon, Mayor of Grenoble, who was fired and sentenced to a term in prison for taking bribes to award Grenoble's water contract to Lyonnaise des Eaux and that company's local partner.

Also symptomatic of the new mood are the committees and reports and recommendations that flowed in mid-decade. One of these reports, from a group led by André Levy-Lang, chairman of the bank Paribas, dealt with stock options. Another came from a committee set up to examine corporate governance in France, this time chaired by Marc Viénot, head of Societé Générale.

Now these developments are perhaps more remarkable in France than they would be in other western countries. France, after all, is strongly elitist (elites have more leeway as well as more money than ordinary people) and is the country of administrative right – what the authorities will, requires no further justification. As a senior civil servant in France once expressed it to one of the authors: 'When we decide to drain the swamp, we don't ask for permission from the frogs.'

Another strand in this newly ethical ethos is the judgements on individual business leaders. In some instances, perhaps ironically, they have been arraigned for their misdeeds 'in earlier life' as politicians and administrators. The most famous of them is Louis Schweitzer, chairman of Renault, who was placed under formal investigation in November 1995, not for misdeeds at Renault, but for alleged involvement in a wire-tapping scandal when Schweitzer had been chief aid to former socialist prime minister Laurent Fabius.

Or again Martin Bouyges, head of the Bouyges construction company, was similarly placed under investigation in late 1995 for alleged influence peddling. André Levy-Lang, just mentioned, was investigated for alleged accounting irregularities in his group's sale of Ciments Français, the cement company. Pierre Suard was forced to step down as chairman of Alcatel-Alsthom in 1995 after he was placed under investigation regarding abuse of corporate funds charges and accusations of over-billing France Télécom.

And so it goes on. Cases and developments indicating a break with the past, perhaps the start of a new accountability.

Tensions or change

We introduced this discussion of 1990s developments in French business life by remarking that while there is a significant change in the business environment, the style, character, and disposition of French managers appear to be rather more stable. There is, however, a possible force for change, rather a bleak one, and this is the spectre of unemployment.

Colin Gordon has noted (1996) that unemployment among *cadres* (French managers) rose sharply in 1991. Indeed, between 1989 and 1993 the rate rose from 3.7 per cent to 6.1 per cent. This is pretty much without precedent, and comes as a nasty shock after the pro-management 1980s when the *cadres* tended to enjoy something of a folk hero status. In the mid-1990s graduates of the *grandes écoles* are not being 'snapped up' and fought over as had previously been the case: some are being offered short-term contract employment, and even engineers are being affected.

At this juncture we are doing no more than formulating a possibility. It is possible that changes in French business and managerial labour markets may have a long-term impact on the mentality and behaviour of the professional class who are the subject of this book – *les cadres*.

2 Cadres: Qui êtes-vous?

> *Les cadres. C'est toujours par défaut qu'ils ont été définis. Tour à tour, ou simultanément 'chiens de garde des employeurs' ou 'intellectuels de la classe ouvrière', ils restent désignés par ce qu'ils ne sont pas.* (Cadres have always been defined by default. Either 'the guard dogs of the employers' or the 'intelligentsia of the working classes', or sometimes both at once, they are always identified in the negative.) (Hubert Boucher, *Le Monde*, 3/2/93)

LITERALLY SPEAKING, *cadre* is a noun meaning 'frame' (of a painting or mirror). In the industrial setting, Harrap's gives the definition, 'salaried staff'; Larousse suggests, 'officials'; whilst Collins opts for 'executives, managers and managerial staff'. It is used in expressions like *cadre moyen* or *supérieur* (middle manager or senior manager), *petit cadre* (junior manager), *elle est passée cadre* (she has been named *cadre*) – and even as an adjective, as in *un emploi cadre* (a management-level job).

What is a *cadre*?

This term *cadre* is one which has no equivalent in other languages (other than Italian where the word *quadri* was adopted by business in the 1970s). Basically, it corresponds to 'manager' in English, though with rather different legal and sociological connotations.

The origins of the term in a business setting date back only to the 1930s. Prior to that, the word *cadre* is only used in a military context, where it denoted the ensemble of commissioned and non-commissioned officers. But in 1937 the word made its first appearance in the title of a professional organization – la Confédération Générale des Cadres de l'Economie (Grunberg et Mouriaux, 1979, 11).

The emergence of the term coincided with the industrial unrest of the mid-1930s (le Front Populaire and the 1936 strikes) and the consequent desire on the part of graduate engineers to distinguish themselves from the employers on the one hand, and the workers on the other. Initially, then, this new socio-professional category was composed essentially of graduate engineers, and was meant to assert their position and status in negotiations. But, over time, it has attracted disparate groups (Boltanski, 1982, 52) in search of status and representation, and has extended its boundaries to include 'others enjoying some level of authority' (NEDO, 1987, 63). Today, the term would even include jobs like researcher, consultant or IT specialist – in other words, individuals who do not necessarily exercise authority over anyone.

The 1930s therefore represent a critical stage in France's managerial evolution. This is the point at which historical forces pushed France into creating a buffer group between workers and employers, rather than attempting to reduce the fissure between the two factions and treating them as mere strata within a unit. Studies at LEST, a famous French research institute at Aix-en-Provence, point to the German model as an expression of the unitary approach (Benguigui et al., 1975, 466). The Germans distinguish only between *Angestellter* (white collar) and *Arbeiter* (blue collar), and endeavour to minimize organizational hierarchies and to reconcile differences through consultation (Lawrence, 1980, 42–49). The French, on the other hand, seem to have opted for a tripartite solution which includes this fleshy intermediary class: *les cadres*.

How to become one

There are basically two ways of achieving *cadre* status: by virtue of educational credentials, or through loyalty to a given company.

Those fortunate enough to graduate from one of the 'super-universities' or *grandes écoles* (*baccalauréat* plus five years of full-time study in higher education[1]) can look forward to immediate *cadre* status on entering professional life,[2] whereas a person with only two years' post-*baccalauréat* education (a vocational course such as DUT or BTS as described in the next chapter) is likely to have to wait five or ten years to *passer cadre*. As for an *autodidacte* (self-taught person), the only real chance of turning *cadre* is to prove him- or herself over several years[3] in a company and hope to be named an *ingénieur-maison* – a title which is company specific. In other words, by changing companies *cadres* of this latter type could expect to relinquish their status.

Qualifications are clearly the favoured currency, and time is the price paid for those who are in short supply of this currency. This trade-off between time and qualifications gives rise to a remarkably stable continuum, with particular qualifications corresponding to an implicit 'apprenticeship' (socialization and selection) period before one can have pretensions to *cadre* status.

Needless to say, this produces two distinct populations of *cadres:* those with educational legitimacy, and those without. This divergence gives rise to mild disdain on both sides: those 'with' will secretly deplore *le manque de culture générale* (that is, the lack of intellectual refinement based on superior education) of those without, whilst those without bemoan the automatic handing out of *cadre* status. One *autodidacte* half-jokingly confided, 'Soon they'll be naming them *cadre* on admission to the *grandes écoles.'*

While a talented and hard-working *autodidacte* can aspire to *cadre* status, the chances of becoming *cadre supérieur* are exceedingly slim:

> *La superbe invention française baptisée 'cadre' est un objet de curiosité pour les managers étrangers qui s'étonnent de la quasi-absence d'autodidactes dans les directions. Car ce statut très convoité nécessite un passeport: le sacro-saint diplôme.* (The unique French invention labelled *'cadre'* is an object of curiosity for foreign managers who are amazed at the virtual absence of *'autodidactes'* at board level. For this much-coveted status requires a passport: the much-revered qualification.) (*Le Nouvel Economiste*, 2/02/96, 44)

Defining the population

Exactly what defines a *cadre*, rather like what constitutes a *grande école*, is a subject of some debate – and depending on the definition used, the population varies between two and six million (*Le Monde*, 7/10/93, 20).

No account of the French managerial class seems to be complete unless it opens with a long and confusing synthesis of the alternative definitions. Most authors seek support from the official texts, but even these offer no standard definition (Grunberg and Moriaux, 1979, 212) – a most unsatisfactory situation from the stance of Cartesian logic. What is more, the static nature of the texts makes them particularly inappropriate for defining what has always been, and remains, a changing category.

In attempting to single out the *cadre* population, we can immediately set aside the categories of shopfloor (*ouvriers*) and office workers (*employés*[4]). However, a more contentious issue is whether supervisors (*la maîtrise*) and directors (*les dirigeants*) belong to the class. This depends on different industrial sectors and even individual firms – some choose to distinguish these categories even though the nature of their work is comparable to that of the *cadres*. Certainly it is more or less impossible to identify the peculiarities of their work as distinct from that of a supervisor or director – and any differences in activity are differences of degree rather than kind.

Our own attempts to get *cadres* to engage in self-definition elicited various responses. Some *cadres* saw their collective identity in terms of general responsibility – *vis-à-vis* the personnel or in terms of completing a task. Others referred to the immaterial and unquantifiable nature of their work, and the consequent need for trust (on both sides of the employment contract). Others still felt that the common denominator was a state of mind rather than a type of activity – as one *cadre* put it, 'a blend of adaptability, *esprit de synthèse* and initiative'.

However valid these answers, they proved rather unsatisfactory criteria for distinguishing *cadre* from non-*cadre*. So the term *cadre* starts to look like a status and a state of mind rather than a set of distinctive and usefully identifiable tasks.

Collectively, the various stabs at definition by French authors are perhaps more interesting for what they tell us about the writers themselves than what they reveal about the *cadre*. In effect, this preoccupation with establishing the contours is perhaps a manifestation of the French obsession with labels and social categories. This national propensity to dissect, compartmentalize and classify is something to which Zeldin (1983, 336) alluded: 'The government's sociologists, not frightened of being schematic, have divided French people up into five different species.' Reynaud and Grafmeyer (1982, 13) also comment on this penchant for taxonomies: '*On célèbre volontiers le culte d'une raison déductive et classificatoire plutôt que le respect de l'expérience et de ses diversités*' ('Our fixation with the ability to classify and engage in deductive reasoning is often at the expense of empirical evidence and its diversity').

Since no formal definition is available, the scope of the term *cadre* must be ascertained through its connotations – by examining the meaning it has acquired over time.

Homogeneous body?

Given the varying backgrounds of the *cadre* population and the confusion over requirements for eligibility, it would seem fair to say that they are a heterogeneous mass. Certainly this is the verdict most French authors have traditionally returned (Doublet and Passelecq, 1973, 121). They point out, for instance, that the national statistical service (INSEE),[5] places *cadres supérieurs* in the same socio-professional category as *professions libérales*, while *cadres moyens* are allotted a separate category, alongside schoolteachers and qualified nurses.

The diversity of the *cadre* population is largely the result of a massive increase in the number of *autodidactes* (self-taught *cadres*) throughout the 1960s (Boltanski, 1982, 48) – and the consequent drift away from any neatly defined population of *grandes écoles* graduates. This is held to have devalued the status.

But, by drawing attention to the internal subdivisions between, for instance, commercial and engineering graduates, between 'divine right' *cadres* and non-graduate *cadres*, between *cadres* with subordinates and those without, indigenous observers give a one-sided view of the situation. As expressed in *Le Monde* (3/2/93, 29):

> *Les cadres constituent une nébuleuse en expansion. Ses contours sans cesse recomposés, son hétérogénéité, n'ont pas invité l'encadrement à se constituer une identité collective propre.* (The notion of *cadre* is like an expanding cloud. Its ever-changing contours, its heterogeneity, have not persuaded the population to forge its own collective identity.)

To an outsider, on the other hand, this claim that *cadres* share no collective identity is nonsense. Certainly, when we asked plant managers about the meaning of *cadre* status they were able to provide an exact list of their *cadres*. Thus the definitional problem is largely academic.

At the same time there is a complication in the fact that all companies do not use the same criteria for admittance to the *cadre* group. But this should not detract from the strong sense of belonging associated with the category – as well as the difficulties involved in gaining access. The barriers to entry mean that for many employees *passer cadre* is a real aspiration or achievement. To cross the threshold involves sacrifice and enhances status.

The *cadre* title therefore has a motivational aspect – and for employers, it represents a means of duplicating available rewards/reprimands. The system of material rewards and sanctions doubles up with a system of symbolic rewards and sanctions. In effect, the *passage-cadre* (transition) is *the* critical transition in the French hierarchy since it represents a change of status (unlike the UK where the manager has no legal status) and allegiances – from trade union to employing company (Maurice et al., 1977, 770–71).

This notion of *cadres* as an entity is implicitly endorsed by French newspapers, which are quick to put an undifferentiated label upon the group: '*Les cadres sont . . .*', '*Les cadres font . . .*', '*Les cadres veulent . . .*' (Boltanski, 1982, 407). A selection of recent headlines may help convey this sense of collective identity:

Le spleen des cadres. (The anger of the *cadres.*) (*Le Monde*, 10/2/94, 16)

Sondage: Les Français prudents, sauf les cadres. (Survey: The French are cautious, except the *cadres.*) (*L'Expansion*, 7/3/96, 73)

Le 'ras-le-bol' des cadres. (Why *cadres* are fed up.) (*Le Monde*, 4/10/95, 6)

Questions d'identité des cadres. (Questions of *cadre* identity.) (*Le Monde*, 3/2/93, 29)

Les cadres se rebiffent. (The *cadres* fight back.) (*Le Monde*, 23/2/96, 10)

Sondage Cadres: Comment vont-ils, que veulent-ils, y croient-ils? (Survey on *cadres*: how do they feel, what do they want, do they believe in it?) (*L'Expansion*, 25/1/96, 38–45)

These quotes clearly suggest a degree of homogeneity unparalleled in the Anglo-Saxon context. The word 'manager' would be an uneasy substitute for *cadre* in the chosen headlines. This suggests that French *cadres* have a much more focused identity than their Anglo-Saxon counterparts. Newspapers talk of them in a way more befitting of a far more restricted group – executives, for instance – and an annual survey of '*Les salaires des cadres*' (*cadres'* salaries) is a must for any self-respecting business magazine.

It appears that in spite of their dispersal in terms of social and educational backgrounds and revenue, *cadres* do share a number of core characteristics which unite them. These distinguishing features are primarily legalistic – their own status, retirement scheme (AGIRC[6]) and placement service (APEC[7]), different probationary periods and fixed monthly income as opposed to variable weekly wage. But there is also an intangible element – the much-vaunted, yet indefinable, *état d'esprit*, as well as an undeniable sense of pride and belonging.

Consumer group

Seen from outside, *cadres* are certainly perceived as a homogeneous group, and referring to them as such enhances their unity. Politicians, for instance, will angle for the *cadre* vote *en masse*, as evidenced by the headline in *Le Monde* (23/4/95, 7): '*Les cadres, une catégorie choyée par les candidats*' ('The *cadres*, a category courted by the election candidates').

In effect, the run-up to the 1995 presidential elections saw each of the candidates appeal explicitly to the *cadres* – not just with the usual promises of tax cuts and increased social protection, but with more emotive pledges. For example, Nicolas Sarkozy, running mate of Edouard Balladur, stated: '*Il faut que les cadres puissent être citoyens de l'entreprise comme ils sont citoyens de la société, qu'ils puissent participer à l'élaboration des décisions*' ('Where decisions are concerned, the *cadres* must have their say as citizens of the company, just as they do as citizens of society'). A lesser-known presidential candidate, Jacques Cheminade, went as far as to refer to the *cadres* as '*la matière grise du pays*' ('the nation's grey matter'). One has difficulty imagining a similar comment about from a British politician about British managers.

Similarly, the *cadre* is the number one target of the media planner. The summer of 1992 saw intense rivalry between the two national commercial radio stations *Europe 1* and *RTL*. In order to attract the biggest advertisers, each station – falsely, according to the other – claimed to be the preferred station of the *cadre* (*Le Monde*, 3/2/93, 29).

None of this is new. *Cadres* have for some time been prime targets for advertisers who, decades before the advent of the 'yuppie', had created an image and ascribed a specific lifestyle to them: '*le mode de vie des cadres*' became a stock phrase which conjured up visions of a voracious and discerning consumer of goods and services.

The notion of the *cadre* as the original yuppie is also not without interest. Both, after all, were manufactured social groups, with their own particular identity and values. It was the *cadres*, in the mid-1950s, who helped introduce and legitimize acquisitive American values in France. As Doublet and Passelecq once put it:

> *La logique du système de consommation tend à lui faire croire qu'il existe un style de vie, un 'standing' qui lui est propre, et que ce serait le déchoir que de ne pas l'atteindre.* (The *cadre* has been hyped up into thinking that there is a certain lifestyle and standing which befits him and which must be attained at all costs.) (1973, 111)

The socio-professional identity of this group was shaped and reinforced by specialist magazines inspired by the American journal *Fortune*. Thus, *l'Express* (1957) dubbed itself '*le journal des cadres*' ('the magazine for *cadres*') – and was followed in 1967 by *l'Expansion* which also specified the *cadre* as its target reader. These journals signalled a change of tack for the French economic press, which until then had provided financial information for owners and shareholders. But from the late 1950s onwards it focused on the *cadre*, and on encouraging a new business-literate generation of managers

(Boltanski, 1982, 184). Today, in addition to the above-mentioned journals, French newsagents carry a wide range of mainstream publications specifically aimed at *cadres*, including: *Le Nouvel Economiste, Capital, Challenges,* and the last-born (in 1995), *l'Essentiel du Management.*

Social esteem

For several decades, then, the *cadre* has represented a kind of social reference point. The collective identity of *cadres* quickly spilt over from its professional confines and took up a social position. The *cadres* became the social group to emulate, French society's trend-setters. The creation of the category offered an unprecedented degree of social mobility in France. Previously, the only bridges between the *petite* and the *grande bourgeoisie* had been via *l'artisanat* and commerce. The new category offered possibilities of upward mobility on a massive scale, in what remains a notoriously viscous social environment (Euriat and Thélot, 1995, 404).

At the top end of the scale the *cadres supérieurs* enjoy a social status which is on a par with the professions − doctors, lawyers, architects. This can be attributed to their education levels which are usually not very far removed from that of their professional counterparts. The *cadre* is the latter-day bourgeois − well-off, known and respected in his neighbourhood:

> *Héritier du bourgeois, le cadre recherche la distinction, il aime le luxe, il est obsédé par le 'standing', et il recherche le classicisme. Un certain snobisme caractérise son comportement.* (As a descendant of the bourgeois, *cadres* are obsessed by distinction, luxury, standing and yearn for refinement. Their behaviour is typically snobbish.) (Blazot, 1983, 157)

Of course, the social esteem enjoyed by *cadres* is also a product of the education system and the general standing of management. The *grandes écoles*, which supply graduates to the blue-chip companies, are able to attract the brightest students, since their label opens the door to virtually any career. But this requires the collusion of French companies which tacitly guarantee immediate *cadre* status and early responsibility. As long as this complicity works, 'We'll select them, you buy them', the *grandes écoles* will continue to attract a very high calibre of undergraduate recruit − thereby contributing to a virtuous circle in the status of the *cadre* (Ardagh, 1982, 43).

Their position as drivers of the French economy, both as actors and consumers, goes unquestioned. It was they who embodied the emerging values of the 1980s − self-actualization through work, competence, individual initiative and collective effort. And their lifestyle, in terms of leisure spending, environmental concern, or holiday breaks, continues to shape the demands and aspirations of the wider population.

Such is their presumed influence, that the downturn in consumption in the early 1990s was even attributed to them. As an article in *Le Monde* (10/2/94, 17) put it:

> *Les cadres ont joué pendant des décennies un rôle de locomotive en matière de consommation et ils sont les premiers, aujourd'hui, à souffrir de cette 'montée des peurs'. Face au bouleversement de leur statut, les cadres – plus 'sidérés' que les autres catégories sociales – rognent sur leurs dépenses. Lorsqu'on parle du changement de comportement des consommateurs, ne décrit-on pas, en réalité, les effets de la mutation des cadres?* (Cadres have for decades played a lead role in terms of consumption and they are the first ones touched today by this 'growing fear'. With the threats to their status – to which they attach more importance than other social categories – they are cutting back their spending. So when we talk of a change in consumer behaviour, are we not, in fact, describing the effects of the changing nature of the *cadre*?)

The changing role and expectations of the cadre are explored in these final two sections.

Role of the cadre

Just as the manager must manage, so the *cadre* is there to *encadrer*. Yet the accepted translation of 'to manage' is *'gérer'*. Benguigui et al. (1975), refer to *'une mission spécifique: gérer – et plus précisément encore encadrer'* ('a specific mission: *gérer* – but even more precisely *encadrer'*). It is possible to infer from this nuance that there is a difference in the conception of French and Anglo-Saxon managers.

The fact that the French term was borrowed from military circles is not without significance. To start with, the verb *encadrer* has a notion of policing, which Horovitz (1980, 86) suggests is reflected in the French approach to management control. That military view was confirmed by an article in *Le Monde* (3/2/93, 29) which described the *cadre* as someone who exercises *'des fonctions d'encadrement ou de commandement'* ('functions of control or command'). Such terms are more reminiscent of classical management than the kind of New Age terms, like coaching or facilitating, which are commonly used in Anglo-Saxon countries.

More importantly, perhaps, the military antecedents of the term have given it a distinctly masculine aura which, it could be argued, inhibits the perception of women in the role. The macho *a priori* was reinforced by the fact that the category was initially composed almost exclusively of graduate engineers, and these male engineers have left their 'virile' imprint on it. This is reinforced by the fact that the term has a masculine tag – *le cadre* – which acts as a perceptual barrier to the inclusion of both male and female in that category. *Un cadre*, is typically assumed to be a man. A woman in that position is *une femme cadre*.

Setting semantics aside, the role of the French *cadre* has always been different from that of the Anglo-Saxon manager. From the outset *cadres* have had a specific mission which went beyond corporate expectations. Initially, in 1936, their role was to act as a stabilizing force in the increasingly confrontational worker/employer discussions. Then, when de Gaulle returned to power in 1958, he put the onus squarely on *les cadres de la nation* to rebuild the French economy, thereby restoring France to her former glory. Justifiably, the *cadres* have come to be regarded as the prime architects (and beneficiaries) of France's economic post-war economic success – as *Le Nouvel Economiste* (10/3/95, 46) dubbed them, '*les enfants gâtés des trente glorieuses*' ('the spoilt kids of the thirty golden years – 1945–75').

This image of the *cadre* population as drivers of the national economy, with a clear social responsibility, even withstood the onslaught of the 1980s, the famous 'me' decade:

> *C'est lui qui fait le niveau de vie de la nation.* (It is they who maintain the nation's standard of living.) (Blazot, 1983, 13)

> *Les cadres sont les artisans de la mutation sociale en cours.* (The *cadres* are the facilitators of on-going social change.) (*Le Monde*, 23/6/87, 44)

> *Il faut nous souvenir que tous les grands élans de croissance ont été conduits par le personnel d'encadrement.* (We have to remember that all the great growth spurts were driven by the *cadres*.) (*Le Monde*, 7/10/93, 20)

An even more explicit description of the *cadre*'s socio-economic mission was encountered in a report by the Fédération Nationale des Syndicats d'Ingénieurs et Cadres (National Federation of Managers' Unions):

> *Il ne suffit pas d'exister; il faut vivre et plus encore avoir des raisons de vivre. Ce sera demain le rôle des cadres de fournir ces raisons, de participer à leur*

mise en place dans la société, d'animer et d'entraîner les autres, de transmettre connaissance et idéal, de s'engager résolument dans l'action civique et sociale afin que le progrès se confonde avec la civilisation dans le coeur des hommes. (Mere existence is not enough. We must live and have a reason for living. And the onus falls upon the *cadres* to provide these reasons, to implement them, to motivate others and show them the way, to communicate, and to take an active part in society, so that progress and civilization may become one in the hearts of men.) (Blazot, 1983, 94)

Such remarks would appear excessive by Anglo-Saxon standards, where the manager has a role as an economic actor, possibly with a responsibility to the organization, but surely not to the nation. But the *cadre* is clearly invested with an augmented role. The French seem to regard their managers as the moral, as well as economic, saviours of the nation. They have a responsibility as role models, and in helping to raise the standard of living of others less fortunate than themselves.

It is difficult to know to what extent this is merely rhetoric, but there does seem to be a distinct awareness of their social responsibility as an example to the workforce, and their contribution to the nation's wealth. This was clearly expressed at the Confédération Française de l'Encadrement (formerly the CGC) conference, which described its members as:

Le moteur économique, le promoteur social et le garant de l'avenir du pays. (The social and economic force which guarantees France's future.) (*Le Monde*, 23/6/87, 44)

The distinctive mission of the *cadre* was recently reiterated by Alain Madelin, a former minister in the Juppé government, who spoke of the *cadre* population as '*un moteur de notre progrès*' (a driver of national progress) and whose help he solicited in reducing '*la fracture sociale*' (the social cleavage) (*Le Monde*, 23/4/95, 7). The question is, is it a role they are still prepared to fulfil?

A growing malaise?

Ironically, the unity of the *cadre* group is further enhanced by the existence of a much-vaunted 'malaise'. Virtually every French text dealing with the managerial population devotes a section to this notion – indeed, phrases like '*le malaise des cadres*' or '*la crise des cadres*' have become something of a cliché.

Ever since their first appearance in 1936, *cadres* have been represented as a population that is 'misunderstood, humiliated, unpopular . . . caught in a pincers between *patronat* and proletariat' (Boltanski, 1987, 244 (Eng. trans.)). Obviously, this has a lot to do with the nature of the group which is, by definition, a buffer group. It was precisely because these graduate engineers did not fully identify with either employers or workers that the notion of the *cadre* emerged. The sense of being shut out, experienced by graduate engineers at that time, was described by Georges Lamirand:

> Abandoned by both sides, engineers discovered that they were neither fish nor fowl, that they constituted a third party imperilled on two fronts, in the sad position of an iron caught between hammer and anvil. (Boltanski, 1987, 40 (Eng. trans.))

To some extent, the situation has still not been resolved. The ambiguity of the *cadre*'s position manifested itself most clearly in 'the events' of 1968. Some *cadres* sided with the workers by striking while others were held 'hostage' by angry workers. This simple antithesis reveals the rival pressures exerted on *cadres* – their divided loyalties were a sign that they still did not know where they stood. The same predicament continues to haunt the *cadre* today – and in a strange way, this ambiguity is a defining characteristic of the group (see Figure 2.1).

Figure 2.1: The *cadre* as 'pig in the middle'. (Extract from Lauzier's album *Les cadres* (© Dargaud, Editeur Paris, 1981, by Lauzier.)

On top of this structural and somewhat abstract unease, the economic events of the last few years have provided considerable grist to the mill. For twenty years or so, while other categories were being ravaged by unemployment, the rate of unemployment among *cadres* remained residual. But with the turn of the decade, the situation changed dramatically. The recession which marked the years 1991–94 brought with it an unprecedented amount of restructuring, downsizing, delayering and re-engineering.

Inevitably this resulted in considerable stress associated with a loss of purchasing power, anxiety over pensions, and loss of job security. And it is not just the prospect of their own redundancy which has generated stress. *Cadres* have also had to make others redundant – this is now part and parcel of their work – and ironically something which helps to distinguish their responsibilities from those of supervisors (if not *dirigeants*).

According to the Human Resources Director of a large French group:

> *Pour l'enterprise, les cadres sont sa propriété. Elle leur demande d'adhérer à ses objectifs, de se défoncer toujours plus, d'avoir, sur la productivité, un langage clair, sans états d'âme. S'il faut supprimer une usine, ils doivent le dire. Pour eux, c'est très dur à vivre.* (Companies looks upon *cadres* as their property. They are expected to buy in to the company's objectives, to be increasingly committed, and to be clear and unflinching on productivity matters. If a factory has to be closed, they have to say so. For the *cadres* it is hard to live with.) (*Le Monde – Initiatives*, 17/5/95, 28)

This view that there has been a marked change in the relationship between employers and cadres is confirmed by one embittered *cadre* who complained:

> *Aux Etats-Unis, ils baptisent les cadres executives, ici il faudra bientôt traduire par exécutants.* (In the US, they call *cadres* 'executives', but here we'll soon have to call them 'executors'.) (*L'Expansion*, 25/1/96, 39)

This new malaise, then, goes beyond the fear of unemployment. It arises from a more profound sense of individual and collective powerlessness – the idea that however well they do their jobs, they remain at the mercy of new competition, technological change, company restructuring or sudden take-over.

Now one could say that the joint forces of global competition and recession had a similar effect on the psyche of managers in many developed countries. But, for cultural reasons, we would argue that the impact on the

French *cadre* was particularly devastating. First, there is the high loss of social standing occasioned by the threat of unemployment. There is also the traditional value attached to qualifications as career guarantees, and the low level of inter-company mobility – themes which will be explored in subsequent chapters – and which rendered French *cadres* especially unprepared for such upheaval.

French careers, to a greater extent than those in other countries, have tended to be fairly linear. This was typified by the model of the

> . . . *jeunes cadres dynamiques des années 80, avec un parcours ascendant, des étapes prévues ou prévisibles, une confiance imperturbable en l'entreprise.* (. . . energetic young 1980s *cadres*, with their upward progress, through predetermined or predictable stages, and their complete faith in the organization.) (*Le Monde*, 11/6/96, 1)

The testimony of one *cadre* who joined Philips (France) in the mid-1980s, reflects what was the prevailing attitude:

> *Philips, je me disais, c'est du costaud, j'en aurais jusqu'à ma retraite. Quelle illusion!* (Philips, I thought, now that's solid, this should see me through to retirement. What a joke!) (*L'Expansion*, 25/1/96, 44)

There is also a more subtle point, which has already been hinted at, and which concerns the heavy emphasis on mutual trust in the psychological contract between *cadre* and employer. The expectation of loyalty from both sides was strong. It was a far cry from the heavily contractual American approach where both parties are free agents if expectations are not met. As one *cadre* quipped: '*Jadis on entrait en entreprise comme en religion*' ('In the past, joining a company was like joining the orders').

Symbolically, then, the unilateral breaking of that psychological contract, by the employer, was especially significant:

> *Cette catégorie préservée, qui s'était identifiée aux objectifs de l'entreprise, relayant le projet et la culture, a découvert les limites de l'entreprise-providence.* (This protected category, which had internalized the objectives of the company, passing on both directives and values, suddenly discovered the limits of the guardian-firm.) (*Le Monde*, Alain Lebaube, 12/4/95, 1)

The net result, then, is a *cadre* population which is more calculating and less naïve than before. There is a generalized sentiment that they won't be caught off guard a second time. It is confirmed by one company head, Philippe Kessler, who understands that,

> *On ne pourra jamais plus exiger des cadres le patriotisme qui avait cours avant la crise.* (We will never again be able to demand the same kind of loyalty which was commonplace before the recession.) (*Le Nouvel Economiste*, 10/3/95, 48)

Notwithstanding a genuine hardening of attitudes, this malaise should be put into perspective. While it is true that the *cadre* category experienced the fastest growth in unemployment – tripling in the early 1990s – unemployment touches only 5 per cent of the *cadre* population compared to 14 per cent of *employés*.

It appears, however, that the problem may be overstated. One *cadre* from our interview sample suggested that the *cadre* has little to grumble about in relation, say, to the supervisor. After all, the *cadre* still enjoys a privileged social position and a high level of material comfort. This was indirectly confirmed in a recent survey by *l'Expansion* (7/3/96, 73). When asked whether they would be willing to work more hours for a higher salary, only 13 per cent of *cadres* said yes, compared to 21 per cent for the wider population. And when asked whether they would be willing to work less for a reduced salary, a massive 59 per cent of *cadres* agreed, compared to 38 per cent for the rest of the population.

So, to what extent should we pay heed to this alleged malaise? One could argue that the much-vaunted malaise is just a journalistic device, albeit somewhat perverse, for promoting group solidarity among a fairly disparate readership of salaried workers.

Overview

The mere fact that all companies do not use precisely the same criteria for admittance to the *cadre* group does not detract from the strong sense of collective identity associated with membership. The barriers to admission mean that for many employees being named *cadre* is a real aspiration. Managerial status in France is not part of a graded continuum as in America or Britain, but rather a quantum leap. And associated with the transition in France is a change of legal status, as well as subtle changes in outlook and self-perception. As French executives see it, management is a state of mind, not a set of techniques. For them, it is the ability to think logically and analyse systematically which sets them apart from the rest of the personnel. So to be named *cadre* is akin to passing an intelligence test – it is a hallmark of intellectual calibre. It follows that the title bestows social as well as professional consideration on its incumbent. A *cadre supérieur* enjoys the same kind of social prestige as a lawyer, architect or doctor.

3 Education: Les jeux sont faits

Les grandes écoles sont rendues abusivement responsables de tous les maux dont la France est affectée et en même temps créditées tout aussi abusivement de tous ses succès. (The *grandes écoles* are falsely blamed for all France's disorders and, just as wrongly, credited with all its successes.) (Conversation with head of l'Ecole Nationale d'Aministration)

The French education system

Any understanding of French management necessarily implies a knowledge of the French education system since there can be few nations in the world which take education quite so seriously. This brief descriptive section sets out to fill in the basic details for readers who may be unfamiliar with the French education system (see Table 3.1).

French schoolchildren enter common or comprehensive schools at the age of 11, the competitive entrance exam having been abolished in 1957. The issue of public or private education does not arise in the same way as it would in Britain since the state education system absorbs 90 per cent of the school population, regardless of social and income level. In France, private school means church school and many children would be embarrassed to admit going there. With tougher discipline and old-fashioned teaching methods, the private school is reputedly a refuge for the *cancres* (dullards) – children who cannot keep pace with the relentless state school system.

An idea of the pace of that system can be gleaned from an anecdote told by François de Closets, a thoughtful chronicler of blockages in French society. Preparing a TV programme on the school curriculum, he went out and bought six textbooks, of the kind handed out to 11-year-olds entering *collège*. He happened to show them to the director of Sciences-Po, one of the foremost higher education establishments. On seeing them, the director joked, 'If all my students knew that, I'd be a happy man!' De Closet makes the point that the French system confuses the education of children and and that of graduates of Sciences-Po (*Le Point*, 23/3/96, 96).[1]

This anecdote also gives a flavour of what the French understand by education. As Ardagh once put it:

	Age
Primary: 5 years	
• CP (cours préparatoire)	6/7
• CE 1 (cours élémentaire 1)	7/8
• CE 2 (cours élémentaire 2)	8/9
• CM 1 (cours moyen 1)	9/10
• CM 2 (cours moyen 2)	10/11
Secondary: 7 years	
• Collège: 4 years	
– 6ème (first foreign language)	11/12
– 5ème	12/13
– 4ème (second foreign language)	13/14
– 3ème	14/15
• Lycée: 3 years	
– 2*de*	15/16
– 1ère (choice of *baccalauréat* options)	16/17
– Terminale *(baccalauréat* exam)	17/18
Higher Education	
• University:	
– 1st cycle: DEUG (Diplôme d'études universitaires générales)	Bac + 2
– 2nd cycle: Licence	Bac + 3
Maîtrise	Bac + 4
– 3rd cycle: DEA (Diplôme d'études appliquées)	Bac + 5
Thèse d'Etat (Doctorate)	Bac + 8
• Grande Ecole:	
– Ecole préparatoire (2 years minimum)	18/19
Entrance exam	
– Admission to *grande école*	20–22
– Graduation	23–25

Figure 3.1: The French education system

Much of the best and the worst in the French national spirit can be imputed to the concept of education as inspired academic pedagogy confined to the classroom walls: its role is to transmit knowledge and to train intellects, not – as in Britain – to develop the full individual. (1987, 453)

Secondary education in France has two cycles: the first cycle is compulsory and is given in comprehensive schools called *collèges*. This lasts from 11 to 15, but at the age of 13 some 12 per cent transfer to a *lycée d'enseignement professionnel*,

LEP or technical school, to take the three-year craft course leading to the Certificat d'Aptitude Professionnelle (CAP). At the start of the second cycle, some 23 per cent, aged 15, join these vocational *lycées*, some to do the CAP, others the shorter and more broadly-based Brevet d'Etudes Professionnelles (BEP). It needs courage, however, in white middle-class suburbia to get off at this stage, enter an LEP and learn a blue-collar skill. It is taken as a sign of premature failure in an academically obsessed country.

This second cycle of secondary education lasts three years and caters for those deemed capable of passing the *baccalauréat* (university entrance exam). Although all the *lycées* have theoretically standardized intakes, they do in fact have different clienteles. The best *lycées classiques* are still largely a preserve of the bourgeoisie while the others, because of geographical distribution and lack of prestige, receive more working-class and fewer bright children. One only has to look at the *baccalauréat* results of schools for confirmation. While an average *lycée* might be satisfied with a 70 per cent success rate, the top high schools (such as Louis-le-Grand or Henri IV) would be uncomfortable with less than 90 per cent. Indeed, in 1995, these two particular *lycées* actually achieved 100 per cent success rates in certain *bac* categories (*Le Monde*, 28/3/96, 9).

There are several *bac* categories, meaning sets of pre-packaged subject combinations. Three of these are 'general' and a further eight are 'technological'. The general ones comprise the *bac S* which is the highly rated maths and sciences option, the *bac L* which is the main literary option, and the *bac ES* which is oriented towards economics and social sciences. Whilst each option has a particular focus, each also carries traces of all the other subjects – French, philosophy, history, geography, mathematics, sciences and modern languages – the aim of the *baccalauréat* being to provide a high level of *culture générale*.

Alongside these mainstream *bac* categories, there are the more specialized 'technological' *bacs* which are more professionally oriented. These include the *bac SMS* (*sciences medico-sociales* for paramedical or social work), the *bac STT* (*sciences et technologies tertiaires* for accounting, management, and IT professions), or the *bac H* (*hôtellerie*). At the age of 15, when pupils have to decide which *bac* to take, few have a clear idea of what they want to do, and so it is easy to succumb to parental pressures to take the more general *bacs* which provide the widest range of career choices.

Of the general *bacs*, the one which opens the most opportunities is undoubtedly the *bac S*. The formalized grouping of subjects has made it easy to make comparisons – and a hierarchy of prestige has emerged which is essentially determined by the maths content of each option, with the *bac S* ruling the roost. Such is the importance attached to some combinations of subjects that parents may prefer to pay for private tuition in their children's weaker subjects, rather than encourage them to follow less demanding courses, for which they may be better suited.[2]

Taken at age 18 or so, *le bac* remains a very classical exam. Repeated demands from parents' associations and teachers' unions to broaden the methods of appraisal, by including projects/dissertations, continuous assessment or even multiple choice, alongside the written exam, have been dismissed for fear of devaluing the *bac* (*Le Monde*, 18/7/95, 8).

Back in the early 1980s, the stated intent of the Socialist government (1981–86) was to increase the number of pupils gaining the *baccalauréat* to 80 per cent of an age group by the year 2000. In 1995, the pass rate for the *bac* had reached an unprecedented 75 per cent. This means that 63 per cent of an age group now obtain their *bac* compared to 30 per cent only ten years ago (*Le Monde*, 28/3/96, 9). This dramatic increase reflects the fact that *le bac* is a guaranteed passport to higher education, and that obtaining the highest possible qualification is the safest protection against unemployment.

Higher education

Higher education is provided in institutes of advanced technology, universities and *grandes écoles* (see Figure 3.2). A *baccalauréat* gives automatic entry to university, where courses comprise three cycles. The first, lasting two years, leads to a general university studies diploma, the *Diplôme d'Etudes Universitaires Générales* (DEUG) which covers both compulsory and optional subjects. After this students may leave or stay on for the second cycle. This also lasts two years, the first year of which leads to the *licence* (equivalent of a BA) and the second to the *maîtrise* (MA). The third cycle involves a research-oriented *Diplôme d'Etudes Approfondies* (DEA) often leading to a three-year doctorate or else a one-year *Diplôme d'Etudes Supérieures Spécialisées* (DESS) in a highly specialized area which is more geared towards organizations.

In an attempt to ease the overcrowding and remedy the absence of vocational training in the universities, the government created Instituts Universitaires de Technologie (IUT) in 1966. These were intended to provide a more practical grounding and fill a manpower gap at middle management level. Like the universities, the IUTs recruit *baccalauréat* holders, but unlike the universities, they offer intensive vocational training (in management, commercial and technical subjects) over a two-year period. Essentially they are an upgraded version of the BTS (Brevet de Technicien Supérieur) offered by *lycées* to pupils who wish to stay on after the *bac*. IUT courses include

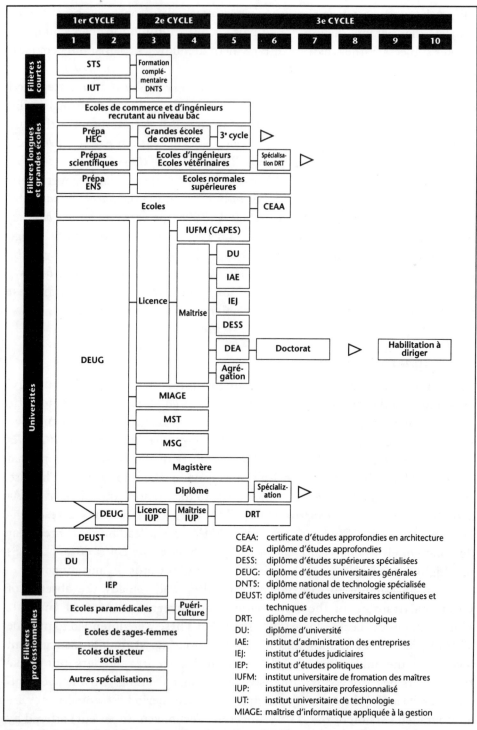

Figure 3.2: French higher education (Source: *L'Etudiant*, March 1996, 14)

industrial placements, and the failure rates are lower than at the traditional universities.

For many years industry did not recognize the qualifications gained in the IUTs because of a traditional bias against semi-vocational education, still considered the poor relation in the French educational system. After initial prejudice against courses of this type, the IUT diploma has now gained recognition in industry. Many employers now prefer it to a DEUG or even a *licence* (see Figure 3.2), the teaching of which, even in science subjects, is perceived as too theoretical.

To combat this perceived deficiency, universities have introduced a trio of two-year professionally oriented masters degrees: a masters in management and information systems (MIAGE), a masters in management sciences (MSG), and a masters in accounting and finance (MSTCF). The universities also offer a three-year diploma known as a *magistère* which is like a compressed *licence-maîtrise-DESS* (see Figure 3.2). For each of these qualifications, candidates are selected by application form and interview, and need to have a level of at least *bac*+2. If readers are starting to get confused, they will understand why parental ability to navigate the French system provides their offspring with a key advantage. And the worst is yet to come.

The *grandes écoles* are a feature of the French educational landscape which has no equivalent in any comparable western country. Students are selected by competitive entrance examinations, having been subjected to two or three years of intense preparation in special post-*baccalauréat* classes. Some of the *grandes écoles* are under the control of the Ministry of Education, for example the Ecole Nationale d'Administration (ENA). Others are sponsored by bodies such as the chambers of commerce, for example the Ecole des Hautes Etudes Commerciales (HEC), while others are controlled by different ministries, for example the Ecole Polytechnique by the Ministry of Armed Forces.

Not all the *grandes écoles* enjoy the same prestige. Perhaps the most sought-after places are at l'ENA which is neither an engineering nor a business school, but a public administration school.[3] Entrance to l'ENA is extremely competitive, and many candidates have undergone training at the Paris Institut d'Etudes Politiques (commonly known as Sciences-Po), a private institution created in 1871 and superseded in practice by l'ENA. The position achieved in the final examination at l'ENA determines the choice of civil service appointment, and the spirit of rivalry is maintained throughout the course, as an individual's whole career may hinge on a quarter of a mark in the final assessment.

While the number of students at the universities has been increasing in an uncontrollable way since the war, the intakes of the *grandes écoles* have remained almost static, and their students have continued, though not so easily as in the past, to find satisfying employment.

The role of education

A long-standing feature of French society is the high premium it places on intellect. Where America extols money, West Germany work and Great Britain blood, France has nailed its flag to the post of cleverness. It is achievement in the educational field which determines inclusion among the decision-makers of French society. The nation is governed by its star pupils, and the higher reaches of management are no exception. One can argue that social eminence based on brains is a fairer basis than either hereditary privilege or the acquisition of wealth. Yet, as will become clear throughout the book, the three are not unrelated.

Educational credentials are ideal props for authority since they are verifiable discriminators of the organizational hierarchy. In France, they indicate status and competence in much the same way as an individual's salary situates a person in the US. Graduates of a prestigious *grande école* are demonstrably 'better' than their organizational subordinates and this justifies inequalities of power (remember the conundrum posed in Chapter 1!). Thus, elitism and the French preoccupation with egalitarianism are reconciled, since the systematic testing of intellectual merit gives everyone (in theory) the same opportunity of access to the elite.

In keeping with this desire for objectivity, mathematics is the central feature of French selection methods in education. From secondary school onwards, a priority is given to the mastery of mathematical tools and to the quality of logical inference. The maths input provides the basis for the pecking order in *baccalauréat* options and determines admission to the top flight *grandes écoles* – both in engineering and, more surprisingly, management.

French higher education is thus based on a two-tier system which is rooted in France's history and distinguishes the exclusive *grandes écoles* from the sprawling universities.

The appellation, *grande école*, is a general and not an official term. The *grandes écoles* are a diversified ensemble of small or medium-sized autonomous establishments which were created outside the traditional university stream in response to precise sectoral needs, notably in engineering, applied science and management science.

The precise criteria for acquiring the precious label are not at all clear. For the same reasons, it is hard to specify the exact number of these schools. Even a call to the Ministry of Education provides only 'ballpark' figures! Some

160 establishments can lay claim to the *grande école* label in that they recruit from the *classes préparatoires* via a nationally recognized *concours*: 50 of these are commercial schools and 110 are engineering schools. They average a mere 400 students each. Their small size explains their lack of international renown. It is difficult to play on a world stage with less than 100 permanent faculty, small intakes, and limited research output. But within France they enjoy tremendous prestige.

In comparison to the *grandes écoles*, the universities have a distinctly lacklustre image. Part of the reason for this lies in the need to cater for too many students of differing abilities. This is primarily due to the fact that universities have little control over the quality of intakes. A *baccalauréat* gives automatic entry to university, as opposed to the highly selective regime operated by the *grandes écoles* – though it is true that the universities do a lot more 'weeding out' along the way.[4] The contrasting systems will be discussed more extensively in the following section.

Management education in France: games people play

Paradoxically, while education in general has been exalted, management education has had some trouble in gaining legitimacy. The universities, which specialized in classical education, were, until the mid-1950s, particularly reluctant to embrace this vocational discipline. The 1980s, however, witnessed the belated emergence of an enterprise culture, in a society which was traditionally hostile to the ethos of wealth creation – and nowhere was this turnaround more apparent than in the attitudes of students. In 1968, they had been busy trying to burn down the Bourse (French stock exchange); 15 years later, every self-respecting business school was setting up its own investment club. There was a new-found willingness to treat business as socially acceptable, and essential to the life of the country.

There is something at once instrumental and idiosyncratic about pre-experience management education in France (the issue of post-experience management education will be dealt with in the next chapter). Each party involved seems more concerned with beating the system than achieving a common end. Students seem to repress their sense of vocation, schools seem more concerned with pecking orders than curricula, and companies pay inflated salaries for raw graduates from the right places. The whole edifice seems founded on premises which are only tenuously linked to the production of well-adjusted managers. Yet, for all their apparent deficiencies, the games in which they engage have a sense of coherence and compatibility. The system works because the parties complement one another and play by the same rules.

Games students play

Devil take the hindmost

In essence, the managerial apprenticeship begins when pupils choose their *baccalauréat* options. Although there are both economics (*bac ES*) and management (*bac STT*) options, pupils with real managerial aspirations will steer clear of these! They will choose instead the maths and sciences option (*bac S*) which affords the best chances of admission (entrance exam permitting), two years after *baccalauréat,* into both engineering and commercial *grandes écoles.* The irony that the management option leads to anything but a high-powered managerial position[5] is compounded by the fact that there are 11 *baccalauréat* options but only one which really counts. This situation has been condemned as the dictatorship of the *bac S*.

On completing the *baccalauréat,* it is accepted that those who can, will proceed to the *prépas* (preparatory schools) to be coached through the *concours* (entrance exam) to the *grandes écoles*. Competition to enter the most successful Parisian *prépa* (Louis-le-Grand) is said to be tougher than the subsequent entry into one of the prestigious trio of management schools (HEC/ESSEC/ESCP), collectively known as *les grandes parisiennes*. Students are kept informed of the relative success rates of the various *prépas* by annual 'hit parades' published by the journals *l'Etudiant* and *Le Monde de l'Education*, thereby instilling an early notion of career strategy.

In the preparatory schools, the students find the same kind of structured environment they left at the *lycée*. They are subjected to an intense work rate, weighted heavily towards maths, and punctuated by written and oral tests, which can make the subsequent pace at the *grande école* seem comparatively slack.[6] For most students *l'enfer préparationnaire* (the hell of the preparatory school) represents the peak effort since, having reached the inner sanctum of the *grande école*, the diploma is *de facto* guaranteed. As one Polytechnique student joked: '*De toute façon, il faut avoir tué père et mère pour sortir sans diplôme*' ('Anyhow, in order to fail one would have to commit patricide').[7] In other words, the gains stemming from admission to a *grande école* are so automatic that students are wont to perceive entry as a landing point rather than a launch pad.

The notion of career strategy manifests itself again in the choice of *grande école*. Students display precocious awareness of their own limitations, so they will only enter exams they feel capable of passing. Evidence of this can be seen in the fact that it is not necessarily the top *grandes écoles* which attract the most candidates. The students engage in a large measure of self-selection to avoid paying costly exam fees where there is a low likelihood of success. They are sensitized early into optimizing their chances and cutting their losses.[8]

Charades

In order to keep their options open, students are best advised to pursue maths to the limits of their potential. Thus, students will renounce vocational preferences in favour of instrumental disciplines. The route to the top is clearly signposted which minimizes the risks of losing potential talent through misinformation. But the price paid is a snubbing of vocational courses and a sheep-like procession towards the same *grandes écoles* because of the tremendous career advantages they confer. This reaffirms a calculating approach to education which seems especially pronounced among French students. Indeed, the student magazine *l'Etudiant* constantly reinforces this notion – with references to tips, short-cuts, success rates and tactics in gaining access to the various establishments (a special issue in March 1996 was entirely devoted to the subject).[9]

This willingness to forgo personal preferences in order to maximize later opportunities extends right through the system, to its very summit. The highest ranked students of Polytechnique, and those of l'ENA, earn the right to choose which of the elite *grands corps*[10] they wish to join – with first choice going to the highest ranked student, and so on down the line. Although presented as a choice, it is virtually unthinkable for the top *énarque* to spurn the *Inspection des Finances*, or for the top *polytechnicien* to turn down the *Corps des Mines*. The *grands corps* also have a strict pecking order. There are 13 of them altogether, but only five which really count: in addition to the two mentioned, there is the *Corps des Ponts et Chaussées* (for *polytechniciens*), and the *Cours des Comptes* and *Conseil d'Etat* (for graduates of l'ENA, known as *énarques*). Admission to these *grands corps* pretty much guarantees career success (for reasons we will explore in the next chapter).

Games educational establishments play

Dressing up

For nigh on two centuries, the top engineering *grandes écoles*, spearheaded by l'Ecole Polytechnique, have groomed their alumni to take up positions as *les cadres de la nation* (the nation's organizers), in spheres as diverse as business, politics and public service. Not surprisingly, the schools' legitimacy as suppliers of the nation's business elite does not rest on the curriculum (albeit generalist in content) but on the type of education they impart. French graduate engineers are not only knowledgeable or well versed in engineering; they are, first and foremost, the products of a mind-stretching system which has nurtured them for leadership positions in industry. More than in other countries, French engineers enjoy a privileged social status, which can be seen by their widespread presence in upper management.

The seal of approval from a prestigious engineering school endorses its holder's capacity for rapid learning and intellectual virtuosity. The quality of the raw material is guaranteed by a highly selective recruitment process, which requires two years' additional schooling beyond secondary education – and the finished product has the added feature of three years of intensive study. In short, the graduate engineer is endowed with the necessary resolve and analytical ability to tackle any problem.

On top of this, the schools provide their students with the social wherewithal and with access to influential old-boy networks to enhance their career chances[11] (discussed in more detail in Chapter 4). For instance, by the time they graduate, *polytechniciens* (students of l'Ecole Polytechnique), have assembled a battery of real or assumed advantages that ensure speedy professional ascent. To add to that, they will have inherited a network of contacts which transcends all sectors. Indeed, the engineering schools have been so convincing in promoting themselves as 'surrogate management schools' that one can understand in part the belated emergence of American-style business schools in France. The success of the engineering schools also explains the tendency for commercial *grandes écoles* to emulate them.

Follow the leader

The first signs of emulation were seen in the explicit attempts by l'Ecole des Hautes Etudes Commerciales (HEC), the foremost commercial school, to model itself on the engineering schools at its inception. The school was set up in 1881 with the express intention of breaking the engineers' stranglehold over large sectors of business in the expanding industrial context of the late nineteenth century. From the outset, HEC espoused what were considered the most prestigious aspects of the state-sponsored engineering schools, notably a socially biased, post-*baccalauréat* recruitment policy. Furthermore, HEC's curriculum rested firmly on the cornerstone of law, a noble discipline which lent commercial education a veneer of academic respectability. In terms of image it looked to l'Ecole Centrale for guidance since this was the only private engineering school which had managed to stamp its identity among the state *grandes écoles* (the very first head of HEC was in fact a *centralien*).

Naturally enough, HEC spawned its own imitators, a network of provincial commercial schools (ESCAE[12]) which, by association, tended towards the *nec plus ultra*, l'Ecole Polytechnique. Perhaps the most striking legacy from the engineering schools was the widespread adoption of maths as the critical entry determinant. This tribute to engineering education is understandable in that maths represents an objective measure of merit for selection. But the link between strength in maths and management potential is more debatable.

The less prestigious commercial schools (mostly private rather than sponsored by the Chambers of Commerce like HEC and the ESCAE network) are also faithful to the HEC model. These lesser schools are forced into reducing the maths content in order to attract those who fail the *concours* (entrance exam) owing to a weakness in maths. But in other respects they do their best to imitate the more prestigious establishments.

The prime manifestation of this lies in their names, which bear more than a passing resemblance to those of the more venerable establishments. They are abetted in this by the French penchant for acronyms, which lends itself to abuse. Lesser schools capitalize on the confusion in order to imply similar status to the provincial commercial schools, the ESCAE network referred to in the previous paragraph. One personnel manager we interviewed speculated that new commercial schools were named by picking out three of the following at random: '*école, institut, supérieur, hautes études, gestion, finance, direction, entreprises, affaires*'. There is undoubtedly an element of deliberate *trompe l'œil* in many appellations – to dupe potential students, their parents and employers alike. The profusion of acronyms can prove quite bewildering, even to the initiated.

The same goes for the popular confusion surrounding the various degrees of state accreditation, which is comparable to trying to decipher wine labels. Some of the less scrupulous schools trumpet the billing *homologué par l'Etat* (state registered), knowing that the uninitiated will equate it with the more exclusive *diplôme reconnu par l'Etat* (state approved qualification) or the intermediary label *reconnaissance par l'Etat de l'etablissement* (state approved establishment). The first merely indicates the level of the qualification, whilst the latter two are attestations of quality. Where the establishment is approved, the state guarantees the calibre of the faculty and resources, as well as the credibility of the directors. Where the qualification itself is approved, it implies a more stringent audit, by the Ministry of Education, which extends to the syllabus, teaching methods, and naming of the Chairman of the Admissions and Examiners' Board.

Further evidence of mimicry can be seen in the necessity for the most embryonic business school, whose future still hangs in the balance, to set a token entrance exam.[13] This is intended to set them apart from the universities and, by implication, identify them with the *grandes écoles*. Generally, the said exam is more than a touch symbolic since meeting entrance requirements has less to do with exam marks than parental funds. The schools demand high tuition fees since they do not have the same ability as the *grandes écoles* to attract financial support from companies (*taxe d'apprentissage*[14]). These private schools have also some difficulty in attracting permanent academic staff and generally resort to a mixture of part-time faculty and visiting staff. They typically encourage placements in industry as it means less teaching hours, while boosting the perceived study period (*bac*+4 looks better than *bac*+3). And they market themselves hard in their brochures, paying particular attention to the features which distinguish *grandes écoles* from the universities, notably their close links with companies, the industrial placements on offer, the membership and scope of their old-boy networks, and the dynamism of their *junior-entreprise* (student-run consultancy).

Universities are limited as to the extent they can copy the *grandes écoles*. For instance, the universities must operate an open-door policy whereby any holder of the *baccalauréat* is eligible for admission. The fact remains that the most successful universities are precisely those which have found a way round these constraints.[15] Foremost among these universities is the management university of Paris IX-Dauphine created in 1968 in response to student discontent and housed in the freshly vacated NATO headquarters.

Dauphine's selection, competition and professionalism give it all the hallmarks of a *grande école*. By law it should not practise selection – yet, in reality, only people with a *bac S* (maths) need apply and 95 per cent of the intake in fact obtained a distinction in their *baccalauréat*. This is deemed preferable to selection '*par la file d'attente*' ('first come, first served'). As a result Dauphine's reputation among employers is enhanced and its students can expect increasing numbers of unsolicited job offers. Although the university clearly flouts the principle of non-selection, the state is prepared to turn a blind eye to uphold the reputation of this jewel in a lacklustre university system.

Dauphine also pays the same attention as the *grandes écoles* to industrial placements – demonstrating full awareness of the importance of these initial contacts between students and companies. In the same vein, Dauphine has followed the example of the *grandes écoles* and organized annual job fairs, as well as a yacht race whose teams are composed of students and executives, and which amounts to a floating job fair. The teaching methods, too, are reminiscent of the *grandes écoles* in that they are based on group work rather than the staple university diet of lectures. Thus, it has taken on many of the features of a *grande école* education as regards length and format of studies, but most importantly in terms of recruitment. It would seem that any university which seeks to emulate this success is destined to follow Dauphine's lead and renounce its university origins in order to gain credibility in the business community. Stringent selection at entry level, based on application form and *bac* grades, is the emerging pattern.

What appears to be universal convergence towards the Polytechnique blueprint even extends to the Institutes of Technology (IUT) which were destined to replenish the ranks of middle managers by providing a shorter and practical apprenticeship to management. Like certain universities, the institutes have resorted to selection by introducing a mini-'*concours*' which, according to a headteacher interviewed, has turned them into scaled down *grandes écoles*.

Moreover, with the top commercial schools extending the period of preparatory schooling to an obligatory two years in order to align themselves with engineering studies, the institutes have found their vocational two-year courses devalued in relative terms. Once again the influence of the top engineering schools has prompted emulation with each educational establishment lengthening its curriculum – partly for image purposes and partly to attenuate student fears of unemployment.

Rather than trying to respond to demand in a pluralist fashion, each establishment strives more or less consciously to attain the Polytechnique ideal. They seem undeterred by its relation to a bygone age and its oblique approach to the acquisition of management skills. L'Ecole Polytechnique remains the archetypal model, the universal *point de repère* which renders comparison between the various establishments easy and apparently legitimate. This gives rise to another game.

King of the castle

The predilection for hierarchies is a familiar feature of French culture and the facile ranking of educational establishments provides the press with an eager readership (incorporating students and their parents, teachers and employers). Each category of establishment is regularly scrutinized and classified in league tables compiled by *Le Nouvel Economiste, Capital, l'Etudiant* or *Le Monde de l'Education*. There are even cross-category (all-comers) surveys conducted by *l'Expansion* based on starting salaries offered to graduates. The higher the league position, the higher the signing-on fee commanded by its graduates. Whatever their initial accuracy, these comparisons tend to prove self-fulfilling since employers use them to align their salaries on market trends, thereby reinforcing findings presented as neutral.

Of course, conventional bases of comparison always favour the same schools, so the lesser schools endeavour to find new criteria which will upset the traditional pecking order and put them to the fore. Certain schools will point to the number of times they are oversubscribed as an indication of exclusiveness. They will publicize the low chances of admission and on this basis will claim to rival the top schools – carefully neglecting to acknowledge the self-selection in which prospective students engage (mentioned earlier).

Another measure which schools are increasingly highlighting is employability on graduation. The lesser schools, in particular, may make much of their high placement rates, neglecting to mention that many of these jobs are in small regional companies, in the retail sector, or in functions such as sales and IT, all of which are disregarded by the top *grandes écoles*.

These constant comparisons fuel intense rivalry among the various establishments. As one observer of the system put it to us:

> *Les responsables des écoles surveillent la moyenne des salaires d'embauche avec une passion comparable à celle des petits porteurs sur les cours de la Bourse.* (*Grandes écoles* directors scrutinize the starting salaries of their graduates with the zest of small shareholders checking stock prices.)

In spite of the jockeying for position, the level of consensus surrounding the intricate pecking order is high and leap-frogging is minimal. Some measure of the immutable nature of the hierarchy can be illustrated by the fact that, when the Raymond Barre government (1976–81) decided to upgrade French technical education, the only policy it could come up with was to make it easier for the best pupils on vocational courses to enter the *grandes écoles*. More recently, there have been similar attempts by the likes of HEC to open up their entrance exam to scholars with an arts background *(Capital,* June 1994, 121). The point remains that there is only one hierarchy in France.

The leading three commercial *grandes écoles*, HEC/ESSEC/ESCP, are closely followed by the regional Ecoles Supérieures de Commerce (led by Lyon) mingled with a few of the private schools mentioned earlier. The attraction of these prestigious schools is that their label is a guarantee of employability. In particular, the stamp HEC/ESSEC/ESCP is a passport to a prosperous career. But the stakes are not negligible. The failure rates in reaching these schools are high and the preparatory system leaves many people bitter or demotivated after two years of sustained effort and not even a concrete qualification to show for it, their only consolation being direct access to the second year of university courses.

Games employers play

Hunt the thimble

Employers tend to have mixed feelings about the merits of the French education system. On the one hand, it saves them considerable effort by systematically ranking people in terms of smartness. On the other hand, they are not fully convinced that the skills nurtured and the knowledge transmitted are especially geared to the needs of business. The tension was neatly captured by an article in *Le Monde* (18/4/95, 9) reporting on employer preoccupations:

> *Le système éducatif français est parfait, disent [les patrons] ironiquement, mais inadapté. Il survalorise le savoir au détriment du savoir-faire. Il conforte les parents dans une recherche frénétique du diplôme, sorte de ligne Maginot contre le chômage, et dans un mépris pour les métiers techniciens.* (The French education system is perfect, say the employers ironically, but ill-adapted. It reveres knowledge at the expense of know-how. It comforts parents in their desperate search for qualifications, as a kind of Maginot line against unemployment, and reinforces their scorn for technical work.)

Or again, consider the mixed verdict of François Michelin, the pragmatic head of the Michelin group, given in a rare interview:

> *Plus les gens sont cultivés, meilleur c'est . . . A condition qu'ils sachent aussi écouter, et ne disent pas 'Moi je sais', mais qu'ils se mettent à côté des gens tout simplement en leur disant 'Qu'est ce que c'est que votre métier? Quelles sont les difficultés que vous avez? Qu'est ce que je peux faire pour vous aider? Apprenez-moi quelquechose.' Or, malheureusement dans les écoles, on apprend l'inverse.* (In terms of education, more is better . . . Provided that those educated people also know how to listen, and don't assume that they know. Provided they stand alongside people and ask them simply, 'What is your work about? What problems do you have? What can I do to help? Teach me something.' Unfortunately, in the schools, they learn the opposite.)[16]

While acknowledging the perceived deficiencies in the French education system, employers seem more than willing to embrace its products. Come graduation time, companies pull out all the stops to attract candidates from the top schools. IBM-France, for instance, has a department specifically concerned with the schools, '*Relations grandes écoles*' (a title which consciously omits the universities). The blue-chip companies will start their pursuit of the best talents early, offering placements, sponsoring events, visiting the schools and conducting presentations. It is not uncommon for the best graduates to receive more than ten offers of employment which enables them to play hard to get. At HEC, the *average* is three job offers per student (*Capital*, June 1994, 121).

With the big companies all chasing the same candidates, it creates a micro-market where the salaries demanded become inflated. Yet companies tend to play along, dangling gilt-edged carrots to attract the brightest available talent. Companies are apt to look upon the *grandes écoles* as elaborate sifting systems rather than purveyors of knowledge – and some make no secret of the fact that they are primarily purchasing the *'concours'* (entrance exam). As Guy de Jonquières once observed: 'The prowess of the *grandes écoles* rests heavily on their admission procedures, which weed out all but the most brilliant candidates' (*Financial Times*, 18/4/90, 13).

Although the salary gap between commercial and engineering graduates is constantly being eroded, companies still broadly favour the engineering schools which are entrusted with the making of French managers, even if they no longer hold a monopoly. In particular, there are plenty of companies prepared to pay back (to the state) the fees of a 'polytechnicien' in order to capture him/her immediately after graduation and spare that person their obligatory two or three years of state service.

As previously noted, universities, with the notable exception of Dauphine, tend to be disregarded by employers because of the alleged inapplicability of their teaching or research. In spite of attempts to become more vocationally relevant, the university system is still tainted by a reputation for authoritarian, non-interactive teaching, which does not lend itself to the demands of management education. As far as many employers are concerned, the products of the universities are still synonymous with the teaching profession and the dole queues.

There is a slightly brighter picture for the IUTs (Instituts Universitaires de Technologie) with their vocational two-year technical or management courses. Their reputations are rising, as witnessed by shortening lead times for their students to reach *cadre* status. Yet, the IUTs remain 'Cinderella' establishments. This makes them a favourite hunting ground for the large retail stores (like Auchan or Carrefour) which are themselves snubbed as *'vendeurs de sardines'* ('sardine sellers') by *grande école* graduates. One might say that the large retailers get their recruits at a discount.

One explanation for the 'conservatism' of employers, in terms of where they recruit, has to do with the complexity of the system. Even human resource managers are unable to keep up with the constant profusion of acronyms, qualifications and course options. When in doubt, they tend to play it safe which, inevitably, reinforces the existing hierarchy. As the recruitment manager of a large metallurgic company puts it:

On est perdu devant cet afflux de diplômes inconnus. On préfère donc embaucher des généralistes dans les écoles que l'on connaît. (We're overwhelmed by this abundance of unknown qualifications. So we prefer to recruit generalists from the schools we know.) (*L'Expansion*, 4/4/96, 89)

No one ever got sacked for recruiting an HEC graduate!

The fact remains that employers seem relatively indifferent regarding the possession of occupationally relevant management skills. Access to business is not associated with qualifications embodying a job-specific content, in the same way as access to architecture, medicine or law. But French companies seem to push this argument to its extreme. Most employers would still prefer products of Polytechnique (engineers) or l'ENA (civil servants) to their HEC counterparts (managers). Strictly speaking, the former were not designed to train managers for private enterprise, but both students and employers treat them as such. Students intent on a career in industry will have no qualms about heading for these schools, whose label is an 'Open sesame' to all careers. This merely endorses the view of qualifications as 'entry tickets'.[17]

Consequences

The complexity and elitism of the French education system has a number of consequences on the profile, career and outlook of senior French managers. Many of these will become apparent in the chapters which follow, but a few need to be unpacked here.

Benefits

First we need to consider whether the French system manufactures good products, that is well prepared managers. In answer to that question, it is worth reviewing a number of the points touched upon in the preceding discussion.

First, we must consider the basis for selection. Maths, as a culturally neutral and precisely quantifiable criterion, is used as an objective measure of merit for entry into the *grandes écoles* – including the top-flight business schools.[18] This raises questions about compatibility of means and ends. Does France really need supernumerate managers? In terms of subject matter the answer is probably no. But if we consider the depth and rigour of the study process, the apprenticeship looks more appropriate.

To start with, maths is deemed a faithful indicator of the ability to synthesize and to engage in complex abstract reasoning, qualities which are highly prized in all spheres of professional life. The mind has been trained to grasp complex problems and assimilate new knowledge quickly. Thus, employers are confident that the specific expertise needed for the job and the graduate's potential as a manager can be brought out by the company's own training and development programme.

In addition to this, the intensity and duration of the *grande école* training equips the would-be manager with essential mental and physical capacities: the ability to cope with pressure and to work long hours, a lengthy span of concentration, an analytical mind and a disciplined approach to work. In advising scholars whether they are suited to pursue a *grande école* regime, *L'Etudiant* (March 1996, 32) suggests that prospective candidates require the following qualities (on top of outstanding *bac* grades):

> *Stabilité psychologique, endurance au travail et résistance au stress, esprit concours, aptitude au raisonnement théorique.* (Psychological stability, the capacity to cope with high work loads and stress, an exam mentality, and an aptitude for theoretical reasoning.)

To fully appreciate the qualities and resolve of the *grande école* graduates, one must consider the obstacles they have overcome, the uncertainty and competition they have faced, and the sacrifices they have made. Their odyssey will also have brought out their tactical awareness and their single-mindedness which will serve them well in the cut and thrust of the business world.

But perhaps the most important psychological asset which the *grandes écoles* confer upon their students is confidence. The atmosphere within the schools prepares its incumbents for leadership. Secure in the knowledge of where they are heading, anticipatory socialization tends to operate. Individuals assume the values, outlook and poise of the 'ruling class' from an early age. They may not be *au fait* with the technicalities and jargon of management, but they have the social wherewithal and psychological authority to take up positions of power.

In terms of concrete advantages, the schools provide their *protégés* with a ready-made network of contacts which can prove especially supportive in times of trouble, notably unemployment. Career-minded students can start to establish links before even entering the fray of the business world, safe in the knowledge that their cohorts are also bound for the nation's executive suites. To a greater extent than most nations, France pools its elite from an early age which fosters the solidarity born of a common educational experience. And that elite fans out into all sectors of French society.

Although the *grandes écoles* were not specifically designed to train managers, that is the role they have assumed. Indeed, it is a role they have successfully fulfilled, though this success is largely a product of their unique evolution in parallel to the great economic surge of the nineteenth century. The likelihood is that they could not be replicated outside the peculiar French context. For instance, if the schools did not benefit from such historically based esteem, they would no longer attract their proper proportion of the cleverest people in each age group. The schools would be unable to sustain their reputations which, to a greater extent than Anglo-Saxon institutions, are based on who attends, rather than on who teaches there, or the excellence of the research output.

Perhaps the best testimony to the quality of their products is that employers will frantically outbid each other to secure the services of a *grande école* graduate. It could of course be argued that a popular product is not necessarily a good product and that the influence of networks might be artificially boosting the continued demand. However, if the schools really were failing to enhance the raw material then employers could easily acquire the same talent by recruiting directly from the preparatory schools. The fact that this is unheard of suggests that the schools do provide considerable added value, which goes far beyond inculcating formal knowledge.

Costs

An elitist system has an effect both on those it selects and on those it sidelines. Those it favours are guaranteed preferential career advancements and can, if they choose, treat their diploma as *une rente éducative* (an educational annuity). For this reason, there is sometimes a tendency to look upon admission to the *grande école* as a swan song rather than a *point de départ*. A manifestation of this is that *grande école* graduates are not generally inclined to risk their talents in entrepreneurial ways to stimulate new business, but exploit them instead to gain authority in bureaucratic hierarchies (the theme is treated in more detail in the following chapter).

Needless to say, if the system puts a brake on the motivation of the sucessful, this is doubly the case for those it rejects. The nation is deprived of the individuals whose talents or disposition are not suited to the strict regime of preparatory schools, notably the late developers, the pragmatic or the artistically inclined who are eliminated from the running at an early stage. Later, they are joined by all those embittered by their failure to meet the exacting requirements of the entrance exam to the *grandes écoles*. This combined population of potentially able managers must resign itelf to impoverished salary and promotional expectations since the top places are virtually reserved to *grande école* graduates – and sometimes to graduates from a particular school.

To a large extent these are costs which are accepted. There is little pressure for the *grandes écoles* to increase their intakes or to change their selection methods, which might jeopardize their prestige. Keeping the supply low, helps the *grandes écoles* to guarantee the marketability of their products.[19] The barely perceptible rise in output of *grande école* graduates is in stark contrast to the continual increases in university subscriptions. The elitist tradition shows no real signs of weakening.

Such a model is perfectly legitimate provided that the elite identified is roughly representative of the wider population – but the French elite is not, either in terms of gender or social background. These issues are worth considering in more detail.

The *grandes écoles* are not only intellectually elitist, they are also socially discriminating, with the chances of access to the different types of higher education being heavily biased.[20] *Le Monde* (6/7/95, 9) reported on a survey comparing levels of education and social origins. It emerged that the proportion of students whose parents are *cadres supérieurs* (senior executives) grows steadily so that: at *baccalauréat* level they represent 29 per cent of the population, at *bac+3* they are up to 35 per cent of the population, and at *bac+6*, they amount to 47 per cent of the population. The reverse effect is visible among students whose parents are '*ouvriers or employés*' (blue-collar or clerical workers). These represent 18 per cent of the population at *bac+1*, but only 9 per cent at *bac+6*.

There is an added twist. Social origins not only influence the length of studies, but also the type of studies. So students whose parents are either *cadres* or professionals (34 per cent) are over-represented in the preparatory schools for sciences (45 per cent) but considerably under-represented (12 per cent) in the practical-oriented STS (*Sections Techniciens Supérieurs*). Conversely, students of modest origins who represent 73 per cent of the school population, account for 69 per cent of STS intakes but only 28 per cent of preparatory school intakes.

The findings are confirmed in a longitudinal study by Euriat and Thélot (1995). While the authors note the massive democratization of access to universities, the same cannot be said of the *grandes écoles,* especially the top four.[21] They conclude their painstaking study with the observation:

> *Il y a trente ans, un jeune d'origine populaire avait 24 fois moins de chances qu'un autre d'entrer dans une de ces quatres grandes écoles [X, ENA, HEC, ENS]; aujourd'hui, il en 23 fois moins.* (Thirty years ago, a young person of humble origins had 24 times less chance of making it into one of the top four schools. Today that person has 23 times less chance.) (1995, 419)

Exactly *how* this discrimination operates is not clear. It is difficult to challenge the fairness of maths as a sifting mechanism. Still, Bourdieu and Passeron (1970) contend that requiring managers to be supernumerate, biases access towards well-to-do students who benefit from an earlier and easier apprenticeship to abstraction. This may be true, but more compelling, perhaps, is the argument that the 'gateways' to power are so few, that intimate knowledge of the French education system is needed to reach them. A parent who has successfully negotiated this tricky system is in a better position to orient his or her child. This would also explain the 'high degree of inheritance of occupational aspirations' noted by Marceau (Whitley et al., 1984, 86). Those familiar with the 'snakes and ladders' of the system are more likely to guide their children along the paths they trod. As Szarka puts it: 'An essential element of the legacy to the offspring of French business families is an understanding of the educational system' (1992, 162).

That social bias is compounded by a gender bias which tends to correlate with the prestige of the institution. For example, women represent 53 per cent of the students in the economic sections of the preparatory schools, 51 per cent of the intake in the provincial ESCAE schools, but only 35 per cent of the intake at ESSEC and 33 per cent at HEC (Frémy, 1996, 661). The situation is of course worse in the engineering schools since women only represent 22 per cent of the students in the scientific sections of the preparatory schools. This would not be a problem were it not for the fact that the engineering schools continue to supply industry with the bulk of its business elite.

There are traditional reasons why women tend to steer clear of the engineering route to careers. The top *grandes écoles* are founded on 'virile' values – decisiveness, networks, hierarchies, camaraderie and dominance. The curriculum too bears the stereotypical masculine hallmark of logic, mathematics and Cartesianism. Boltanski explains:

> *Les valeurs viriles inculquées dans les grandes écoles conduisant traditionnellement a des positions d'autorité dans l'industrie, comme l'Ecole des Arts et Métiers ou l'Ecole Centrale, sont fortement exaltées et recherchées.* (Qualities of leadership and other manly virtues inculcated by schools such as the Ecole des Arts et Métiers and Ecole Centrale, whose graduates have traditionally assumed positions of authority in industry, are highly sought after and valued.) (1982, 325)

The foremost school, l'Ecole Polytechnique, did not even open its doors to women until 1972. Predictably, the annual intake of women at Polytechnique rarely exceeds 12 per cent, while the 'barrier' for its chief rival, l'ENA, is around 25 per cent – this in spite of the fact that the percentages of women candidates far exceed these figures. The indications are that the entrance exams somehow militate against female success, thus denying women access to these seed beds of top management positions. The heads of the schools claim to be baffled, but there is little incentive for them to change the system given the 'lower value' of women as alumni. The fact that a woman may interrupt her career to have children weakens the school's network and potential influence. Under these circumstances, why interfere with admissions policies?

France remains what Vincent (1981) termed a 'high-viscosity' society, where upward mobility is a generally slow process. The educational system plays a key role in making sure that it stays that way.

4 Careers: La force du destin

Si le diplôme n'est plus le passeport garantissant le succès qu'il était jusqu'à la fin des années 80, il reste en France le sésame indispensable pour accéder aux grandes carrières de managers. (Although qualifications no longer represent a meal ticket as they did until the end of the 1980s, they remain an essential entry ticket for those heading for the corporate boardrooms.) (*Le Point*, 28/9/96, 79)

CAREERS ARE A SUBJECT of tremendous interest for *cadres*, as witnessed by the popularity of salary surveys and 'career pull-outs' published by the likes of *l'Expansion, le Nouvel Economiste, Le Point, l'Express, Challenges, Capital* or *l'Essentiel du Management*. This chapter sets out to examine the various influences on a managerial career in France. Of course, the differences which exist between France and the Anglo-Saxon countries, are of degree rather than kind. Themes like qualifications, performance, mobility, training and functional choice automatically affect an individual's career, but their relative weightings vary between corporate and national cultures.

Recruitment procedures: reading between the lines

By way of introduction, it may be worth taking a look at the French recruitment process, which contains a number of tell-tale signs regarding ways to the top in France. The form and substance of career advertisements, CVs and covering letters all provide insights into the critical influences on career success.

Job advertisements

A cursory glance at managerial job advertisements in *Le Monde* or *Le Figaro* reveals a number of surprises (see Figure 4.1 below). First, a piece of information considered vital by Anglo-Saxons – what the post pays – is conspicuous by its absence in France. Rather the advertisement will speak coyly of 'appropriate salary' and, although there may be general references to fringe benefits, they are not likely to be itemized. This is in contrast with Anglo-Saxon ads which typically state the salary, often in the headline, and also list other material inducements, including company car, bonus, relocation expenses, stock options, health care and other benefits. In France, a reference to '*substantiels avantages sociaux*' would be considered indecently explicit.

Two explanations can be advanced for this reticence over salary and perks. First, it can be seen as part of a wider stigma that still surrounds money in Roman Catholic France. Second, it reflects a different emphasis in deciding

---

Important groupe de Sociétés
dans le domaine du Bâtiment

recherche son

DIRECTEUR DU DEVELOPPEMENT

Formation HEC, ESTP . . .
+ expérience confirmée
secteur Bâtiment

Paris/Région Parisienne

Rattaché au Directeur Général, de formation supérieure HEC, ESTP . . . âgé d'une quarantaine d'années, vous assumez le développement des différentes sociétés du groupe.

Autonome, vous avez développé votre sens de l'initiative ainsi que vos qualités de rigueur, d'analyse et de synthèse. Vous disposez de bonnes aptitudes relationnelles et du goût des négociations de haut niveau. La dimension internationale du Groupe nécessite de fréquents déplacements à l'étranger et une excellente maîtrise de l'anglais.

Vous maîtrisez les techniques d'analyse des marchés, l'évaluation des coûts et des risques et la gestion administrative et financière de l'activité. Vous possédez une excellente connaissance du réseau relationnel du secteur.

Votre dynamisme et votre sens de l'initiative vous ouvriront de larges perspectives de carrière au sein du Groupe.

Merci d'addresser votre candidature (lettre manuscrite, photo et CV) à: TRP Conseil, 20 rue Treilhard, 75008 Paris.

Figure 4.1: Example of a French job advertisement

salary. In Anglo-Saxon countries, the salary tends to relate closely to the nature of the job, its responsibilities, and the results obtained. In France, it has more to do with the individual's credentials, and particularly his or her qualifications – but also age, experience and even contacts.

If French adverts are vague on material rewards, they are more precise about educational attainments. Typically, advertisements specify a particular type of education identified by the number of years the course lasts after the *baccalauréat*: for instance, *bac*+2 for DUT, BTS (short vocational courses) or DEUG; *bac*+4 for a *maîtrise* (masters) or some business school diplomas (increasingly *bac*+5); and *bac*+5 for the best business and engineering *grandes écoles* and the university-based Diplôme d'Etudes Supérieures Spécialisées. The required credentials are generally given prominence in the text, sometimes even featuring in the sub-heading. All this is in stark contrast to the rather vague call for 'graduates' (or 'graduate preferred') which prevails in Britain.

French companies are precise in their requirements and at least give the impression that they will get what they are asking for, typically demanding 'a degree in . . .' not simply, 'a degree', and their advertisement may even mention a particular set of awarding institutions. Quite often an advertisement specifies: '*Formation supérieure (HEC, ESSEC, ESCP . . .)*'. Or it may ask for '*Formation ingénieur généraliste (A et M ou autre)*' (*A et M* being shorthand for Arts et Métiers). In France, few blue-chip companies go in for anything as untargeted as 'graduate recruitment'.

In Britain and the US, prolonged studies on the part of applicants tend to make potential employers nervous, but in France five or six years of intensive post-*baccalauréat* study at a *grande école* is considered an ideal apprenticeship. Nor is the accumulation of qualifications viewed ambiguously. For example, a recent issue of *l'Expansion* profiles the latest generation of graduates to arrive on the job market. It refers to one individual who was snapped up by the French subsidiary of an American consultancy: he boasted qualifications from Sciences-Po (1991), ESCP (1995) and a DEA (in law). This suggests that French employers do not share the Anglo-Saxon view that long-term students are either 'work shy' or 'impractical'. In France, there is not the presumption that qualities of reflection and action are mutually exclusive.

This difference shows through in the desirable qualities required of candidates. Anglo-Saxon ads stress drive, enthusiasm, pragmaticism, team orientation, and social skills, as in this ad from the *Sunday Times* (26/5/96, Appointments): 'Mature, forward-thinking, self-starter with hands-on approach and previous exposure to corporate reorganisation. Energetic and ambitious team player with excellent communication and interpersonal skills.' And this company was looking for Finance Director!

French ads are much more likely to emphasize cerebral qualities: *l'esprit critique, la rigueur, la capacité de synthèse* (analytical mind, intellectual rigour, ability to synthesize). For example, where a British employer pledges that it is recruiting only 'people of the highest calibre', its French equivalent seeks out *'les éléments les plus brilliants'*. The nuance is significant. The French are not looking for hands-on, sleeves-up operators. They are looking instead for formally sanctioned cleverness, for people who can grasp complex issues, and analyse problems. Relatively, French employers tend to focus on qualities of reception (a capacity to assimilate new knowledge quickly, to analyse problems, and to conceive solutions) at the expense of qualities of emission (charisma, pugnacity, ability to communicate and motivate). They seem to adhere to a rather different conception of management – primarily as an intellectual challenge rather than an interpersonal one.

French ads also tend to be more informative than Anglo-Saxon ones. French ads are less likely to open with a catchy headline along the lines, 'Turn a new page this autumn', or 'An outstanding development opportunity'. They are less likely to try to appeal to the 'winner' in you. Their tone is more subdued. They provide details of the size and scope of the company, and describe who you will report to (*rattaché à* . . .).[1] These details indicate the status of the position, in much the same way that the package on offer, the number of people reporting to you, and the development opportunities would do in Anglo-Saxon countries.

Job applications

French advertisements generally close with a request for, *'lettre manuscrite, CV, photo'*. Closer examination of these artifacts is also revealing. US readers may be shocked by the fact that a photo is often requested. For US employers this would merely lay the company open to accusations of discrimination. But French employers have few such qualms, and legal pursuits on the grounds of discrimination are rare. By the same token, French CVs typically open with the personal situation of the candidate: nationality, age, sex, number of children – details considered irrelevant in the US. The content and format of the CV provide further clues. The example shown in Figure 4.2 is fairly standard.

The most striking feature of the French CV is its brevity. Perhaps French job searchers are discouraged from 'stretching out' their CVs by the need to come across as focused – a concise CV being proof of one's *'esprit de synthèse'* ('ability to synthesize').

Certainly by Anglo-Saxon standards, the contents are fairly dry and impersonal, stating qualifications, language skills and work experience but

Martin LEPELLETIER
Né le 15 mai 1972 (24 ans)
87, avenue Gambetta
75020 PARIS
Tél: 01 43 43 32 93 (répondeur)
Célibataire
Service militaire effectué.

FORMATION
1995   ESCP – Ecole Supérieure de Commerce de Paris
1992   Concours commun de la banque HEC
1990   Bac S, mention Bien

LANGUES
Anglais: lu, parlé, écrit
Allemand: bonnes notions

EXPERIENCE PROFESSIONNELLE
1995/96   Service national dans la coopération: adjoint de l'attaché
d'ambassade, chargé du commerce international à Brasilia:
- Etudes de marchés (Jacobs Suchard, CCIP, CFCE)
- Participation aux séminaires de développement;
- Rédaction de trois mémoires pour l'OFCE et le CFCE.

1994   L'Oréal (Paris)
préparation d'un plan pour le lancement d'un produit. 3 mois

1993   Artouni Récré, fabricant de jouets (Paris)
assistance export, mise en place d'un nouveau système. 3 mois

1992   Chambre de commerce français (Londres)
études marketing sur le marché des jus de fruits en
Grande-Bretagne. 1 mois

DIVERS
Fréquents séjours en Angleterre
Bonne pratique de WORD, EXCEL et POWERPOINT
Sports pratiqués : ski, golf, tennis.

Figure 4.2: Example of a French CV (compiled from several CVs to which we have had access)

dispensing with details of travel experiences or involvement in social, charitable or sporting activities. Such activities are of lesser interest to French employers. Compared to Anglo-Saxon employers, they are less concerned with 'the whole person'. What they want is someone with an extra 15 points on the IQ scale.

The importance of brains over 'character' is echoed in the style of the CV. Where British candidates strive to show their drive and motivation, French candidates are content to 'state the facts' in a low-key way. They use the passive voice, not the first person as in Anglo-Saxon CVs. For example, the sample CV in Figure 4.2 reads, '*études marketing sur le marché . . .*', where a British candidate might have written, 'undertook market research . . .', which suggests a far more pro-active approach. In France, there is less onus on recent graduates to prove their initiative and ambition. The rigour of their educational experience generally speaks for them – indeed this may explain why French CVs make no mention of referees. The qualification itself is a sufficient gauge of credibility.

The importance of the qualification is clear from the sequence of the CV, which starts with the education section and, by reversing the chronology, manages to place the most impressive qualification up front. Candidates can give even more prominence to their qualifications, as suggested by *Rebondir* (November 1996, 127). It advises recent graduates to broadcast their qualification and specialization in the heading. So where Anglo-Saxons might state their career objective, French candidates would write: '*ESSEC, promotion 1991 – Spécialisé en commerce international*' ('ESSEC, graduated 1991 – Majored in international business').

It is exceedingly rare, in France, for candidates to opt for anything other than a chronological presentation. Reworking their experiences either by function (personnel, management, training, sales) or else by theme (grouping similar competences acquired in different jobs) would not be considered interesting; it would merely raise suspicion. French recruiters are particularly attentive to gaps and non-sequitors in a candidate's personal history. Time spent travelling abroad will have to be justified, and is less likely to be interpreted favourably than it would in Britain or the US. A chronological CV emphasizes the candidate's itinerary, and the logical progress through various checkpoints. This says more about a candidate's reliability and commitment than can be inferred from character traits or behaviour.

As regards the covering letter, the same kind of themes emerge. Again the style is more understated and deferential than is the norm in Anglo-Saxon countries. According to Tixier (1987, 63), candidates tend to refrain from using action-oriented verbs, such as 'organizing', 'leading', 'deciding', much less 'spearheading' or 'driving'. Instead they opt for verbs which are passive in their form or meaning: '*être embauché comme*' ('to be placed as'), '*chercher un emploi de*' ('to seek employment as'), '*collaborer, aider*' ('to be involved, to assist'). Getting employed in France is less about presenting oneself as action-oriented.[2]

The fact that a handwritten covering letter is often requested implies that it will probably be subjected to the scrutiny of a graphologist. Recourse to handwriting analysts is surprisingly commonplace in France. Several major companies including Cap Gemini Sogeti, Le GAN, La Redoute or Sony France readily admit to using it, but others prefer to say nothing. One consultant claims that only one or two of the French top hundred companies do not use the services of graphologists, and his comments are supported by the fact that over 500 certified graphologists work exclusively for recruiters. (*Capital*, November 1993, 120).

Ostensibly this contradicts what we have said so far about the lesser interest in personal characteristics as recruitment criteria. Yet, French companies *do* need to have insight into the personality of the candidate and to assess his or her fit with the company.

Irrespective of the merits of graphology, where this practice differs significantly from Anglo-Saxon recruitment procedures, is that the resulting analysis is not discussable. It is not a joint conversation regarding the significance of past choices and activities. It is a third party's interpretation of the person's personality which the candidate cannot defend. As the recruitment manager of Sony France puts it, '*L'avis du graphologue nous permet de valider nos impressions sur un cadre*' ('The graphologist's opinion allows us to validate our impressions on a manager') (*Capital*, November 1993, 120). It also paves the way for justifying the recruitment of a favoured candidate over similarly qualified others.

Even selected candidates will not get to see what was written about them. Their assessments will be slipped into their confidential file for the exclusive use of the company. As one American manager working in France recalls, 'Employees who request copies of their analysis are usually refused access or else made to jump through legal hoops to get at it' (Johnson, 1996, 77).

The spectre of education

The allusions we have already made to the importance of qualifications as a recruitment criterion are confirmed by a senior German manager, working in France, who observes: '*C'est la première question qu'on vous pose dans un entretien*' (It's the very first question you'll be asked in an interview) (*Le Nouvel Economiste*, 2/2/96, 44).

Having gained admission to the managerial corps or *encadrement* one would expect that educational credentials would be eclipsed as a criterion for further promotion. Ostensibly that is the case, with one corporate recruiter telling us: '*Franchi le cap du démarrage, le rôle du diplôme tombe vite à zéro*' ('Having cleared the first hurdle, the power of the diploma soon disappears').

Many of the *cadres* interviewed corroborated that idea, the general consensus being that a prestigious qualification cannot be relied upon for more than about three years. That is true insofar as the mileage derived from the qualification *per se* is concerned.[3] But there are numerous indications that qualifications have a lingering influence.

To start with, one's educational background will be of considerable interest to one's new work colleagues. When a French manager asks, '*Qu'est-ce qu'il a fait?*' ('What has he done?') or '*D'où elle sort?*' ('Where has she come from?') – the question is not about what jobs they have done or what company they were with, but what degrees and where from. One Spanish manager is astounded at the curiosity elicited by the topic of education:

> *Ici, même en privé, on vous demande toujours quelle école vous avait faite. Et si vous êtes X ou énarque, votre vie est toute tracée dès 25 ans.* (Here, even outside the work setting, people want to know what school you graduated from. And if you happen to be a *polytechnicien*[4] or an *énarque*, your life is mapped out from the age of 25.) (*Le Nouvel Economiste*, 2/2/96, 44)

Such questions are not just idle curiosity. One's academic pedigree determines how colleagues position you and relate to you. Are you to be considered a rival, an ally or insignificant? Should they be nice to you because you might end up as their boss one day? Should they co-operate with you because you have heavyweight sponsors (possibly from the same school) higher up the organization? And this questioning accompanies every transfer, promotion and new job, throughout one's career.

Respect for qualifications can be further gauged by scanning the high-level career switches reported in the press. A look at the weekly *L'Usine Nouvelle* or the financial daily *La Tribune des Fossées* is especially revealing. When reporting on a new appointment, diplomas gained several decades past feature prominently in the sequence. The fact that these are mentioned at all might surprise Anglo-Saxons; the fact they are placed ahead of the executive's penultimate position, even more so. For example:

> *Vincent Maurel, 48 ans, ancien élève de l'Ecole Polytechnique, diplômé de l'ENST, est nommé directeur général du groupe centrales énergétiques. Il*

reste PDG de GEC-Alsthom Electromécanique SA. (Vincent Maurel, 48, graduate of l'Ecole Polytechnique and of L'Ecole Nationale Supérieure des Télécommunications, is named director general of the energy generators group. He remains CEO of GEC-Alsthom Electro-mécanique SA.) (*L'Usine Nouvelle*, 31/10/96, 20)

The blue-chip company to which the new appointee also happens to belong is almost included as an afterthought. In France, people are measured primarily by their intellectual achievements – even if they date back 20 years – rather than their most recent job. An almost perverse example of this is Jacques Maisonrouge who retired as head of IBM World Trade Corporation in 1984 and went on to become a Minister of Industry. Yet in his autobiography, entitled *Manager International*, something clearly bothers him. Several times he mentions that he 'only' went to Centrale. His considerable achievements can never quite erase the fact that he never made it to Polytechnique at the age of 20. The comments of the French politician and writer, Alain Peyrefitte, two decades ago, still ring true:[5]

> *Il n'y a sans doute pas de pays au monde où les diplômes soient mieux respectés, leur validité aussi persistante.* (I cannot think of any country in the world where qualifications have greater power or longevity.) (1976, 320)

Part of that power comes from the influence of alumni networks. In many schools the durability of school links is institutionalized. At l'Ecole Polytechnique, for instance, all graduates high and low call each other *camarade* whether they have met before or not, and the lowliest X *(polytechnicien)* can write out of the blue to a high-placed colleague and be sure of help and sympathy. Having such an extensive network of contacts from the very start of one's active life is an immeasurable advantage.

A similar situation exists at l'Ecole des Arts et Métiers, which reputedly has the most efficient old-boy association to which graduates are automatically affiliated. Members receive regular journals and newsletters on salaries or career paths to supplement the annual directory listing alumni by name, region and company. One consultant in the interview sample admitted that before visiting any company he would check the association directory for a fellow 'Gadzarts'[6] in that firm to fill him in on the prevailing situation. One production manager from the observation sample even confessed to having illicitly invited a colleague from a rival firm into the plant to show him how to solve a recurrent production problem. The graduates' freemasonry can clearly transcend corporate allegiances.

The purpose of alumni associations is basically three-fold: to promote the school's reputation, to help out in the search for a first job, and to facilitate mobility. Each association therefore runs a careers service which offers jobs to new graduates and restless alumni alike. More impressive still are the efforts made when alumni fall on hard times. The association will pull out all the stops to find a job for (*recaser*) an unemployed member.[7]

Likewise when it comes to promoting the school's name the associations can prove very helpful. For instance, the INSA (Institut National des Sciences Appliquées) association put pressure on the French electricity corporation (EDF) so that the company would recognize in its recruitment salaries the fact that the school had lengthened its curriculum to five years. Similarly, the Arts et Métiers association managed to persuade the French railways (SNCF) to open up certain posts previously reserved to the highest rated schools.

Bereft of these close-knit ties, 'mere' university graduates find it difficult to infiltrate the higher reaches of business. Their lack of business contacts works against them when they seek industrial placements which means they fail to gain an initial foothold. Thereafter, their absence from positions of authority in the more traditional companies becomes pathological. In contrast to this, the 'gadzarts', say, are renowned for their stranglehold over the automobile industry. As the head of one university explained to us:

> *Souvent, dans les grandes entreprises, les mafias d'anciens des écoles sont pour nous un mur infranchissable.* (The old-boy networks in the large companies often represent an insurmountable obstacle for us.)

It would be simplistic to suggest that *grande école* graduates simply free-wheel to power. Our aim here was rather to establish education as the cornerstone of one's career. The rest of this chapter will consider how this start-up capital is carefully invested and leveraged.

Career strategy: where to start

The question of which functions, companies or sectors to target is partly answered by the previous section. *Grande école* graduates head where they find helpful contacts willing to guide them – or simply, where their schools are most heavily represented in the organizational charts. These companies are well known. For example, *Le Nouvel Economiste* (21/3/96) presents the recruitment strategies of 38 major industrial firms in France, separately highlighting the commercial and engineering schools they tend to target. So we learn that if you went to Sciences-Po, a well-known feeder into l'ENA (the civil service school) you will be particularly appreciated at Renault and Schlumberger. Or again, if you went to l'Ecole Centrale, you can apply to l'Air Liquide or Michelin, but perhaps not Elf, where *polytechniciens* rule the roost.

Different companies offer different salaries, different career tracks and different responsibilities. Some promote on seniority, others on profits recorded. Ambitious young graduates therefore have to pick their way through a complex field of profferred opportunities – which sector, which function, and is a foreign subsidiary better than a French company? Yet one question which seldom arises is whether to opt for a large corporation or to chance their hand in a smaller company where they may be given wider responsibilities.

Essentially, those who *can* will always opt for the safety of the large company for the simple reason that it is status enhancing, opens more doors, and provides greater opportunities to exercise the skills learned at the *grande école*: the ability to engage in analytical discussion, to write succinct and probing reports, to make thoughtful presentations, exploit networks and so forth.

The prospect of joining a small company, on the other hand, brings with it numerous disadvantages: primarily, because the notion of risk-taking does not correspond to the educational experience of *grande école* graduates. They have followed a course charted by others, and succeeded by conforming, albeit brilliantly, not by taking initiatives. As one cynic put it to us:

> *Ne réussissent que les élèves un peu placides, tenaces, avec un seul objectif: obtenir le diplôme. Les grandes écoles forment des gens doués d'une formidable force de travail et de concentration, mais peu préparés à prendre des risques.* (Those who succeed are generally calm, tenacious and focused on obtaining a degree. The *grandes écoles* produce individuals with a tremendous work rate and concentration, but ill-prepared to take risks.)

Moreover, *grande école* graduates are aware that joining a small company is virtually an irreversible move. One HR manager interviewed, explained that opting out of the race for top positions in major corporations is tantamount to admitting that one is not cut out to work in an overtly structured and competitive environment. And it is not just a matter of mentality, but also one of geography. Small- and medium-sized companies are associated with the provinces, and therefore imply isolation from influential networks. Of the large French companies, only Michelin is headquartered outside Paris. As the partner of a consulting firm explained to us: '*Dans un pays centralisé comme le nôtre, il ne faut pas rester trop longtemps en province*' ('In a country as centralized as France, you shouldn't stay too long in the provinces'). The theme is echoed by Johnson:

> A career minded French person has few options but to make a go of it in Paris. If the job goes sour, often there is no alternative but to put up with a sour life. Relocation to Bordeaux, Lille, Metz or Marseilles is seen as professional withdrawal or plain failure. (Johnson, 1996, 18)

Of course, not all large companies have the same appeal. First, there is the question of which sector to target. The most prestigious sectors have traditionally been those responsible for driving France's technological progress; sectors with a high capital intensity and long-term perspectives in which the problems of manufacture are secondary to those of conception, such as aerospace, nuclear energy, telecommunications, and electronics. Social prestige (*noblesse*) is an important notion in French industry.

Companies which service mass markets, such as Carrefour (retailing) or Accor (hotels and leisure), may be highly successful but they do not tend to attract the highest qualified graduates – partly because these companies generally demand a field apprenticeship and contact with ordinary customers (as opposed to industrial clients), which is considered demeaning.[8] Similarly, in the food or textile industries important groups such as Danone, Damart and Dim struggle to overcome the perceived lack of 'nobility' of their products.

There are signs of change with sectors like broadcasting, multimedia, advertising, fashion, entertainment and luxury goods – long dismissed by France's technocratic managers – generating their own elites. But for many *grande école* generalists *what* the company makes remains more important than *how much* it makes.

A similar ethos manifests itself at functional level where the perceived nobility of an activity, its interest and its variety often outweigh remuneration factors. Conception functions, which are cerebral rather than operational, have higher status than execution functions. The prestige of a function corresponds closely to its 'immateriality'. In engineering, electronics has a higher element of abstraction and therefore of purity and nobility, which places it above electrical engineering with its high currents, and way ahead of mechanical engineering, which requires brute force! The same goes for other functions. Hence finance, which deals exclusively with figures, carries more kudos than purchasing which deals with tangible bought-in components; corporate communications, which produces words, is more esteemed than manufacturing which produces things; and marketing which sells 'concepts', is more prestigious than sales which shifts produce. The point is reinforced by Boltanski:

The highest positions are those in which one need not be aware of labour, labourers, or production but only of such abstractions as commodity and cash flows, high technology processes, and investments. (1987, 249, English trans.)

British readers might justifiably question whether France is any different from the UK in this respect. After all, the view of production as low status and finance as high status is not exclusive to France. This is true, but we may posit that different causes lie behind the same reality. What is valued in France is abstractness as a concomitant of intellectuality. Thus, finance has high standing because it is associated with maths and strategic choices while production is a victim of its perceived lack of intellectual challenge, requiring resourcefulness (*débrouillardise*) rather than cleverness. In Britain, on the other hand, a similar pecking order has a very different basis. The pecking order is determined by traditional anti-industrialism. It follows that the most prototypical industrial functions such as production, evoking the 'dark satanic mills' of the industrial North, are devalued. And at the other end of the spectrum, functions like finance, with their professional affiliations, are high prestige.

Grandes écoles graduates also tend to be wary of joining foreign multinationals where they know their qualifications will count for less. But they also know that a spell with a foreign multinational may be valued by French companies later, particularly in those domains where French companies lack strength. For example, companies such as Unilever, Procter and Gamble, Xerox, and Mars are particularly strong on commercial functions (sales, marketing) and HR functions (recruitment, training, compensation and benefits management). Similarly the major foreign consultancy firms are considered ideal springboards for acquiring the coveted 'generalist' label without having to manoeuvre between functions.

Getting ahead

One of the first priorities for management trainees, especially if they are engineers, is to establish their generalist credentials. French managers we interviewed explained that an engineering education is highly valued, but that one must quickly develop a general management perspective. Someone who stays too long in a specialist function is likely to become typecast as an 'expert' or worse still a 'technician'. As one engineer explained to us:

Si vous restez à la fabrication trop longtemps, on vous enferme dans un ghetto. Aucune chance de faire partie un jour de l'état-major de l'entreprise. (If you stay too long in production, you get locked in to a ghetto and you can wave goodbye to your chances of ever reaching the higher echelons of the company.)

Mostly, human resource managers will attend automatically to the needs and expectations of their *grande école* recruits. The latter will be rotated through various functions and given challenging assignments, sometimes in other countries. It is considered natural that they should receive privileged career advancements simply on the strength of their entry credentials. The quasi-automatic distinction made between their careers and those of others is noted by the HR director of a bank:

Les dipômés de grandes écoles de niveau 1 évoluent très vite vers des postes de chefs de projets et de responsables d'application, puis quittent l'informatique pour des postes de responsabilité dans les métiers de la banque . . . tandis que les ingénieurs spécialisés travailleront à la production et à l'exploitation des systèmes de l'entreprise. (The graduates of the top *grandes écoles* quickly move on to positions as team leaders and project managers, then leave IT for managerial positions in the bank's various activities . . . whereas the specialist engineers work on the company's design and implementation systems.) (*01 Informatique*, 24/5/96, 67)

How one performs in these various assignments is important, but it is almost exclusively from this restricted population that the future *dirigeants* are drawn.[9] The capabilities of the management recruits are assessed and those earmarked as high potentials are placed on carefully prescribed career paths destined for top management.

A study by Derr and Laurent (1987) on what it takes to get ahead in different countries confirms the distinctiveness of the French model. For American managers, the single most important criterion for career success is considered to be 'ambition and drive'. The French managers see things quite differently. For them, the single most important determinant is 'being labelled as having high potential'. Those who fail to gain this label early on need to revise their career expectations or else change firms.

From this point on, those identified as fast trackers enjoy an informal apprenticeship system that gives them a relatively secure setting in which to acquire the necessary leadership skills. They are given training missions, encouraged to visit plants in the provinces or abroad, often working as personal assistant (*attaché de direction*) to a senior manager. At l'Air Liquide, for instance, brilliant young managers are given strategic observation assignments by the PDG himself. This guarantees high visibility, gives them privileged insights into the workings of the group, and establishes contacts in other units.

Educational capital is thereby converted into more orthodox career capital in the form of broad experience. This skilful conversion strategy enables the holder to cast aside the crutch of education and point to an 'authentic' track record.

In the next sections, we will consider to what extent mobility, training and performance can upset this established order.

Mobility

There are various forms of mobility – across functions within a company, across companies, across sectors and across nations – and French attitudes towards these typically differ from British or American ones.

For example, it is widely accepted in Anglo-Saxon companies that once a job is mastered, managers need a change of scenery to avoid stagnation. That is not necessarily the case in France. Consider the view of the HR director of the luxury group, LVMH:

> *Si un cadre reste au même poste pendant dix ans, ses fonctions deviendrons plus intéressantes au fil du temps.* (If a manager stays in the same job for ten years, the functions will become more interesting as time goes by.) (*Challenges*, November 1995, 56)

This comment seems to be confirmed by an APEC survey[10] which shows that more than 50 per cent of French managers aged between 35 and 49 are in the same post as they were five years ago. Such figures may seem surprising to Anglo-Saxon managers who, if they have reached a plateau, are accustomed to frequent rotations simply to stimulate them and 'keep life interesting'. This reflects the different view of managerial motivation and performance which prevails in France. Effectiveness is perhaps less a question of providing fresh challenges than one of establishing contacts and developing trust.

Similar patterns are visible in terms of mobility between companies or sectors. Americans generally regard such mobility as a proof of ambition, drive and readiness to adapt – and a slightly diluted version of that ethos tends to prevail in Britain. The French, on the other hand, stress the positive aspects of stability – loyalty, esprit de corps and particularly trust which, as we discuss in Chapter 5, takes longer to build up in France. The difference in attitude is captured by Betrand Collomb, head of the Lafarge group, the world's second largest cement producer:

> In the US cement industry people move around. If you need a plant manager, you hire him from the competitor next door. So you're not encouraged to develop your own people. In France, it was – and still is – in bad taste for an executive to leave one cement producer to go to another. You just would not hire the guy. (Thulliez, 1989, 30)

An American manager with the same company observes:

> *En France, vous dites 'chez Lafarge' un peu comme on dit 'à la maison' . . . L'idée que vous pouvez passer toute votre vie chez le même employeur est encore vivace ici.* (In France, you say 'at Lafarge' a bit like you might say 'at home'. The idea that you could spend your career with the same employer is still conceivable here.) (*Le Nouvel Economiste*, 2/2/96, 43)

The tie with the company is stronger. Traditionally, in France, the psychological contract has been based on the idea of employer protection in exchange for employee loyalty, rather than rewards in exchange for performance. Notwithstanding this French peculiarity, there are clearly different norms between sectors and companies.

The perception of executive mobility in France is largely dependent upon the prevailing norms within the sector or company. Personal mobility may be interpreted unfavourably in sectors such as heavy industry, banking or nationalized companies. On the other hand, it is generally viewed positively by PR firms, consultancy, IT, 'Americanized' companies and, generally speaking, in the sales function. Whilst this pattern of behaviour is similar to that in Britain, there is perhaps an underlying difference between the countries. The UK attitude, coloured by American views, is favourable in principle to mobility. In France, on the other hand, there is a more ambiguous attitude.

Mobility is not automatically regarded as a sign of professional success and ambition. It will often be construed as a sign of restlessness or even unreliability, possibly the result of successive failures, as suggested by the rather disparaging reference of one headhunter interviewed to *'les papillons aux CV tourbillonants'* ('butterflies with whirlwind CVs'). Bright young graduates are warned not to respond too readily to the offers of headhunters since they may get a reputation for instability. For example, one manager in his 40s with a wealth of experience in ten companies, returned to France only to find himself 'unemployable' in French companies (despite graduating from a business school):

> *Je trouve de plus en plus difficilement, et seulement dans des entreprises étrangères qui ont des difficultés à s'implanter en France.* (I find fewer and fewer opportunities and only in foreign companies which are having difficulty establishing themselves in France.) (*Le Point*, 28/9/96, 81)

Even where mobility is known to be motivated by ambition rather than 'flightiness', it may be regarded negatively. For instance, the career-minded financial director at one large company visited was described to us as '*un escargot*' ('a snail'). The implication was that he had 'no fixed abode' which made him slightly suspect and placed a question mark over his corporate loyalty.

Of course, the recruiter's interpretation of mobility also depends on the age of the candidate. Early on in a career, playing the field will probably be viewed positively, particularly since a young *cadre* may be anxious to shed the new graduate image by changing companies. However, later on (after 35), mobility is likely to be frowned upon.

Few of the middle managers interviewed envisaged a change of company (or even function) as part of their career strategy – an impression confirmed by a survey in *L'Expansion* (25/1/96, 39) which showed that only 25 per cent of the managers interviewed anticipated having to change companies more often in future. Mobility tended to be regarded as a last resort, when there was no other way out, rather than a positive means of gaining promotion or greater responsibility. They seemed unwilling to take a risk and relinquish the protection afforded by length of service in a company. It is not uncommon for *cadres* to pass up salary or promotion opportunities which demand mobility.

There is a paradox here which is worth exploring. Countries which favour generalism in management usually favour manager mobility as well: the US is the obvious example, and these American norms are reflected in Britain. France, on the other hand, is unusual in favouring generalism, but not on the whole favouring mobility. Other countries which, like France, are negatively oriented to mobility – Germany, for example, and to a lesser extent the Netherlands and Scandinavia – tend to have a more specialist view of management, expecting individual entrants to be qualified to work in a particular function or department, and either to make their whole career in this function, or to rise to general management on the basis of experience in a single function.

The answer to this French enigma lies in dual norms regarding mobility. The tendency to stay put, described so far, is generally associated with lesser qualified managers, including university graduates. For this population, mobility is something which tends to be imposed rather than chosen. Without a prestigious qualification to certify their value to prospective employers, their chances on the job market are severely reduced. That is particularly the case of those who have climbed up through the ranks (*autodidactes*), for whom changing company would entail loss of responsibility, salary and status. The fate of the *autodidacte* is basically tied in with his/her employer's and promotion relies on the firm's growth. This is in stark contrast with the US or Britain where the self-taught individual would first get credit for having done the job, and second, be less disadvantaged in a culture that is not so self-consciously intellectual.

Quite a different mobility norm applies to the *grande école* graduates whose label and contacts allow them to roam more freely in the job market. Again we see the ubiquitous effect of qualifications which enable their holders to multiply experiences in different companies. The net result is that their breadth of experience outstrips anything other *cadres* of their age could hope to have accumulated. Subsequently, this provides justifiable grounds for discrimination when they apply for more senior positions, as confirmed by a report in *Le Point* (5/10/87, 54) which cites a diversified career as a common trait among French directors. The widespread immobility at middle management level ends up legitimizing the access to power of the few who are mobile. So, whilst French managers cannot make a career out of mobility alone, mobility can assume the role of distinctive competence which justifies a senior position.

We should also draw attention to a peculiarly French form of mobility, at least in comparison to Anglo-Saxon norms; the mid-career transfers from the public to the private sector, known as *pantouflage*. In France, added value may be obtained from entering public service and using one's privileged knowledge of its workings as a springboard for a second career in industry. It is a sign of their relatively smooth transition that the extent of the phenomenon is so little known. The irrigation of the business elite by civil servants is eased by the social and educational proximity of the two groups. The French tend to regard it as professional mobility rather than sectoral transition.[11]

The most sought-after civil servants are the members of the *grands corps*,[12] known as *corpsards*. These are brilliant generalists *par excellence* and represent a tiny pool from which the major French companies are eager to recruit their leaders (see Chapter 7). What they have to offer, besides outstanding intellect, is a wealth of experience, early exposure to responsibilities, and a pivotal position in the networks of political, administrative and industrial power.[13] When asked why he recruits from the ministerial cabinets, the CEO of Banque Lazard explains: '*Parce qu'aucune autre fonction ne permet d'accéder aussi jeune à des responsabilités aussi importantes*' ('Because no other job gives young people such early access to such heavy responsibilities') (*L'Expansion*, 7/12/95, 98).

Actually, the headline-grabbing instances of *pantouflage* associated with nationalized or recently privatized companies and changes of government are only the tip of the iceberg. Beneath the surface there is a steady migration from the public sector to the private sector. Ex-civil servants have numerous trumps to play with a prospective employer. They possess intimate knowledge of the rules and regulations. They have colleagues in high places and can facilitate dialogue with those who administer and even if they cannot play on personal contacts, they are familiar with the way political and governmental networks operate; they know how to lobby and, having themselves been on the receiving end, know when and where to apply pressure. What is more, their high-level training permits a rapid grasp of complex problems. In the French context, then, largely as a result of the historical involvement of the state in company affairs, ex-civil servants clearly have something to offer most employers.

Training and development

Besides mobility, another way of giving one's career added momentum is to retrain or develop additional competencies. Here again one witnesses a difference between French and Anglo-Saxon attitudes. Consider, for instance, the comments of a French manager with Apple Europe, overwhelmed by the profusion of training possibilities on offer.

> It's help yourself time. It's self-help taken to the ultimate. But unless someone tells me that I'm going to be a good marketeer or sales guy or finance man by going on this or that course, I don't know which to go on. (Evans, 1986, 24)

Apple's approach is in tune with the American belief in self-improvement – nothing is predetermined at birth and it is never too late to change. So managers are expected to assess their own training needs and seek out training opportunities. This proactive approach has tended to rub off on Britain, but in France employees are less accustomed to taking responsibility for their own development. As a spokesman for the management employment agency (APEC) put it: '*Beaucoup de cadres qui sont à la recherche d'un emploi ont été des acteurs passifs de leur histoire professionnelle*' ('Many of the executives who are now unemployed simply failed to take their own careers in hand') (*Le Point*, 28/9/96, 79).

There may be an explanation for this apparent difference in personal initiative. Anglo-Saxon managers have for some time been encouraged to develop a portfolio of skills that will enhance their 'employability'. Individuals respond because they understand that they cannot expect to remain in the same job, function or even company for long. The psychological contract between employer and employee, especially in the US, is essentially a transaction in which each party preserves their exit rights. As mentioned previously, this has not generally been the case in France where a 'moral' contract has prevailed based on long-term employment in exchange for loyalty; and where career progress was more predictable, based essentially on educational credentials. While downsizing and restructuring activities have weakened this 'moral contract', many of the underlying assumptions remain embedded – and the notion of *un parcours professionnel* (where one accumulates competencies) as opposed to *une carrière* (where one chalks up seniority) is only just starting to gain currency.

It follows that many French managers still rely on the company to 'tell them' what it needs from them. They are more accustomed to a top-down system of training, with the company (line or HR manager) conventionally nominating people to go on courses. Indeed that top-down system extends beyond the company, since companies are compelled by law (since 1971) to devote just over one per cent of their total wage bill to training.[14] Setting compulsory spending levels underlined state enthusiasm for training, as well as providing annual statements of progress and a database to fuel the long-term thinking of government, corporations and educational institutions. However, creating a legal requirement to spend was hardly a declaration of faith *vis-à-vis* the companies, since it implied that they would not undertake training on a voluntary basis.

Another explanation for the lack of personal initiative among managers in terms of training, has to do with the anticipated pay-off. *Cadres* who do upgrade their skills by attending management training courses, know that such efforts will have little impact on their career progress. In France, no label earned at post-entry level will really make up for 'inadequacies' in pre-entry education. Even the most prestigious establishments for senior executives such as the INSEAD, ISA, CEDEP, CPA, ISSEC or CRC will only partly compensate a 'second-rate' education. As the head of the CEREQ[15] (national agency which monitors qualifications) puts it:

> *Les diplômes restent la monnaie forte sur le marché du travail, par rapport aux certificats de qualification professionnelle, trop souvent assimilés à une monnaie faible.* (Compared to professional training qualifications, too

often regarded as a weak currency, educational qualifications remain very much the strong currency in the job market.) (*Le Monde*, 20/11/96, 2)

This is not an indictment of the pedagogy of these executive development establishments but is a sign of the deference accorded to the top *grandes écoles*. Those who emerge from these schools are considered *formés à vie* (trained for life). By virtue of the intellectual qualities brought out in them, they are deemed capable of confronting any problem. Their polyvalence does not stem from the lifelong acquisition of new management skills and techniques, but the fact that they are 'intellectually finished products'.

It follows that, for high flyers, being sent on external seminars is probably less valued for what they may learn, than for its symbolic aspect. As we mentioned earlier, French managers consider it essential to be identified early as having high potential, and being sent on a costly training course is a clear signal. That such courses often serve more to confirm managerial potential than to develop it, is hinted by two ambitious managers who described one prestigious course as:

Un événement professionnel. (A professional watershed.)

Un peu répétitif mais très valorisant. (A little repetitive but a great personal endorsement.)

The distinctive view of training which prevails among French executives is confirmed by executive instructors who teach both Anglo-Saxon and French groups. Talking with a number of instructors, a common complaint is that groups of French executives often have a higher threshold of resistance to management education. They are described as 'more cynical', 'less willing to play the game', 'slower to buy-in' and 'unwilling to make the necessary leap of faith'. Practically, this resistance manifests itself in a tendency to question the process of learning, rather than the actual content, to raise 'philosophical' objections which prevent the development of a fruitful discussion, or simply to dismiss the premises as 'too American'.

Based on some of our previous observations, we can perhaps advance an explanation for this behaviour. It has to do with the 'confessional' nature of much executive education. The process often involves accepting one's weaknesses or biases as a preliminary to developing a different outlook. For French managers, whose authority is based on superior intellect, such self-revelation may be more threatening – particularly in the company of peers of different ranks. They enter the training situation knowing that it represents an implicit confirmation of their career prospects, and they do not expect to come out of the process in any way diminished. Where senior Anglo-Saxon managers might get credit from colleagues for 'leading by example' or having the 'character' to own up to faults, French managers are more conscious of the risk of exposing contradictions in their thinking or actions – and thus undermining their authority. The potential loss of face is therefore greater in France.

What is more, French managers are conscious that the *real* training does not happen inside the classroom. Formal training is largely irrelevant, reserved primarily for the lower echelons. The high flyers know that their development will be organized by rotating them through various activities and will be guided by a mentor who will help them make contacts and oversee their leap from specialist to general management. As noted by Derr in his cross-cultural comparison of management development systems: 'The French give the impression that they value external executive education the least among the national groups' (1987, 76).

Performance and aspirations

In terms of career influences, the constant counterweight to education is, of course, job performance. Any managerial selection system involves an implicit trade-off between performance in professional life and performance prior to entry (as measured by qualifications). As readers may suspect from our description so far, French companies differ considerably from Anglo-Saxon ones in their chosen point of equilibrium.

Talking with French HR managers reveals what, by Anglo-Saxon standards, is a lower emphasis on performance in strict terms of measurable output. This can be seen in the pay systems where the seniority bonus often outweighs the performance bonus. Salary surveys show that the proportion of variable compensation remains small in France – shockingly so, by American standards. For example, a study by l'Insee in 1994 showed that the average performance bonus for individual French managers, amounted to 1.4 per cent of their gross pay – and that only three *cadres* out of ten receive an increase exclusively based on performance (*L'Essentiel du Management*, November 1996, 85).

Or again, consider the sales and marketing function, traditionally associated with results-based compensation. The fixed portion in France, for a director of marketing and sales, amounts to 91 per cent of salary, as against 86 per cent in Italy, 81 per cent in Germany and 78 per cent in Britain (MOCI, 21/12/95, 83). And this tendency is confirmed by a salary survey of senior managers in France which shows, for example, that: the variable component for plant managers is 8 per cent of total salary, for export directors 8 per cent, for finance directors 4.5 per cent, for technical directors 4 per cent, and for quality directors and communication directors only 2 per cent (*L'Essentiel du Management*, November 1996).

This resistance to performance-related pay has several explanations. First, it can be attributed to a low cultural tolerance for uncertainty, noted in Chapter 1. Second, it is a function of the French approach to management control. While the focus of Anglo-Saxon companies tends to be drawn to output controls – making sure that people deliver on budgets, deadlines and objectives – French companies focus more on input controls – making sure that they select the brightest individuals and give them the necessary opportunities to develop the overview they need to make the 'right' decisions. A third explanation stems from the belief that the real value of a manager – incorporating intellect, loyalty, and integrity – cannot be objectively measured.

This last point perhaps explains why the French often regard the appraisal process either with distrust or else as an insult. According to one French manager: 'The French get offended by positive or negative feedback. If you question my job, you are questioning my honour, my value, my very being' (Orleman, 1992). For Anglo-Saxons, feedback is considered to provide information on how they are doing. In France it is more likely to be experienced as a commentary on who they are. This may account for the fact that only 38 per cent of *cadres*, according to a survey of managers belonging to the CFDT union, have an annual appraisal interview with their immediate boss (*L'Essentiel du Management*, November 1996, 86).

The lesser importance of quantifiable performance is confirmed by a cross-country comparison, mentioned earlier (Derr and Laurent, 1987). Looking at the perceived determinants of success, the researchers found that 'achieving results' was considered critical by 88 per cent of American managers. On the other hand, only 52 per cent of French managers placed it in the top 20 determinants of success. Or again, 81 per cent of Americans selected self-confidence while only 42 per cent of the French did; and 73 per cent of Britons and 71 per cent of Americans selected job visibility and exposure, while only 38 per cent of the French did.

What do these findings tell us? They reinforce the view that for French managers things are largely played out in advance. Those earmarked for success have to worry less about selling themselves, looking good, image management, or getting noticed. They can focus more on making the right long-term decisions for the business. That is the up-side. The down-side is that those disadvantaged by lack of education at the start are very unlikely to make up for lost ground. A disillusioned American manager working for a French group observed: 'Becoming a *cadre* through hard work alone does not seem to be part of the system – or if it is, it is highy unusual' (Coale, 1994, 57).

This observation is confirmed by the striking absence of *autodidactes* (self-starters) in French corporate boardrooms. As one *cadre* puts it:

> *A quelques exceptions près, les autodidactes n'ont guère de chance – sauf dans les PME, par nature plus souples et plus innovantes.* (Self-taught individuals have very few opportunities – except in small and medium-sized companies, which tend to be more flexible and innovative.) (*Le Point*, 28/9/96, 79)

In short, the chances of becoming an 'unqualified success', at least within a large company, are virtually inexistent.

There are some signs of change. For example, l'Oréal caused something of a stir in the business press when it announced that it would be paying particular attention to the applications of *autodidactes* (*Le Monde*, 15/3/95, 2). Andersen Consulting also hit the headlines when it decided to allocate 75 posts in 1996 to university (as opposed to *grande école*) graduates with the aim of diversifying its recruitment (*Le Nouvel Economiste*, 21/3/96, 3). But the disproportionate coverage accorded to these initiatives merely confirms their exceptional nature. The real trend in France is towards greater selectivity, not less. Posts previously open to *baccalauréat* holders are now reserved for people with two years higher education, typically from an institute of advanced technology (IUT). And for posts previously filled by people with *bac+2*, companies are increasingly demanding *bac+4/5* (*L'Expansion*, 4/4/96, 63).

So, the 'intellectual discrimination' is not limited to *autodidactes*. A multitude of candidates are discouraged from applying for posts simply because they have 'inappropriate' qualifications. The discrimination becomes self-fulfilling, with individuals not applying for jobs formally open to them but, *de facto*, reserved for *grande école* graduates. They learn to tailor their expectations to organizational realities. As one French engineer explains:

> *Ici les carrières sont décidées par le diplôme. Un ingénieur maison n'ira pas plus loin que chef de secteur, les supélec deviennent chef de département et les X directeurs généraux.* (In my company careers depend on qualifications. A company engineer won't go further than head of sector, graduate engineers from the Ecole supérieure d'électricité become heads of department and *polytechniciens* become directors. (*L'Expansion*, 25/1/96, 44)

While the level of correlation in this firm is perhaps extreme, the French model is characterized by what Szarka (1992, 163) described as 'the tight coupling between specific tiers of the French educational system and career opportunities in management'. Managers know from the start of their careers that certain positions are simply inaccessible. Anecdotal evidence of this abounds. For example, there was the case of a senior executive with CCF who walked out of the company for the simple reason that – although the holder of an MBA and an HEC diploma – his career was blocked by the fact that he was not an *énarque* (*L'Expansion*, 7/12/95, 99) .

So, far from attenuating educational pecking orders, French companies accentuate them – to those who have, more is given. There are no real second chances. Inevitably, such an approach to management development means that some managerial careers are prematurely curtailed. Many of the French managers interviewed felt that their careers had been mapped out for them on the day they completed their higher education. They could foresee how their careers would unfold and where their *bâton de maréchal* (promotional ceiling) would be located, irrespective of their career aspirations. Performance matters, but mainly in determining how quickly individuals reach their allotted station.

This lack of career opportunities for middle managers is well known in France. There is much criticism of the fact that access to the corridors of power is on a one-shot basis. For those who miss the boat as adolescents, the chances of subsequent recovery are remote. Yet the system is tolerated because the criteria are unequivocal and known to all. And while a prestigious qualification is no longer a sufficient condition for career success, it remains, to a greater extent than in other countries, a necessary one.

Overview

From the preceding description of career influences, it is clear that education is the linchpin for French managers. Personal characteristics, such as interpersonal skills, resourcefulness, and drive are no doubt gaining importance, but they remain '*un critère de partage entre les diplômés*' ('a means of distinguishing between the highly qualified') (*Le Nouvel Economiste*, 21/3/96, 66). In other words, they intervene only as a second filter. A surfeit of energy and experience can never make up for a deficiency of formal education – at least, not in a large company.

After graduation, the development of French managers continues along inegalitarian lines. Those recruited on intellectual merit are then helped to trade in their qualifications for more legitimate career trumps such as wider experience and 'healthy' mobility. The playing field is not levelled. The educational high flyers simply become the organizational fast trackers.

French recruiters steadfastly maintain that the value of qualifications quickly evaporates. What remains, however, is an unassailable head-start and the acquisition of rapid and varied experiences which the qualification helps to procure. These factors supersede educational credentials as promotion criteria but serve to promote the same population. What is more, *grande école* graduates who find themselves unemployed or blocked in their careers can rely on alumni networks to help them find new opportunities. So the claim that diplomas count for nothing, after initial recruitment, is disingenuous to say the least.

Our aim here is not to criticize the French system but rather to consider its distinctiveness, not least in order to highlight the scope for choice in the realm of management development. The key feature of the French system is that it relies heavily on pre-experience education as an indicator of management potential. This allows the brightest prospects to be creamed off early and no doubt facilitates their apprenticeship to general management. Not surprisingly, France's top executives are reputedly the best educated in Europe. Moreover, the policy of using the *grandes écoles* to consitute pools of versatile talent obviously promotes mobility and facilitates dialogue between educational, business, financial and public sectors.

The flip side of the coin is, of course, that the system sidelines people at a very early age. Companies are blamed for rubber stamping a pecking order established by the educational system. Even if that ranking system is accurate, and even if it is meaningful for business – neither of which are proven – should it be irreversible? Without belittling the outstanding qualities of those promoted by the system, French companies run a risk in focusing on too like-minded a population. Uniformity of perspective can facilitate co-ordination, but it can also result in impoverished information search and reality testing, incomplete attention to alternatives, failure to consider risks, and premature agreement – collectively known as 'group think' (Janis, 1971).

More specifically perhaps, the distinctive management development system helps to account for two features of French management – one highlighted earlier in Chapter 2 and one to be discussed in the next chapter.

Back in Chapter 2, we referred to the longstanding malaise, often highlighted in the press, among middle managers. The relative lack of unexpected opportunities and the fact that many enthusiastic and entrepreneurial managers find their career paths blocked certainly contribute to this sense of unfulfilled ambition.

Moreover, the fact that French managers realize earlier where their promotional ceiling will be, plus the fact that many of them stay longer in post

(French companies not believing in systematic rotation), helps to explain the *baronnies* (fiefdoms) one often hears about in French companies. If money and promotion are not available rewards, then managers typically seek out other payoffs, such as autonomy. Deprived of other outlets for their energies, French managers may be more inclined to devote their energies into building empires – as we shall see in the next chapter. And in a more general sense, big company respect for educational rankings also sets up our discussion of work relations in France which tend to be characterized by a certain formalism and interpersonal distance.

5 Work relations: Entente (pas très) cordiale

C'est sûr qu'à l'égard des rapports de travail les Français sont plutôt constipés.
(There's no doubt that in terms of work relations, the French are somewhat constipated.) (Conversation with Vice-President, Conseil d'Administration, L'Air Liquide)

THIS CHAPTER TAKES ITS CUE from the seminal work of Michel Crozier on work relations in a bureaucratic context in France. Crozier identified a number of themes which he believed characterized French organizational interaction, notably the isolation of the individual, the avoidance of face-to-face relationships, the compartmentalization of the organization, the struggle for privileges and the lack of constructive solidarity. The aim here is to put our view side by side with that documented so well by Crozier in the 1960s.

Formality

Our immediate impression of the ambience of the traditional French office is that it is less chummy and relaxed than the equivalent in Britain or the USA. Work colleagues are regarded as just that, rarely as friends or even 'fellow sufferers'.

An obvious manifestation is the relative absence of joking around (ribbing, running jokes, self-deprecation). Where there is humour, it is less self-revealing. It may draw attention to the incongruency between someone else's words and actions, but rarely one's own.

French managerial humour is often based on intellectual or linguistic *finesse*. A witticism will be judged as being a 'second-degree' or 'third-degree' allusion, which refers to its layers of obscurity. Likewise, the *jeux de mots* (puns) demand a high level of linguistic accomplishment which excludes most foreigners, even the most fluent. Humour, in the French workplace, is not generally meant to facilitate bonding. The repartee is intellectually discriminating. It distinguishes who is in and who is out – and because of the close link between classical education and organizational rank, humour tends to reinforce the hierarchy. Understanding a joke in France sometimes feels like passing an intelligence test.

The fact that joking seems to play a smaller role in French work relations has been discussed more extensively elsewhere (Barsoux, 1993). The prime reason would appear to be that, at work, the French put a heavy emphasis on keeping up appearances, on being *sérieux*: that is, both conscientious and credible. As described in the previous chapters, French managers largely owe their position to their cleverness. The consequences of fouling up in public are more damaging. The average British manager, on the other hand, can laugh off a mistake because he or she has been selected on the basis of 'character' – indeed the ability to handle failure may be seen as affirmation of managerial robustness.

In many countries managers feel they can relax more as they climb the ranks. In France, the opposite tends to happen. Bosses rarely spice up their presentations with anecdotes or jokes. Executive behaviour is restrained because authority is not something to be taken lightly. The phrase, *'Ce n'est pas sérieux'* springs easily to French executive lips to admonish unprofessional behaviour. Appearances matter.

For the same reason, French executives are less likely to relax their dress or posture. Jackets are less likely to be removed, ties loosened or sleeves rolled up. For the French, these are signs of relaxation, not 'getting down to business'. 'Slouching' (sitting on or putting one's feet up on desks) is also uncommon. Interestingly, the only 'French' manager we saw who actually provided evidence to the contrary was a trainee store manager at Carrefour, who turned out to be an English expatriate and readily rested his feet on the nearest available surface. This theme of non-verbal expression is explored in much detail by the American sociologist Lawrence Wylie, who maintains that the French are far more upright in their posture and controlled in their movements than the Americans: 'The French have a sense of vulnerability about their bodies that is greater than that of Americans who are less worried about their body boundaries' (in Santoni, 1981, 38).

This physical restraint has a psychological complement. Unless talking to a close colleague, French managers do not tend to appreciate inquiries into their personal lives, their family circumstances or how they spent the weekend. The fear is that once you get on these kind of terms, you expose yourself to the kind of personal obligations one might expect of a friend or relation. This was the experience of one American manager sent out to head up a French subsidiary:

> Making small talk, I once proposed to one of my most senior deputies that the two of us organize an evening with our wives. His reaction was non-committal. When I asked him a few days later to remind me of the name of his wife, his icy reply was unmistakable: 'Her name is the same as mine.' (Johnson, 1996, 69)

There is a certain wariness towards informality, especially when it comes from above. In particular, corporate efforts to engineer friendship, trust and commitment are regarded as manipulative.

Consider the example of a French medical equipment maker, taken over by General Electric in 1988. GE decided to boost the morale of its new French employees by calling a training seminar for the French managers. In their hotel rooms, the company left colourful T-shirts emblazoned with the GE slogan 'Go for One'. A note urged the managers to wear the T-shirts 'to show that you are members of the team'. The French managers wore them, grudgingly, to the seminar, but as one of them recalled, '. . . forcing us to wear uniforms was humiliating' (*Wall Street Journal*, 31/7/90, 4).

The French are very sensitive to actions which risk encroaching on their freedom – even if the initiative is claimed to be for the 'greater good'. They are inclined to share the view of the French philosopher, Camus, who observed that when deprived of choice, the only freedom left is the freedom to say no. It follows that overt attempts at team building may create a sense of 'forced comradery' and may be resisted rather than welcomed.

As we will argue towards the end of the chapter, social interaction in France makes a clear distinction between personal and professional relations. The role played in the office can easily be kept distinct from the person occupying the role[1] through the use of a battery of props (explored in Chapter 6). This is indeed one of the paradoxes highlighted in our first chapter.

That lesser investment of the 'self' in one's job is developed by Desmond Graves, who suggests that the French tend to regard authority as residing in the role not the person. According to Graves, it is by the power of position that a French manager gets things done (what Chester Barnard termed structural authority). This is in contrast to the Anglo-Saxon view that authority is vested in the person (personal, charismatic or moral authority). The distinction between the two cultures implies that a French manager will accept responsibility so long as it is attached to the role but will not actively seek responsibility, as a British manager might, for it adds nothing to one's stature. As Graves puts it: 'He is "*le responsable*" – but not, as in our culture, "the person responsible"' (1973, 293).

For a French manager, extra responsibility without extra compensation, offers little *intrinsic* satisfaction. Indeed, those who accept this may be regarded as dupes. Retaining one's independence, by whatever means possible, is the objective. Responsibility does not lead to a higher level of self-actualization. It simply ties in your ego to corporate objectives, and co-opts your soul. It is therefore *un piège a con* (a trap for fools).

It follows that 'empowerment' – the idea that people can be developed through work, by giving them more space to exercise their initiative, and to take decisions – may not be well received in French companies. This so-called autonomy makes individuals accountable for decisions previously taken by their bosses – and that is not what the French call freedom.

This can cause considerable problems for international companies trying to introduce notions of empowerment in France. The head of one French subsidiary explained to us:

> Empowering our business managers, as has already happened in Britain, Germany and Italy, is proving a real struggle. Their initial reaction was enthusiastic. They thought they would become *les rois du pétrole* (the oil kings). They had no trouble accepting the increase in power, but they are still resisting the additional responsibilities. It's understandable. There has always been a tendency to push the blame upwards or onto the system, when things go badly. But when you are individually responsible, that becomes more difficult.

The desire to keep function and personality separate has repercussions on the nature of organizational interaction. Formal (as opposed to personal) authority is not especially conducive to convivial relations.

Working with others

The low level of social openness and desire for independence described above find spatial expression in the office layout where personal space seems to be a matter of some importance. Open-plan offices remain rare at *cadre* level and can cause quite a stir if they are imposed. One American manager recalls his struggle to get such a layout accepted:

> When I announced the plan, a groan arose in unison from the staff. They were not convinced. When moving day came six weeks later, they were even less convinced. The parade of protesters through my door in the first days was a chastening experience. A long list of demands included more lights, different light fixtures, more air, more windows, open windows, and more partitions. (Johnson, 1996, 64)

In the end, the manager had no choice but to order a dozen partitions to break up the space, thus diluting the intended effect of the design. Work relations are both a consequence, and a determinant of the physical layout of companies.

The French like to have a 'territory' to call their own – and the impregnability of the sanctuary tends to increase with organizational status. Three of the PDGs (CEOs) observed had soundproofed doors, great unwieldy things which were almost permanently closed and which simply encouraged people to seek access via the secretary's office. At lower levels glass partitions tended to be blocked out with posters, and doors were generally closed – and one maintenance manager even had a spring-loaded door which shut automatically. Such clues tend to indicate low emphasis on informal exchanges, teamwork, confrontation of opinions as well as a negative view of open conflict.

This general theme is spectacularly highlighted by the head offices of l'Air Liquide in Paris. When it was built, in 1932, the building was designed to double up as a hotel should the existing business turn sour. This may have been a wise precaution on the part of the founder, but it has left a legacy of mazy corridors and isolated offices. The physical geography of the building does not lend itself to easy communication – either spoken or physical. What is more, the sumptuous, marbled *décor* (reminiscent of a museum or ministerial office) seems to militate against any sort of informal contact – the only coffee point, for instance, is in the basement. While this is an extreme example, it does highlight French attachment to classical management principles and the rejection of continuous quick-fire exchanges as a legitimate means of communication. The French attitude to work is based on the ideal of intellectual effort.

A similar pattern emerges when one considers the way French managers structure their days. Relative to Anglo-Saxon cultures, they have a more classical conception of management which favours work in isolation (often reading internal reports), punctuated by formal meetings. Such an approach restricts exchanges to a more codified framework which diminishes the need for personal involvement. This is in striking contrast to America, where managers take a much more interactive and unstructured approach to management work (Kotter, 1982, 88). The cut-and-thrust, say, of Management By Walking Around does appeal to French managers.[2] It is not where most of them excel.

A number of *cadres* in the sample commented on their preference for getting things done through formal meetings. One PDG (CEO) went as far as to say, '*C'est la seule façon de faire avancer les choses*' ('It's the only way to get things moving'). The French penchant for meetings is understandable in that these are occasions for planning and reflection. As French managers see it, that is primarily what they are paid for – not persuading, supporting or motivating. Meetings are also seen as an opportunity to bring conflicts to a head ('*déclencher l'orage*' – 'to start the storm') or to obtain firm commitments from individuals thanks to peer group pressure.

There is a case for suggesting that French *cadres* are meetings specialists, in much the same way as their Anglo-Saxon counterparts might be considered adept troubleshooters. In meetings, the agenda is known in advance as are the people attending, and the exchanges are formalized. The structure of the situation reduces uncertainty and provides a perfect stage on which *cadres* can display their oratory skills; organizational status can be enhanced by skilful advocacy and stylish expression or lost through poor eloquence and reasoning. Relatively speaking, French meetings are more ideas-oriented, than people- or action-oriented.

French managers like to talk. In meetings, they have no qualms about advancing the discussion on several fronts at once. Rather than treating one item at a time, they prefer to consider the issues together, the rationale being that these may well be inter-related: why take a decision on item 1 when item 3 may well impinge on it or help to clarify it in some way? In international meetings, this is liable to frustrate American managers, in particular, who see time passing and no decisions being made on any particular agenda item. They become restless sitting through what looks like talk for the sake of it. An expatriate Briton who headed the French textile group DMC, observed:

> *Dans ce pays, on adore le débat intellectuel, les discussions et les remises en question, quitte à tergiverser et à repousser le moment où il faut enfin trancher.* (In this country, they love intellectual debate, discussion and calling into question, even if it means equivocating and pushing back the actual moment of decision.) (*Le Nouvel Economiste*, 2/2/96, 45)

Such frustrations are largely based on different notions of time. The French see time as expandable. They do not expect the clock to control events. Rigid agendas are perceived as inhibiting creativity, and it is more acceptable for several people to talk at once without this being experienced as chaos. This is in stark contrast to the more sequential view of time which prevails in Anglo-Saxon cultures, where agenda items are expected to be dealt with systematically, decisions taken, deadlines respected and where one person speaks at a time.

These different views of time also lead to different interpretations of what is considered 'acceptable behaviour' in meetings. To start with, the agreed start time is just the signal for the keenest people to *start* making their way towards the meeting room. Once the meeting gets under way, French managers may not instruct their secretaries to hold calls nor ask unscheduled visitors to wait outside. Similarly, French managers may engage in side conversations, leave to make calls or attend to paperwork if the discussion is not immediately relevant to them. Announcements for meetings in France specify a start time, but rarely mention an end time – so French meetings don't *actually* overrun.

An additional reason why French meetings tend to be drawn out has to do with different views of what constitutes a good decision. In Anglo-Saxon cultures, when divergent solutions are proposed, the parties may quickly agree to 'split the difference' – this being justified by the time saved, the fairness and the increased likelihood of buy-in from both parties. While managers from the US and Britain generally place a high value on compromise, the French tend to interpret the word negatively. For them, it typically signifies a threat to opportunities or plans. By French reasoning, why go for a second-rate or improvized solution if the perfect solution is available,[3] either through clever synthesis or by achieving consensus on which is the better idea? Persuasion, in France, is about beating the opposition into intellectual submission. And that can take time.

In several companies, there were complaints that the number of meetings was in fact becoming excessive. These companies were deemed to be suffering from *la réunionite* (meeting-itis). One PDG (CEO), whose American MBA gave him different terms of reference, posited that meetings were in fact status-lenders since they reduced access to the person in question – as he put it, *'ça meuble une journée'* ('it fills up a day'). For French managers it is important to be considered one of those whose views matter.

Hierarchy

Another sign of French attachment to the classical principles of management can be seen in the continued distinction between thinkers and executors. This shows in the way many French companies have implemented the kinds of discussion groups which were first introduced as quality circles. As a complement to the established hierarchical channels, these new forms of participation were intended to tap the knowledge resources of the entire personnel. Unfortunately, these groups have rarely had the expected impact. Mostly they have simply reinforced existing hierarchical relationships rather than opening up the way for wider involvement. Instead of using these informal work groups to designate their own leaders, many companies imposed hierarchical heads – thus underlining from the start a lack of faith in the personnel to elect sensible leaders and the fear that it would give rise to *une hiérarchie parallèle* which might undermine the so-called *hiérarchie naturelle*.

Furthermore, French managers still seem unconvinced by the capacity of those at the base to think for themselves. The entire management group at one company we visited attended an in-house seminar on empowerment. The organizer started by detailing a handful of 'irrefutable' principles, along the lines 'We can improve productivity if we increase worker commitment'. When he reached the principle about each worker being an expert in his/her own work, the meeting hit a sticking point. A protracted discussion ensued about the validity of the statement, and the outcome was a redefinition which did away with the word 'expert'.

This was not simply a one-off case of linguistic 'nit-picking'. It represented a serious lack of faith in worker aptitudes; something which was reiterated by the reaction to a subsequent statement: *'Il existe des réserves d'intelligence inemployées'* ('There are untapped reserves of intelligence'). Here too, the *cadres* felt they could not let the proposition pass unchallenged and suggested that *'réserves d'intelligence'* be replaced by *'ressources'*.

Or again, consider the case of two Michelin tyre workers who came up with a simple solution to a complex problem. Their boss, an *ingénieur*, marvelling at their ingenuity, commented: *'On ne m'avais pas appris dans mon école que les ouvriers pouvaient être aussi intelligents'* ('They didn't teach us at engineering school that workers could be so intelligent').[4] This kind of attitude explains the harsh verdict of a non-French senior executive working in one of the large French groups:

> *Beaucoup d'entreprises traitent leurs salariés comme aux XIXe siècle, bref, comme des illettrés!* (Many companies treat their employees like in the nineteenth century, in short, like illiterates!) (*Le Nouvel Economiste*, 2/02/96, 44)

The heavy distinction between *cadre* and *non-cadre*, first noted in Chapter 2, is regarded by some as an obstacle to the economic and social progress of companies. In particular, it is contradictory to the current emphasis on shortening hierarchical distance and devolving responsibility. The advent of IT has not helped matters. The requirement that *cadres* learn new skills like typing has thoroughly confused the traditional 'intellectual/manual' boundary.

Segregation could also be seen in the existence at most companies of separate canteens for workers and management, common enough in Britain, of course, but unusual in Germany, Swizerland and Scandinavia. And even where there was a single dining-hall, it was not uncommon to see unofficial 'territories'. This 'intellectual apartheid' was sometimes cloaked in practical considerations – for instance, one company had a notice which designated one canteen for 'people in civilian clothes', the aim being to avoid mixing overalls and suits. Yet it transpired that production managers would change out of their overalls while secretaries would eat with the workers. Perhaps more striking was the fact that in the canteens people would generally eat in small groups rather than fill up tables with spare seats – again with very obvious layering by rank.

It becomes clear that the gross distinction between thinkers and doers is but the tip of the iceberg. Within each category – *dirigeants, cadres, employés, ouvriers* – relative status is a matter of some importance. The notion of a professional pecking order permeates every stratum right down to the base. Even workers think in terms of more or less honourable professions. Skilled workers are referred to as *l'aristocratie ouvrière* (the manual aristocracy) in relation to unskilled workers. Thus, the workers are merely echoing the distinction higher up in the hierarchy between, say, graduate engineers in the 'noble' speciality of electronics and graduate engineers in the 'common' field of mechanics. Of course this stratification rests upon more than the historical distinction between what is 'noble' and what is not. The French researcher Marc Maurice drew particular attention to the qualification hierarchies and salary structures with the evocative *'grilles de classification'* ('classification matrices') which pit manual versus non-manual, skilled versus unskilled, supervisory versus non-supervisory and line versus staff *cadres* (Maurice et al., 1986, 252).

This keen sense of hierarchy has quite an impact on work relations and activities. To start with, it tends to inhibit informal communication between levels. Office colleagues do not often try to meet each other socially, and there are few signs of fraternization between staff of differing grades. For instance, the decision by a senior *cadre* we observed to take his son skiing on a works council holiday was greeted with much surprise by colleagues and subordinates alike. Such trips are theoretically for the benefit of all personnel but hitherto no senior managers had ever 'deigned' to mix with subordinates on such an intimate exercise.

Nor is openness particularly encouraged by the companies. For example, one company visited refused to send senior managers and middle managers on the same training courses. The logic behind that decision was that the benefits of training might be lost if the participants felt inhibited by the presence of superiors or subordinates – particularly in view of the potential loss of face which accompanies the learning situation. The Anglo-Saxon view, that this would be an ideal opportunity to surface and reconcile communication problems, is not widely shared by the French.

The difference in approach is neatly summed up in a cross-cultural experiment conducted by former Insead professor Owen James Stevens (in Hofstede, 1991, 140–42). He presented an organizational problem to separate groups of MBA students from Britain and France. The problem hinged on a conflict between two department heads within a company. The British saw it as an interpersonal communication problem between the two department heads which could be solved by sending them for interpersonal skills training, preferably together. The majority of French MBAs simply referred the problem to the next level up, the president.

French managers with problems that fall outside their immediate sphere, generally look upwards for guidance. An Anglo-Saxon boss would typically react by dumping the problem straight back: 'My job is not to decide for you. I'm only the boss.' But in France, there is a higher expectation of the boss to have the answers, partly by virtue of the boss's superior education. This expectation is confirmed by Laurent who asked managers of different nationalities to react to the following statement: It is important for a manager to have at hand precise answers to most of the questions that subordinates may raise about their work. Only a minority of US managers (13 per cent) agreed with the statement, compared with a moderate 30 per cent of British managers and 59 per cent of French managers (Laurent, 1986, 177).

Similarly, in meetings, the senior person is expected to chair the sessions and have the final word on any decisions. The French expect strong control from the chair regarding the agenda and the flow of the discussion. French managers have difficulty believing that a group can make a decision. That is the boss's job.

Hierarchical deference is also visible in certain assumptions. For example, a senior manager with l'Air Liquide, who happens to be a New Zealander, observes: 'French top managers don't often worry whether their direct reports are otherwise engaged, when they call them for an *immediate* meeting' (*Le Nouvel Economiste*, 2/02/96, 44). It remains more acceptable to 'pull rank' in France. There is little pretence of equality between levels. For this reason too, the idea of 360 degree feedback – whereby the team gives constructive criticism to the leader and the leader accepts it – has made very slow progress in France. The loss of face occasioned by such a process and the risk of reprisal makes it difficult to envisage in French companies.

This respect for hierarchy is reinforced by constant references to *la voie hiérarchique* (the formal chain of command). Urging managers to go through the 'official channels' would sound very bureaucratic in America, but in France it is a perfectly reasonable request – even if it is often contravened. Back in the early 1970s, Desmond Graves noted that the actual contacts of the French manager were very much in line with what one would expect after examining the organization chart. This, incidentally, was in stark contrast to British managers, who showed few qualms about breaching organizational protocol and whose 'patterns of communication bore no relation to the "official" organization charts' (1973, 296). While workplace interaction has grown more flexible and unpredictable since then, relatively speaking, the French pattern remains hierarchic. For example, skip-level meetings, where managers meet with employees two or three rungs below them, are uncommon.

Now, we are not claiming that the French work only through official channels. That would be impossible. What we are saying is that short-circuiting intermediary levels is not officially sanctioned in France as it is in Britain or America. In France, circumventing is only permissible if the person who 'should' have been informed does not hear about it – or else it occasions a loss of face.

This field observation is supported in the research findings of André Laurent. An international comparison of managers' willingness to bypass the hierarchical line (Laurent, 1983, 86) showed that French managers were particularly inhibited. As French managers see it, if the most efficient way to do things is to go over or around the boss, then there may be something wrong with the hierarchy.

This attachment to a formal and unambiguous structure has been advanced as an explanation for the relative failure of matrix structures in France. For the French, matrix structures violate the principle of 'unity of command' and clear reporting relationships. The view of organizations as hierarchical systems makes the idea of having to report to two bosses, as required in matrix organizations, difficult to tolerate. It is undesirable as it creates divided loyalties and causes unwelcome conflict (Laurent, 1981, 113).

Partitioning

Differentiation within French firms is not merely vertical but also horizontal. This is perhaps a collective manifestation of the way individuals seek a personal 'territory'. There were numerous allusions to le cloisonnement (partitioning) at the firms visited. The clannish nature of interpersonal relations is epitomized by the alumni of prestigious grandes écoles who tend to congregate in particular companies. But the practice is not restricted to the elite. Indeed, François de Closets (1982, 280) cites taxi drivers, bakers and pharmacists as three of the prime offenders in the perpetuation of *numerus clausus* (closed shops). And Crozier supports this view when he says: 'At all levels of society the French, once they gain entry into an influential group, instinctively try to keep others out' (Beer, 1982, 26).

The French propensity for forming cliques was mentioned spontaneously by a number of interviewees. They alluded to *l'esprit de clan* (clannish mentality), *les chasses guardées* (preserves), *les petites bastilles* (small fortresses), *les querelles de chapelles* (warring factions), *les castes* (casts), and *les fiefs* (feudal estates). The head of one small company in the study explained how he was forced continually to reshuffle the personnel around the offices in order to break down cliques. Little wonder that one German director working in France regarded French companies as 'a throwback to medieval times, made up of fiefdoms and warlords, where each individual feels like a proprietor and aspires to autonomy' *(Le Nouvel Economiste*, 2/02/96, 42).

The essential function of the above-mentioned cliques, based essentially on shared interests rather than personal affinities, is to protect their members. It was noticeable, for instance, that once a right had been gained by a group, there was no way it could be abolished – it became *un droit acquis* (an acquired right). Two examples from our study involving bonus payments may serve to illustrate the point: one PDG (CEO) was trying to rename a *prime de période de pointe* (bonus for rush jobs) since the label no longer corresponded to reality. Another head was tackling a similar misnomer – *une prime qualitative* (a quality bonus) which had become institutionalized and had lost its exceptional nature. In both cases, suppressing the bonus was out of the question since it would be equated to a drop in salary. They had become acquired rights, and the only option was to rename them in order to show awareness of the situation.

So in spite of the much-vaunted egalitarianism associated with the French Revolution and the First French Republic, the French are deeply attached to the accumulation of privileges and distinctions which divide them – a tension that was introduced at the end of Chapter 1 with our provocative hexagon. René Remond described it as: *'L'attachement à l'égalité et la course aux privilèges'* ('A passion for equality and a race for distinction') (Reynaud, 1982, 37).

Yet, what appears to be a contradiction between values and behaviour is neatly reconciled by the French philosopher, Henri Laborit:

> *On parle d'égalité et plus récemment d'égalité des chances. Mais chances de quoi? Tout simplement de devenir inégal.* (We talk of equality and more recently of equality of opportunity. But the opportunity to do what? Why the opportunity to become unequal, of course.) (Laborit, 1992, 209)[5]

Within firms, the cliques often correspond to functional boundaries. Relatively speaking, professional relationships between colleagues are founded on rivalry rather than collaboration. So, what starts off as a personality clash between rival directors easily spreads to conflict between whole departments. This is understandable if one considers the channelling of communications through *la voie hiérarchique* (the formal chain of command) as mentioned above. The boss's protective powers are considerable, and it would be unwise for managers to show split loyalties. As one *cadre* put it: '*C'est lui qui fait la pluie et le beau temps de ses cadres*' ('He determines the lot of his managers'). So the boss is less likely to be tolerant of what Americans might call 'boundary spanners', people who have an informal liaison role. In French companies, it is best to choose your camp.

The following interfunctional complaints are culled from observation and interviews:

> *La production s'en fout.* (Manufacturing doesn't give a damn.)

> *Le personnel fait du social sans mesure.* (The personnel department is obsessed with social considerations.)

> *Les ventes ne pensent qu'à faire du volume.* (The sales department only think about their sales figures.)

> *Le marketing crée ses produits sans écouter l'avis du terrain.* (Marketing pays no notice whatsoever to those in the field when it dreams up its products.)

An actual example, from our research, concerns the well-documented rivalry between manufacturing and maintenance. At the production plant in question, efforts were being made to integrate the two functions in order to ease authority problems. These problems stemmed from the fact that maintenance operators were geographically isolated from their boss, and unaccountable to the manufacturing supervisors – which meant they did very much as they pleased. As one neutral *cadre* explained, '*le médecin se fait attendre*' ('everyone awaits the doctor'). The manufacturing manager in that plant reiterated the point by referring to the maintenance department as '*l'état dans l'état*' ('a state within a state') – suggesting that little had changed since Crozier's classic study from the 1960s.

The problem with such rivalries is that they tend to inhibit co-operation across functions. As the head of an IT department ironically explained to us,

IT was actually the only department which generated any kind of consensus from the other departments: '*Ils peuvent tous se mettre d'accord pour dire du mal de l'informatique*' ('Criticising IT is about the one thing they can all agree on').

Clearly, co-operation across functions cannot be taken for granted. As discussed in Chapter 3, the French approach to education does not place much emphasis on learning to collaborate to solve problems. When this is added to the hierarchical differences mentioned previously, it helps to explain resistance to working in *ad hoc* teams. Such teams, drawn from different functions, units and levels within the organization, seem to experience greater problems in France – not least because of their temporary nature. Why on earth would someone want to commit to a temporary team which offers little protective power? As one American manager concludes from his experience heading a French company:

> Even primitive teams in France can falter because the taste for groupwork isn't there . . . Trust is a requirement for such partnerships, and trust does not come easily to the French. Relations between equals are suspicious, wary, watchful. Relations between workers and management are the same only more so. (Johnson, 1996, 28)

This is not to say that teams do not exist. There *are* high performing teams. The difference, compared to Anglo-Saxon teams, is that team spirit does not materialize spontaneously from facing a common challenge. In Anglo countries there is a stronger presumption that trust is handed out 'up front' and withdrawn only if abused. In France, trust has to be earned, and team spirit is something that builds up, over time, independently of the task. Once it exists, high performance will follow, but one should not expect the task to serve as catalyst for successful co-operation.

While new allegiances and constructive solidarity take time to build up, generating negative solidarity is more straightforward.[6] Rival factions will quickly set aside their differences when faced with a threat to their shared interests. Thus, an international company can expect swift and concerted resistance to more or less any proposal which challenges the established order in its French subsidiary. Sometimes the defensive line taken, is simply, 'France is different, and this won't work here. Take our word for it.' But sometimes, the resistance is more subtle. Consider the example of the French subsidiary of an American multinational.

The American parent had decided to implement a different organizational structure throughout its European operations – one designed to be more responsive to markets and better aligned with the US operation. The

French subsidiary, dominated by what one *cadre* labelled 'a *Troika* of rival barons' volunteered as a pilot site for this new design. Some months later they reported the successful implementation of the new structure, gaining much credit with head office in the process. Two years later, with results slipping, a new subsidiary head was appointed from Germany. By this time, two members of the *Troika* had been promoted to better positions outside France. The incoming subsidiary head soon realized that the earlier 'reorganization' had been mostly superficial. It had been implemented in a way which preserved the power of the three foremost directors, the result of a pact between them and the former subsidiary head.

This example paves the way for a wider discussion of the political dimension (in the Machiavellian sense) of French business.

The informal system

The image we have so far painted of work relations in France suggests that business is conducted 'by the book', in an orderly and professional way, unobstructed by personal relationships. That is only superficially the case. Below the surface, there are complex networks of personal relationships and alliances through which much of the real work gets done. The difference with Anglo-Saxon cultures, is that such relationships are not likely to be cultivated over a drink outside work, nor based on personal chemistry and shared pursuits. In France, they are more likely to be founded on educational allegiances (*grandes écoles*), professional solidarity (*cadre, ingénieur*), or vested interests.

The weight of the informal system can be seen in the importance accorded to 'the grapevine' as a means of communication. A survey in *Le Nouvel Economiste* (12/5/80, 47) actually placed rumours ahead of one's immediate superior as a means of gaining information. And several of the managers observed spontaneously referred to *les bruits de couloirs, le téléphone arabe*, or *radio moquette* (slang terms for the grapevine). As one of the German directors of Lafarge Aluminates explains, it took some getting used to:

> *Je consacre une heure, chaque jour, aux conversations de couloir, car ces mécanismes de consultation informels peuvent déboucher sur des blocages désastreux si on n'y prend garde.* (I devote an hour each day to hallway conversations which, if neglected, can lead to disastrous blockages.) (*Le Nouvel Economiste*, 2/02/96, 42)

The importance of this form of information in the French context may be a reflection of the relative inefficiency or rigidity of standard channels of communication. As discussed above, the communication patterns in France are more dictated by the formal structure of the organization. Communication in France tends to be on a 'need to know' basis – it tends to be serial and secretive rather than open and multiple. To give a caricatural example of how far this can go, a highly rated project manager working for Dumez learnt of the merger between between his company and a subsidiary of Lyonnaise des Eaux, thanks to a radio announcement (*L'Expansion*, 25/1/96, 36).

The informal channels of communication therefore compensate for the centralized, formalized and limited participative nature of organizational communication. It is only natural for rumours to flourish when there is an imbalance between the demand and supply of information. The rumour in France has a democratizing influence in an otherwise elitist system of communications – as one *cadre* put it, '*c'est le marché noir de l'information*' ('it's the information black market'). The speed of propagation easily outstrips official channels and responds to the dual needs of the personnel: to be informed early and to make out that one is privy to 'inside' information.

It is from these two needs that rumours derive their efficiency. Rumours serve as early warning systems to *cadres* who fear there may be another wave of redundancies (*plan social*) or to union representatives who wish to mobilize action against impending changes, such as a proposed modification to the bonus structures. Rumours also serve as social currency. Managers take a risk when they defy organizational protocol or break expectations of confidentiality by passing on information. Trading information therefore serves to nurture and reinforce their network of relationships. But information only has a social function in a context which lacks transparency. As one French manager put it to us: 'Information which is widely distributed is obviously useless.' This is in marked contrast, say, with Swedish managers who show willingness to share information with anyone who has an interest in it and for whom information has an instrumental, rather than a social value (Lawrence and Spybey, 1986).

In French companies, then, getting things done means using informal, personal networks to circumvent the hierarchy as well as the rules and regulations. This is what the French call *le système D* (resourcefulness). According to Michel Crozier (1964), it is this informal system that gives the French 'bureaucratic model' its short-term dynamism and flexibility. Were it not for this invigorating subculture, based on informal networking, and characterized by flexibility, scepticism, and energy, the formal system would quickly prove unsustainable. Yet this is not America where the existence of a parallel system would provoke questions about a need for change in the official system. In France, the rules and procedures are constantly distorted, manipulated and ignored if they do not serve the purposes of those using them. As one *cadre* once told us, '*S'il y a une règle, c'est qu'il y en a qui le font. Alors pourquoi pas nous?*' ('If there's a rule, it's because people break it. So why shouldn't we?'). The trick is to know which rules can be broken and how. It is another aspect of French managerial initiation. As Laurent puts it:

> French managers perceive the ability to manage power relationships effectively and to 'work the system' as particularly critical to their success. (1986, 179)

While French managers also 'wheel and deal', scheme and manipulate, it would be true to say that manifestations of political behaviour are less overt than in Britain or the US. There was plenty of evidence that it was going on. For instance, over lunch, we heard executives at one company talking about a former high-flyer, over at head office, who had suddenly become more cautious:

> *Il n'y a pas longtemps il fonçait, jusqu'à ce qu'on a commencé à lui glisser des peaux de banane.* (He used to rush headlong, until they started putting a few banana skins in his path.)

Nevertheless, the examples cited by the French managers invariably referred to other people. During observation, they did not typically let the observer in on an impending political manoevre, nor did they seem to derive the same sort of pride as their Anglo-Saxon counterparts in divulging successful past manoeuvres.

There is a possible explanation for this guardedness. As with their view of organizations, the French seem to hold a more classical conception of the role of managers. Theirs is to reflect, to ensure consistency of implementation, to uphold equality and even, as pointed out in Chapter 2, to serve as a kind of role model. The 'honour' of the businessman, the engineer, and the administrator is an important factor (d'Iribarne, 1989). As Sorge points out: 'It is constituted by his or her ability to achieve high professional standards and to do justice to norms of taste, sophistication and logical rigour' (1993, 72). None of this fits in with political machinations. The need for intrigue clashes with the need to project integrity.

It follows that political behaviour is not considered legitimate in France as it is in Anglo-Saxon countries. In the US and Britain, political astuteness is widely accepted as part of the manager's skills; it is taught as a subject in business schools and discussed openly in the memoirs of corporate heads. In France, it remains an underground activity. Besides which, openly discussing such matters might give others insight into one's real motives or personality.

Work versus social relations

The tendency towards formality, described at the start of this chapter, reflects a strong distinction between work and social activities. This is perhaps the main reason why, as we noted in Chapter 1, frequent holiday visitors to France may have little idea of the character or workings of French business.

French managers tend to regard their professional life and their personal life as quite separate domains. As the Scottish head of a French property company observed:

> *La convivialité professionnelle n'existe pas en France. En Angleterre ou en Ecosse, tout le monde va prendre un verre à la sortie du bureau, ensemble, avant de se quitter; les agences concurrentes organisent même entre elles des compétitions de fléchettes, de golf, de football . . . Impensable ici.* (Professional conviviality is non-existent in France. In England or Scotland, everyone goes out for a drink together after work, before heading home; rival agencies even organize darts, golf or football matches. That's unthinkable here.) (*Exportation*, October 1990, 32)

A striking example of this was the case of a French executive who, in two years of working for Disneyland Paris, had not once brought his family to visit the park – this, in spite of the provision of free passes and the staging of 'events' for family members. Nor was this due to lack of time. He simply had no intention of mixing family and work even though the corporate culture actively encouraged it.

Attempts by foreign managers, in particular, to blur this line between the private and the professional realm may meet with some resistance. Consider the difficulty experienced by an incoming American manager in getting hold of the home telephone numbers of his 14 reports. He charged his secretary with the task, but she reported back two days later with only two answers. The other 12 finally gave in when the manager made the request in person – and only after pledging not to use it unnecessarily or pass it on to third parties (Johnson, 1996, 69).

In France, activities like the Friday night 'beer bust' or the team picnic, which seem perfectly natural in the US, may fail miserably in their team-building goals. Similarly, the prospect of taking on the boss at tennis or golf at a weekend retreat can be daunting in that it will not be considered 'equal' competition. And while the French could not be accused of prudery, the idea of mingling with colleagues from work (and their spouses) in shorts or swimsuits may cause further discomfort. Anyone who has attended a French company 'do' outside the work setting will know the meaning of resentment. The enforced bonhomie of such activities is likely to be seen as manipulative.

The reason for maintaining this distinction between work and non-work, is hinted at by Johnson, from his first-hand experience:

> French employees, conditioned by a lifetime of distance from their superiors in all spheres, will hang back, believing that the less is known about them, the longer they can safely hide in their cocoon. (1996, 46)

The idea is supported by Wylie, who studied a French village in the Vaucluse. He describes a boy who wasn't bright, never got into trouble and worked very hard. Why? *'Pour qu'on me laisse tranquille'* ('So I'll be left in peace') (in Santoni, 1981, 60). The desire for independence, even at the expense of not doing what you want, seems important in France.

The relative impersonality and formalism found in organizational relations is echoed in French social life. If one looks at the traditional pattern of interpersonal relations inculcated in the basic associative life of a village, one can see the roots of the work relations described above.

The principles that indiscriminate friendship exposes one to manipulation, that property should be enclosed, that outsiders are not to be trusted – these defensive solidarities are all legacies of the village mentality which still has a strong hold over French social relations. As Wylie points out, the basic social arrangement in France is the circle – a person is responsible only to people in his own *cercle* and indifferent to people outside it.

Overview

Whilst it would be foolish to suggest that the above description is universal, it certainly prevails in French companies. French work relations are, on the whole, more highly structured and more detached. As described in the chapter, these cultural characteristics have often inhibited the introduction of new organizational forms (such as matrix structures) and practices (such as management by objectives and empowerment).

From an Anglo-Saxon stance, all this may appear like a tremendous indictment of the French organizational model. However, in the French mind this lesser investment of the self is considered a means of preserving personal choice, independence and individual dignity – a way of protecting oneself from abuse and exploitation.

It is noticeable in France that those companies which do try to impose a more informal style of work relations are often unpopular. There is a widespread belief that convivial relations merely serve as a means of motivating (and manipulating) employees, of dismantling hierarchical and functional cleavages, and of encouraging a certain freedom of expression which facilitates decision-making – in other words, as an instrument which cleverly subordinates the interests of the individual to the interests of the firm.

This resentment towards informality as a manipulative device may explain the relative flop of Kenneth Blanchard's worldwide best-seller *One Minute Manager* in France. The transparency of his proposals was rather too much for French managers. Indeed, one *cadre* maintained: 'I would not take kindly to being patted on the shoulder – not in the professional context at least.' This was considered '*un geste déplacé*' ('an inappropriate gesture') which reinforces the idea put forward earlier in the chapter that the French do not like their personal space unexpectedly violated – except, as we shall see in the next chapter, in highly codified rituals.

Clearly, in the French context, the desire to avoid conflict and to be protected from arbitrary decisions and manipulation are more important than the immediate gratification provided by social contact or 'enriched' (more autonomous) work. This points to an interesting difference between the Anglo-Saxon and French versions of freedom at work. For Americans, and Britons to a lesser extent, autonomy means the freedom *to* act in a self-determining way; for the French it means freedom *from* dependence on others – hence the attachment to bureaucratic structures.

The organization is not considered a place for self-expression. However much discretion individuals are given to change structures or exercise initiative, that is not where they expect to find their 'real selves'. French managers may work long hours, but they do not derive their identity from work, and their work colleagues are rarely their friends. And if the company wants to develop the 'human capacities' within the organization, French employees do not regard themselves as the prime beneficiaries. They, and indeed French researchers (Amado, 1991), do not tend to share the American view that the development of the firm and the individual go hand-in-hand.

This chapter basically concurs with Crozier's view of French work relations as impersonal, formal, compartmentalized . . . in short, predictable: consider here the low tolerance for ambiguity in France, discussed in Chapter 1. There is certainly an undercurrent of informal action which helps to 'oil the wheels', but that influence is better concealed than it is in Britain or America.

We have now set the scene for the following chapter on business rituals – the desire for ritualization being a manifestation of the desire to preserve distance and independence.

6 Rituals: Beaux gestes et faux pas

L'informalité est un aspect du management à l'américaine qui n'a pas achevé la traversée de l'Atlantique. (Informality is one aspect of the American managerial model which has not quite made it across the Atlantic.) (Conversation with PDG of Treifus-France S.A.)

ANY ATTEMPT TO CHARACTERIZE French management would be incomplete without an examination of the country's business rituals. They are reassuringly conspicuous, often physiological, manifestations of differences between cultures. They are concrete not abstract, and are accessible to simple observation. This adds to their intrigue. They go more or less unquestioned by insiders – only an outsider is likely to be struck by their distinctiveness.

Closer examination suggests that these ceremonial singularities of French management in fact represent the visible part of the proverbial iceberg. They are supported by particular beliefs and values, which can be accessed by asking managers to explain behaviour the researcher has witnessed. But beneath these beliefs and values, there are more profound assumptions which are far harder for managers to articulate, since they are taken for granted. It is up to the researcher to infer these deeper meanings (Schneider and Barsoux, 1997).

Rituals are not trivial. They actually serve to reinforce many of the deeply rooted traits of French management – and can only be interpreted in the light of wider issues such as hierarchy, education, networks and cliques, formality, the boundary between work and private life and the role of women in organizations. In this respect, the investigation of rituals provides a focus for several of the themes already discussed.

Greeting

Perhaps the most striking ritual for the business visitor to France is the frequent shaking of hands. This gesture, together with kissing as a form of greeting[1] are renowned as typically French customs.

Handshaking in France is not merely a one-off gesture that accompanies introduction. It is a daily ritual on meeting and parting which is regulated by fairly rigid conventions. In the vernacular of the etiquette guide, the hand should not be squeezed, brandished or slackly dropped; nor should the shake be too brief (discourteous) or prolonged (familiar). It must be straightforward and without brusqueness.

Protocol demands that the boss stretch out his or her hand first,[2] as pointed out in a recent guide:

> *Il convient de se lever quand votre supérieur arrive dans votre bureau; attendre, que vous soyez homme ou femme, qu'il vous tende la main.* (You are expected to rise when your boss comes into your office; and whether you are a man or a woman, to wait for the boss's hand to be profferred.) (Le Bras, 1995)

If the individuals are of equal hierarchic status, the onus is on the entrant to approach the others and they are required to make some semblance of rising to greet or bid farewell. In practice, individuals only rise when confronted by very senior executives (or visitors); colleagues are treated to a summary lean forward or nod of the head, and a token hand on the arm of the chair (as if to rise).

At the start of a meeting, it is customary for *cadres* to go round the table and shake everybody's hand in turn, starting with the most senior person. Exemption from this ceremony would only be granted to the person chairing the meeting (by virtue of his or her authority) and to late-comers (to avoid disruption). The answer in such circumstances is often to perform an abridged version of the ritual – clasping one's own hand, mimicking the handshake, and making a circular motion to symbolize movement round the table. This collective handshake might be accompanied by the phrase, '*Le bonjour à tout le monde*' ('Hello everyone').

Ostensibly a plain dichotomous (either performed or not) gesture, handshaking in fact offers managers considerable scope for passing on messages which reflect transient moods and relationships. Consider the following examples all witnessed during research in French companies:

1. A maintenance manager offered his hand to one of his foremen. The latter responded by holding out his wrist, indicating that he had a dirty hand. The maintenance manager symbolically insisted on shaking his hand. In doing so he enhanced his image as a robust manager who, in spite of his *grande école* education, was not too proud to dirty his hands alongside his subordinates. An interesting twist on the theme was witnessed at another factory where a disgruntled worker displayed a

subtle lack of respect for his superior (and the visiting researcher) by knowingly stretching out a dirty hand, which the manager (having instigated the salutation) was committed to take.

2. A popular *cadre* returning to see old colleagues following a promotion to another department was greeted with an 'augmented handshake'; in other words, a double-handed clasp which went beyond the expected formality of a simple handshake, thereby expressing closeness after a lengthy separation.

3. A maintenance manager carried out systematic tours of the works three times a day with the 'sole' purpose of shaking hands with every supervisor on each of the three shifts. He did not have to concoct some pretext for dropping in on them since *pour faire un tour de mains* (to shake their hands in turn) was reason enough. Needless to say, it also helped him to manage proactively since it both allowed him to *prendre la température* (test the water) and to pass on messages *entre quatre yeux* (face to face).

4. After losing face in front of his boss because of a peer's criticism, a head of department marked his anger the following day by delaying his handshake with the *provocateur*. The rules governing salutation are so compelling that even a minor transgression is highly significant; and by momentarily withholding acknowledgement on entering the office, the offended party had clearly registered his displeasure. Ostracism in France is not to be shaken by the hand. Boltanski quotes a graduate engineer who engaged in political activity embarrassing to the firm. His colleagues made their feelings known to him through exclusion: 'After a while some guys refuse to shake your hand' (1987, 262, English trans.).

The importance of this mundane ritual explains why the refusal to shake the boss's hand constitutes the epitome of insubordination. Consider the following example:

> A new department head felt the sting of confrontation on her first day. One of her staff took an instant dislike to her, and refused to shake her outstretched hand or speak to her – a kind of declaration of war against her own boss. When the employee was satisfied she had made herself clear, she turned her back and stalked off. (Johnson, 1996, 42)

This 'slight' of hand constituted such an attack on the head of department's authority that it was the latter who eventually resigned in frustration.

All this seems to reflect a wider cultural need, in France, to acknowledge the existence of people around you. The satirical comments of Pierre Daninos, observing a harried French journalist trying to meet a deadline, still hold much truth: 'Five times in five minutes I saw him shake hands with people who said "Please – don't get up" but who would have throught him very stand-offish if he hadn't upset all his notes and mislaid his pen in order to bid them "Good evening". The French are extremely touchy on this point' (Daninos, 1954, 31).

Since the handshake is deemed a mark of respect towards the individual, it would be equally remiss to shake the hand of the same person twice. This may cause offence in much the same way as failure to shake a person's hand since it implies that the initial encounter was immediately forgettable!

In a similar vein, Theodore Zeldin cites a teacher who complains, 'In my *lycée* the headmaster shakes the hands of the *agrégés* (highest qualified teachers), holds out two fingers to the *certifiés* and merely nods distractedly to all the other teachers' (1980, 386). Less caricatural versions of this 'physiological differentiation' were witnessed with people greeted more or less cordially, with more or less eye contact, depending on their rank. Favouritism based on intellectual pedigree or longstanding association, was explicit in terms of the people a top manager would deign to acknowledge.

Clearly, the handshake acts as a channel for expressing moods or reinforcing authority in relationships which go far beyond the basic signal of lack of hostility – though it has retained this essential aspect of partnership or conciliation at the end of a tempestuous day. It also signifies respect for colleagues and enables the boss to boost morale among employees who rarely see him or her and set much store by *la poignée de main du chef* (the boss's handshake).

In this respect, French managers are blessed with what amounts to an uncontrived point of contact. Unlike their Anglo-Saxon counterparts, they do not have to make up an excuse to see someone, or wait vigilantly to 'catch them doing something right' as Ken Blanchard once put it (1983, 41). The French manager can legitimately go and see a colleague simply *pour lui donner le bonjour* (to bid him or her good day) – the handshake needs no ulterior justification. What is more, because it requires the participants to invade each other's personal space and look each other in the eyes, it provides an ideal opportunity to pass on confidential messages, and to pick up early-warning signals. One PDG (CEO) in our study looked upon it as a fairly accurate psychological barometer. He recalled an occasion when he had gone to introduce himself to the staff of a newly acquired company: on shaking hands with the personnel he had consciously noted two individuals who did not look him straight in the eye. On enquiring, he later learned that they had been the most vociferous opponents of the takeover.

Used wisely, the handshake can prove an invaluable tool for proactive management. This is especially important in France since, as noted in the previous chapter, French employees are not very appreciative of Management By Walking Around, tending to regard it as *flicage* (surveillance). The daily round of handshakes therefore provides an opportunity for managers to pick up and pass on informal messages, and to pre-empt future problems.

Yet the handshake is also a channel for less 'salutory' messages. For instance, it reflects and perpetuates that distinctive feature of French management, the hierarchy. Touch is traditionally related to dominance. Paradoxically, while handshaking reduces the physical distance between individuals, it reinforces the organizational distance between them. The distinct set of rules which govern the salutation display leave those involved in no doubt as to who has 'the upper hand'.

It is a power gesture insofar as it is instigated by the superior and, if carried to extremes, can be a faithful guide to the rank of the various parties. Thus, French managers neatly side-step the problem of asserting their authority. They are provided with the means of doing so without having to invest their personality – simply by displaying the trappings of authority. In cultures where handshaking is not the norm, managers have to resort to other, less tactile means (such as tone of voice) to convey the same messages.

This physiological manifestation of inequality is compounded linguistically by the *tu/vous* distinction.

Form of address

For all its egalitarian claims, even the French Revolution had no lasting impact on formalism. The *vous* form of address was briefly abolished (along with *Monsieur* and *Madame* which were collectively replaced by the androgynous *Citoyen*) but soon reinstated. This was inevitable – *vous* and *tu* are power pronouns that signal status and reflect a society which accepts social inequality as natural, and where there are subtle distinctions between insiders and outsiders. Depending on the intonation, the *vous* form can be a sign of respect, of distance, or of contempt.

Of the European countries which retain the formal/informal distinction, France remains perhaps the most 'miserly' with its *tu* – in contrast, say, with Sweden where the polite form is virtually obsolete, or even Spain. As one Spanish manager working for the Lafarge group puts it:

> *En espagnol, nous réservons cette marque de respect aux personnes âgées et aux personnalités. Dans les réunions espagnoles, tout le monde se tutoie.* (In

Spain, this is used exceptionally, as a mark of respect for VIPs and the elderly. In Spanish meetings everyone is on informal terms.) (*Le Nouvel Economiste*, 2/2/96, 44)

In France, the *vous* form of address is *de rigueur* in business circles. Like the handshake it is subject to a number of rules – the basic one being that it is up to the superior to determine which form of address to use, since this defines the relationship. As with the handshake, one of us has actually witnessed an instance where an 'irreverent' subordinate (who foolishly tried to instigate a more familiar relationship) received a firm put-down with an emphatic *vous* in the superior's response to accentuate the social and hierarchical distance between them.

A more subtle, but equally effective, snub is attributed to François Mitterrand (*L'Express*, 1/3/85, 33). On emerging from a particularly successful party congress, a fellow Socialist ventured, '*On se tutoie?*' ('Shall we drop the formalities?'), to which the President replied distantly, '*Si vous voulez*' ('If we must') – or, to put it another way, 'No!' Mitterrand was in fact renowned for his aloofness and one of the claims to fame of François Dalle (the former PDG of the cosmetics company, l'Oréal) is that he was one of the very few people to use the familiar form of address with the late President.

Fortunately, most subordinates know their place and would no more dream *de tutoyer le chef* (of being familiar with the boss) than refuse to shake the boss's extended hand. Many of the *cadres* spoken to, confessed '*J'ai du mal à tutoyer*' ('Familiarity does not come easily to me'), notably with regard to older or more senior colleagues. The resilience of this norm can be gauged from the reaction of one secretary to our hypothetical suggestion that she employ the familiar form with her boss. She was adamant that even with his blessing, she really could not 'bring herself' to do so. Her boss in fact corroborated this by admitting that he would not address her as *tu* for fear of undermining his authority. He felt that a familiar relationship would leave him vulnerable because 'people' were prone to take advantage of it – and use it as a lever for favours. The French believe that friendship obliges, exposes the 'friend' to manipulation, and creates dependence – a fundamentally intolerable situation for them, according to Crozier (see Chapter 5).

Basically, there is a profound apprehension that a relationship will degenerate if one reveals too much of oneself, so distance is artificially maintained using the polite form. Many *cadres* made it a rule never to use the *tu* form downwards. This was particularly so among the older *cadres*, for whom familiarity made reprimand difficult. The use of the *vous* form was primarily motivated by the future need to sanction or, worse still, make a subordinate redundant. Censure is regarded as far more *sanglant* (scathing) in the *vous* form.

Subordinates feel the same way about it. Allowing their boss to *tutoie* them would give him or her some claim on them. The presumption of familiarity makes it far easier, say, to ask someone to work late. Subordinates also resist informality on the grounds that it inhibits candour. Consider the comments of a *cadre* with the Hachette-Filipacchi publishing group, where the boss insists on the generalized *tu* form of address:

> *A première vue, cela facilite les rapports, mais, en cas de conflit, il est beaucoup plus difficile de s'affirmer revendicatif ou de laisser exploser sa colère dans ce genre de contexte consensuel.* (Supercially, it facilitates relations, but when there is a conflict, it is much harder to make a stand or to vent one's anger in such a consensual environment.) (*Le Nouvel Economiste*, 7/4/95, 88)

Thus, to use the *tu* form one has to be fairly confident of not needing subsequent recourse to the *vous* form since back-peddling is out of the question. It is a one-way move, though we observed rare exceptions: for instance, two *cadres* on familiar terms reverted back to the *vous* form when one of them was promoted to be the other's boss – though in private they remained on *tu* terms. This use of *vous* as a face-saving device was also encountered during one of our interviews. We were interrupted by a *cadre* who addressed his colleague as *vous*. It later transpired that the two were on familiar terms but that the 'intruder' had refrained from showing this out of respect for his colleague in front of an unknown party.

As a rule, people of the same generation or organizational/educational status are likely to use *tu* more readily with one another. One *cadre* listed those colleagues with whom he was on familiar terms and mentioned one '*que tout le monde tutoie*' ('that everyone calls by his first name'). This at once implied a certain lack of authority (you do not say *tu* to someone you respect) and a congenial disposition (or to someone you dislike). From his own experience, the *cadre* recalled that the turning point had often been an event (long car journey, overseas negotiation . . .) whose relative intimacy rendered the *vous* form absurd. This would prompt an anxious (for fear of rejection) '*C'est bête quand même . . .*' ('It's a bit silly after all') and a transition to the familiar form. It is striking that the watershed for relaxing these formalities was frequently when those concerned were away from the rigid setting of the workplace.

The widespread use of *vous* means that any derogation of the practice is all the more significant. In other words, the *tu* form of address derives its political power precisely from the fact that *vous* is the norm in business. Thus, the accelerated, or in some cases obligatory, use of *tu* is a powerful means of signalling tribal identity and warding off unwelcome intruders. Mutual *tutoiment* effectively seals a clique in a highly 'visible' way – and numerous old-boys' associations, as well as less formal networks, employ this device to their advantage.

France's top *grandes écoles* (l'ENA, Polytechnique, HEC, Arts & Métiers . . .) are particularly fond of the ruling that their alumni should address their cohorts as *tu*. This, according to one cynic, in spite of the fact that they did not know one another at school and would probably have despised one another heartily if they had.[3] He continued, '*Le seul fait d'avoir posé ses fesses sur les mêmes bancs*' ('The mere fact that they had sat on the same benches') is regarded as reason enough for familiarity.

It is said that ex-Polytechnique students must *tutoie* anyone who was up to seven years above or below them – a ruling presumably designed to spare the sensibilities of senior members. In other schools the rules are equally binding, even at official functions. For instance, at one international conference we attended, the guest speaker, Yvon Gattaz, acknowledged the chairman's introduction with '*Je te remercie . . .*' ('Thanks a lot'). Many of the foreign guests were visibly taken aback at this sudden injection of informality – unaware that the two speakers were both graduates of l'Ecole Centrale.

Directories lend weight to this peculiar form of exclusion rite by listing alumni according to occupation, company and position. Every self-respecting association publishes a directory, thereby reinforcing the popular image of alumni networks as *les mafias*. The directory of the Ecole des Arts et Métiers actually includes a bookmarker-cum-advertisement which addresses members informally: '*As-tu payé ta cotisation?*' ('Have you paid-up your subscription fees?'). The clubbishness of this approach is replicated in a recruitment poster for the communist-based union, the Confédération Générale du Travail (CGT). The poster urges workers to renew their membership: '*Prends ta carte CGT*'.

All this reflects the exploitation of the familiar form of address as a utilitarian device rather than to denote friendship – but its 'misuse' is not confined to institutionalized solidarity. Any coalition can use the informal form of address as a powerful barrier to entry. Consider the experience of a provincial PDG (CEO) who was invited to a product launch by the manufacturer of a complementary product. He accepted the invitation as a useful opportunity to make a few new contacts but was disappointed to find that everyone knew (or pretended to know) everyone else. He was made to feel awkward, an outcast, simply because '*ça se tutoyait à tours de bras*' ('they were all "in" with each other'). The conspirators had rendered the clique 'impregnable' simply by using the *tu* form. Their familiarity with one another, whether genuine or, as he suspected, cosmetic, excluded him from the proceedings. The informal approach acts as an expression of group membership – and as such constitutes one of the pillars of French tribalism (this propensity for forming clans and *cloisonnement* is discussed in the previous chapter).

Having seen what it is like to be on the outside looking in, it may be interesting to quote a boss who happened to be plugged in with the people that mattered. He took great pride in explaining:

> *Je suis personnellement ami à tu et à toi avec tous les présidents de ligue. Aucun de nos concurrents n'a ça. Aucun. Ils viennent là en spectateur.* (I am on close terms with every single head in the confederation. There's not one of our competitors who can make that claim. Not one. They all attend as spectators.)

An interesting twist on the protective use of *tu* was provided by the senior management at a car plant. The personnel manager, who was part of a so-called *organigramme en rateau* (where all heads of department are on the same level), was *de facto* the plant manager's right-hand man. Now this was probably fully justified insofar as his detachment from operational problems, and his regular contacts with outside constituencies, made him a valuable adviser. However, it was reinforced by a psychological barrier which set him apart from his 'peers' – he shrewdly insisted on remaining on formal terms (like the boss) with his colleagues (who all addressed one another as *tu*), thereby asserting his 'authority' over them and keeping potential usurpers at bay.

Another amusing variation on the political use of *vous* was revealed by a young *cadre* who envisaged rapid promotion and took the precaution of addressing everyone as *vous*. This was a conscious decision based on the reasoning that subsequent promotion might prove embarrassing for people with whom he had previously been on familiar terms. The anticipated promotion materialized and the transition was smooth, thus confirming this useful tip for potential high-flyers. As already mentioned, a rather less elegant solution to the same problem resulted from the promotion of one *cadre* as boss of his previous colleague. In order to avoid embarrassment to the senior *cadre*, they agreed to revert to the formal *vous* – in public at least.

Further nuances in relationships are revealed by the way in which people are addressed – such as the title used. The French seem very keen on formality: the referee is *Monsieur l'Arbitre*, just as the policeman is *Monsieur l'Agent* and any ex-chairman expects to be addressed till his death as *Monsieur le Président*.

Even graduate engineers will be referred to ironically as *Monsieur l'Ingénieur*. Older people especially like being called by their titles both in letters and speech. And it was striking that even in the more homely environment of a firm *à dimension humaine* (of human proportions) that we visited, the boss still insisted his staff call him *Monsieur*.

This may be a sign, as suggested by a *cadre* with 20 years' experience in America that, *'on se prend trop au sérieux'* ('we take ourselves too seriously'). Others regard this deference, not so much as a sign of acceptance of the hierarchy, as a mark of respect for the individual. Either way, formality seems to result in a bolstering of the traditional hierarchy.

There is no doubt that French managers are socially reserved by Anglo-Saxon standards – especially in comparison to their American counterparts, who value informality and at least the appearance of equality in human relations, and are quick to seize upon first names. In France, such behaviour may not be welcome, as noted by a senior manager from New Zealand working in Paris:

> *J'appelle tout le monde par son prénom . . . mais les interlocuteurs n'osent pas en faire autant avec moi.* (I call them all by their first name . . . but they don't dare to reciprocate.) (*Le Nouvel Economiste*, 2/2/96, 44)

This difference in approach was especially striking when companies we visited received incoming telephone calls from abroad. The direct manner of Americans in particular often jars in France. On a number of occasions the caller provoked a stir at the reception by asking for 'Philippe' or 'Pascal'.[4] Some French *cadres* have taken this as a cue to modify their own communications with other countries by making the weighty concession of including their first names when signing letters.

In France, close relations between *cadres* are indicated by use of the surname – without *Monsieur*. The secondary importance of the forename can be seen on envelopes where addresses bear the surname followed by the initial (or name), rather than vice versa – a habit which is ingrained at school and perpetuated by the administration. The relative redundancy of the first name was emphasized by the difficulties faced by secretaries when attempting to fill out forms requiring the forename. On more than one occasion colleagues of the *cadre* in question were unable to help the secretary. This French preference was made explicit by one *cadre* who was at a loss to respond to an American request for full names (to fill out hotel reservations) and could only offer a sheepish, 'In France people do not call themselves by their first name'.[5]

As with the predominance of the *vous* mode, the almost exclusive use of surnames loads the use of forenames with significance – they can even become prized rewards if used sparingly. According to one Air Liquide *cadre*, the PDG called only five or six people by their first names[6] – they did not reciprocate, but it was nonetheless considered *'une marque d'estime extraordinaire'* ('a real honour'). One of the privileged few was Pierre who was more important in the company when the current PDG had started out 22 years ago; in this case it was a mark of affection for a senior employee.

A fascinating reversal of this trait is practised by workers who prefix the PDG's first name with *Monsieur*. This is particularly the case in traditional family firms which harbour several family members bearing the same surname, such as Michelin where the current *patron* is known as 'Monsieur François' while his son and presumed successor is 'Monsieur Edouard'. While this signifies a certain closeness, it also smacks of paternalism.

The qualifying prefix *Monsieur* is reserved for superiors or visitors and is generally abandoned with colleagues and subordinates. However, it will be used if the superior seeks to emphasize a point (usually negative). For instance, *'J'ai quelque chose à vous dire, Monsieur Dupont'* (which is reminiscent of the way a mother might signal disapproval by calling out her child's full name).

It can also be used ironically as in the case of a young manager appointed to the personnel function of Yves Saint Laurent. The manager in question upset one of the senior executives (not his boss) by failing to go and introduce himself on taking up his functions:

> *J'ai provoqué un scandale. Il a diffusé une note officielle, j'ai dû m'aplatir. Après, il me lançait des 'Monsieur' longs comme le bras . . .* (It generated a real scandal. He sent out an official memo, and I had to grovel. After that he made a big deal of addressing me as 'Sir' all the time . . .) (*Le Monde*, 6/1/93, 27)

Another example of *Monsieur* deliberately being used the wrong way, was in the case of a boss who had to reprimand a junior *cadre*. On their next encounter the boss made a point of showing there were 'no hard feelings' by mimicking subservience, *'Très bien Monsieur, je m'en occupe'* ('Very good, Sir. I'll take care of it'). The essence of this joke-cum-reconciliation lay in the reversal of the formality expected in hierarchical relations.

The French organizational context provides its players with the means to assert their authority without having to reveal their personalities. There are numerous physiological and linguistic rituals which signal their authority. Their Anglo-Saxon counterparts are bereft of such messages and have to project authority in their tone of voice or attitude – both of which are more open to misinterpretation.

This finding also seems to fit in with Theodore Weinshall's view (1977, 248) that French managers see authority vested in the role as opposed to British managers who see it vested in the person. In France then, authority requires a lesser investment of the 'self' – the handshake, the title and the form of address are stage props which help maintain authority whilst simultaneously protecting the real individual. In short, business etiquette allows *cadres* to assert their authority, whether or not they have the personal attributes to back it up. This perhaps corroborates Crozier's belief that the French are uncomfortable in face-to-face relationships and use organized rituals to cover the anxiety.

It would seem that the French have concocted a system of authority relations which minimizes the personality element. Their 'right to lead', as we shall see in the next two sections, is further reinforced by their familiarity with written and social niceties.

Written rituals

On presenting an English secretary with a draft copy of a letter to be typed up in French, she gave it a cursory glance and immediately remarked on the apparent absence of a closing salutation. It had to be pointed out to her that the whole of the last paragraph, beseeching the receiver to accept the assurance of our most distinguished sentiments, was the French equivalent of 'Yours faithfully'.

Furthermore, there are infinite possibilities for signing out depending on the impression one seeks to make on the receiver. For instance, a senior civil servant will send a lowly colleague *l'expression de ma considération distinguée*, an equal his *haute considération* and a high-ranking superior his *très haute considération*. In the business world, the formalities are not quite so strictly defined, but similar rules operate. The sender can bestow anything ranging from the basic *vive considération* to the more lavish *sentiments respectueux* or even *entier dévouement*, depending upon the perceived relationship with the receiver. The permutations are full of nuance and secretaries generally need an etiquette guide at hand to avoid a regrettable *faux pas* – in other words, to ensure that the signing out phrase conveys sufficient deference given the relative status of sender and recipient. What is more, the courtesy and status-consciousness bear up even under the utmost pressure of deteriorating relations. This can lead to a signing out phrase which is in striking contrast to the tone of the letter (see Figure 6.1).

Another feature of French business correspondence is its impersonal nature. Letters open rather stiffly with *Monsieur* or *Monsieur le . . .* (plus a title),

Paris, le 2 Septembre 1996

Monsieur,

J'accuse réception de votre courrier en date du 29 juillet, qui ni ne me surprend, ni ne m'attriste, mais par contre m'irrite au plus haut point.

En effet je ne peux pas accepter le ton que vous vous croyez autorisé d'utiliser.

Il me semble que je suis celui qui est en droit de demander des explications, et que vous tentez bien maladroitement de renverser cette situation.

D'autre part, et pour que les choses soient claires, sachez que j'entends m'entretenir avec Monsieur Durant tant que lui et moi y trouverons convenance et que je n'envisage pas d'utiliser les services de quelconques intermédiaires pour ce faire.

Enfin, puisque Monsieur Durant a été informé de notre différend tant par vos soins que par les miens, je pense qu'il serait heureux qu'il accepte d'assister au prochain Conseil d'Administration. Je compte en effet sur cette occasion pour aborder aussi précisément que vous le souffrirez la situation pesante que je vous soupçonne, ainsi que ce Monsieur Artois, de créer volontairenent.

Je terminerai en vous précisant que m'écrivant en qualité de Président du Conseil, celui-ci peut et doit être informé de notre litige, la mention 'Personnel et Confidentiel' me paraissant déplacée.

Vous souhaitant bonne réception de la présente, et dans l'attente d'une convocation pour le courant septembre, je vous prie d'agréer, Monsieur, l'expression de mes salutations très distinguées.

J.-P. COIMET

Figure 6.1: Contrast between tone and content in a business letter

and end with the stylized formality mentioned above. There is no presumption of acquaintanceship. By convention, even the content is disconcertingly cold from an Anglo-Saxon standpoint. The aim seems to be to preserve anonymity. There is no sign of the breezy and familiar approach which characterizes Anglo-Saxon correspondence. Even if the individuals parted on the warmest of personal terms, the follow-up correspondence is unlikely to make reference to that cordial meeting. In fact, the only discernible evidence of individuality is the written style of the letter. The letter is an opportunity to parade one's education and impress both secretary and recipient(s) by one's *tournure* (expression).

The French clearly indulge in what, by Anglo-Saxon standards, is excessive formality. French business correspondence seems to prize inordinately complex set phrases such as those quoted by Zeldin (1980, 352), '*J'ai l'honneur de vous prier de bien vouloir*' (to mean 'please') or '*Il ne saurait être question d'apporter à cette demande une suite favorable*' (to mean 'no'). These *formules* do not add to the core message and, if anything, actually serve to conceal it. Thus, for example, in our own correspondence with a French firm, we were led to expect a favourable response until, upon reaching the twelfth line of the letter (see Figure 6.2), it was finally stated that a visit to that company had not been approved.

It would seem that the French sometimes indulge in voluntary long-windedness. One *cadre* admitted as much by saying, '*on prend plaisir à tourner autour du pot*' ('we relish beating about the bush'). Certainly, they do not always seem anxious to get to the heart of the matter. This would seem to bear out the traditional portrayal of the French as a people overly concerned with style, sometimes attaching more importance to means than ends, to form than content. It would appear that the French managerial model has not fully embraced the American managerial values of explicitness, directness and utility.

Yet this lack of directness can be interpreted differently. Their elegant meanderings display respect for the individual and a desire to avoid inflicting unnecessary loss of face. The coded nature of French business correspondence gives it a sense of abstraction which takes the sting out of even the most virulent personal attack. Similarly, a request which is turned down is made far more palatable if the sender takes the trouble to compose a courteous and personalized refusal – the brusqueness of the negative message is attenuated by a veneer of grace and humility which provides a psychological refuge for both sender and recipient. There is also a residual fear, mentioned previously, that informality may be abused, may be used to extract favours or to imply commitments. Thus too cordial a tone might be compromising if on the record.

Paris, le 21 janvier 1994

Monsieur le Professeur,

Vous voudrez bien ne pas me tenir rigueur du retard avec lequel je réponds au courrier que vous m'avez adressé en décembre dernier avec la recommandation de Monsieur le Ministre Conseiller chargé des affaires économiques et commerciales à l'Ambassade de France en Grande-Bretagne.

Ce délai me pemet cependant de vous répondre en meilleure connaissance de cause car mes collaborateurs ont pu ainsi étudier votre proposition avec une attention réellement bienveillante, ainsi que je les y avais invités.

En réalité, nos structures d'accueil pour les étudiants doivent faire face à de nombreuses demandes et nous tentons de satisfaire le plus grand nombre d'entre eux. Malheureusement aujourd'hui, nous ne voyons pas la possibilité d'accueillir votre élève le temps suffisant pour entreprendre valablement une étude en profondeur sur les méthodes de gestion pratiquées dans notre entreprise.

Croyez que je regrette de ne pouvoir vous apporter l'aide que vous sollicitiez et je vous prie d'agréer, Monsieur le Professeur, l'assurance de mes sentiments très distingués.

Monsieur G. de LAMARTINE

Président directeur général

Monsieur Peter LAWRENCE.

cc: Monsieur le Ministre Conseiller

Figure 6.2: Elegant meanderings in a letter of rejection

This preoccupation with form has additional implications. In particular, it serves to uphold the distinction between those who know the rules and those who do not. Besides the rules of etiquette there are also those of grammar and spelling. The importance of these can be gauged from the popularity of a French spelling competition, instigated ten years ago by Bernard Pivot, the editor of a weekly literary magazine, *Lire*. Each year the *dictée* (dictation) is televised and viewing figures are massive. In 1996, there were some 400,000 officially registered candidates along with a handful of celebrities. The dictation itself consists of two or three paragraphs of excrutiatingly complex prose and the correct version (together with explanations) appears in the quality press the next day (see, for example, *Le Figaro*, 16/12/96, 37). Now although this is a recent institution, it has taken hold of the national consciousness in a way which highlights the obsession with writing perfect French.[7]

Of course, mastery of writing skills is only one barrier among others, but it supports the claim of the better educated to hold high positions in organizations. Simultaneously, self-taught individuals are discouraged in their bids to infiltrate this graduate preserve simply because they are not *au fait* with the written niceties of business correspondence. Emphasis on correctness – *faire les choses comme il faut* – in written expression as elsewhere, lends weight to the French conviction that educational credentials are the proper means for determining managerial eligibility.

This was strikingly confirmed in one company we visited run by an *autodidacte* (self-taught) PDG. According to a senior executive, the PDG had always appointed graduates as his personal assistants in order to make up for his ineptitude in matters of formal written communication. Attracting personnel of this calibre invariably meant paying twice the market rate for personal assistants, but this was the price of maintaining credibility *vis-à-vis* the banks, customers and suppliers – and of course, the respect of employees.

Further evidence of the importance of educational qualifications for business legitimacy can be found in the business card. These bear the name of the *grande école* attended (notoriety permitting) and are therefore vital in establishing the status relationships, since there is widespread consensus on the implicit pecking order of schools. Thus, the ritual exchange of business cards enables each party to know which role to play and will ensure that each receives the proper consideration.

Feeding rituals

Meals

The French enjoy talking about food in much the same way as the British find diversion in the weather. These are topics which unify a nation. When General de Gaulle complained that it was impossible to govern a nation which produces 250 varieties of cheese, he missed the bigger point. A love of gastronomy is about the one thing the French have in common. Social, occupational or hierarchical divisions are forgotten once the subject of food is invoked: what goes with what, where you can get it, how it should be cooked. And this preoccupation with food has infiltrated the organizational setting.

First, it is observable in the business language. Where Britons and Americans are more naturally drawn to sporting or military metaphors, the French readily employ food imagery. For example, the 'top brass' are *les grosses légumes* (big vegetables) or *le gratin* (cheese topping); a cushy job is *un bon fromage* (a mature cheese) and making someone do any job going is *mettre quelqu'un à toutes les sauces* (to try someone with every sauce). A *cadre* involved in negotiations rounded off his sales pitch with the aside, '*J'ai vendu ma soupe*' ('I've sold my soup') – it only remained to see if they took the bait, '*si la mayonnaise prend*' ('if the mayonnaise sets'). On the other hand, a favourable situation which deteriorates is said to *tourner au vinaigre* (turn sour) or *se gâter* (going off). Or, if negotiations appear to be leading nowhere (paying 'homage' to German cuisine), *ça patine dans la choucroute* (we're pedalling in sauerkraut) – possibly a sign that a compromise is needed and that the time has come to *mettre de l'eau dans son vin* (dilute one's wine) – or else that a bribe, *un pot-de-vin* (pitcher of wine) may be required.

The importance of food is echoed in the business press. A striking example was the issue of the business magazine *L'Expansion* (13/7/93) devoted entirely to '*Gastronomie*'. It included articles on the best restaurants for clinching deals (where good food and discretion are guaranteed); a comparison of staff restaurants in ten well-known companies; and the difficulties of finding good food when travelling (on planes, trains and motorways). A similar issue of *Fortune*, say, or *Management Today*, is inconceivable.

Nor was this a one-off. Business magazines devote regular columns to wine, restaurants and food. For example, an article in *Capital* tackled the tricky issue of which wine to drink with which cheese, explaining:

> *Vouloir proposer à tout prix un grand vin n'est pas forcément judicieux: un vin trop puissant 'tue' un bon fromage, de même qu'un fromage trop fort peut masquer les saveurs d'un grand vin.* (It may unwise to opt automatically

for a vintage wine: a heavy wine will 'kill' a good cheese, just as too strong a cheese may overpower the flavours of a vintage wine.) (October 1993, 176–77)

A more recent article in *L'Expansion* surveyed the gastronomic delights of private presidential dining rooms across different sectors, rating the atmosphere, the quality of the food and the quality of the wine cellar. Banks and insurances came out top, while communication companies were written off as:

> *Trop pressés, trop américanisés, pas très portés sur la gastronomie.* (Too rushed, too Americanized, not very concerned with gastronomy.) (10/7/95, 122–23)

This obsession with food can also be seen in their eating habits. For instance, the office working lunch with sandwiches is rare. Food is not fuel. It is something which deserves respect, at every level, from factory worker to company president – the ceremony varying only in the details of refinement. The availability of wine at meal times is also considered important. While many opt for water, taking a glass or two of wine is perfectly acceptable. Such is the importance of wine to accompany a meal, that IBM was forced to lift its 'no alcohol' restriction, especially for its French subsidiary.

In terms of duration, the French are conditioned from school days to take a two-hour lunch break which means staying relatively late in the afternoon to compensate. This pattern for the working day carries over into adulthood (and is examined further in the following section). A one-and-a-half-hour lunch break is not unusual – and we are talking here of a standard lunch, not a *repas d'affaire* (business meal). Of course, not all that time is spent at table. It provides a chance to chat, to wander round, and to drink a leisurely coffee to ward off the soporific effects of the meal – *'un petit jus pour me remettre en route'* ('a quick boost to get me going again').

If meal times seem somewhat ritualistic, business entertaining takes the ceremony to new heights. A lavish *repas d'affaires* (business meal) will last anything up to two or three hours and although lunch hours are supposedly shortening, getting in touch with senior French managers between 12:00 and 14:30 remains problematic.

Hospitality is an important element in the business dealings of the French. They may not be inclined to entertain at home, for reasons of privacy explored in the previous chapter, but restaurants are considered important arenas for extended business discussions. Considerable thought is given to the choice of restaurant which should be noted for its fine cuisine rather than its *décor*. The meal itself should be carefully composed and accompanied by particular drinks at specific points. And payment should involve minimum fuss – the epitome being to leave casually immediately on finishing, thus indicating an open table.

So what do all these eating rituals tell us about French management? In many ways they confirm the sense of ceremony which characterizes work relations in general. *Le savoir manger* (knowing what to eat and drink, and how) is important, especially for those in contact with clients. Where Anglo-Saxon sales managers might be sent on courses to improve their presentation skills, their French counterparts are sometimes sent off by employers to improve their knowledge of wine. One sales manager attending such a course explained:

> *Ne pas avoir l'air complètement néophyte au cours d'un déjeuner avec un client, c'est le B.A.-BA d'un bon début de négotiation.* (Not knowing about wine, at a business lunch with a client, is likely to set the negotiation off to a bad start.) (*Capital*, August 1994, 56–57).

Of course *le savoir manger* also demands a capacity to cope with alcohol and to stave off its debilitating effects. This was supported by a commercial director who confessed to resorting occasionally to consuming a tin of sardines prior to important negotiations in order to delay the absorption of alcohol. French managers are not averse to using their international reputation as *bons vivants* as a means of 'softening up' their adversaries – particularly when dealing with foreign visitors.

The expectation of *le savoir manger* also increases with rank. An awareness of etiquette and a certain familiarity with food and wine is a reflection of one's *éducation*, meaning both academic background and upbringing. The higher a manager climbs, the greater the expectation of polish. And while refinement alone won't get you far, those who lack it may find their advancement curtailed. To criticize a *cadre* as *mal élevé* (ill-mannered) in France is far more damning than it would be in American and even British business circles. This perhaps goes back to the point made in Chapter 2 that a *cadre* has a kind of social status which goes beyond the strictly functional role.

Eating rituals therefore tend to reinforce the pattern of hierarchic relations noted in the previous chapter. Besides the issue of how you eat, there is also the matter of *with whom*. Meal times are loaded with social and political significance. In France, lunching with the boss is often regarded as a real privilege. Bosses knowingly use it as a means of routinely 'rewarding' subordinates. This reward draws its value from the prestige of being seen with the boss. One *cadre* in our study went as far as to suggest that the length of the meal was critical since competing *cadres* would compare the time accorded to one another. Of course, the issue of access would not be considered so critical if, as in Britain and America, it were less regulated – but in France the right of access to people or information is not a basic democratic principle. Having access is equated with power.

Being invited to lunch by the boss may therefore be politically motivated, rather than a simple matter of 'keeping in touch' with the prevailing mood. Besides placating disgruntled subordinates, it may serve to 'butter up' external parties like clients, suppliers, prospective business partners, works' inspectors, or representatives from the employment agency and the town hall. They will be flattered by the time accorded to them and the attentiveness to their preoccupations. As one *cadre* explained:

> *C'est une façon de reconnaître l'importance sociale de votre interlocuteur. Un moyen de partager quelque chose qui soit au-delà de la conversation et du café.* (It's a means of acknowledging someone's social standing, of sharing something more than a conversation and a coffee.)

Thus, a private lunch is considered a mark of real respect. It confers a qualitative difference to the encounter. Contrast this with Britain or America where 'Let's do lunch' has become a tired cliché. Sometimes it is used figuratively as a painless way of disengaging. At other times, it means 'I've no time now, but I can fit you in over lunch.' Lunch is seen as 'lost' time and meeting over lunch increases productivity. It is a matter of convenience. In France a lunch invitation promises a different type of conversation. Office interactions being fairly formal, *la table* is a privileged arena for getting to know others and exchanging more confidential information.[8] It is no coincidence that the French refer to insider trading as *'le délit de dîner en ville'* ('the offence of dining in town') (*L'Expansion*, 4/4/96, 123).

In a restaurant the two parties shift from a desk-width apart to within touching distance – in other words, from a work relationship to a social relationship. This facilitates communication, both psychologically and physically. The actors can see and hear each other perfectly and non-verbal communication is less 'showy' and stylized. Reflecting on his experiences in France, Johnson observed:

> More good or bad can be done to a business relationship in the two hours at the table than in two months of ordinary business dealings across a seven-foot mahogany desk. (1996, 86)

This increase in self-disclosure helps to determine who a person *really* is, in much the same way as playing golf or tennis with someone might in Britain or America. In matters relating to food and wine, is this person a bluffer, knowledgeable, entertaining? Is he or she well mannered? As guards are dropped, it may be easier to discuss mutual objectives and intentions. Eating together is regarded as the best means of facilitating open communications and building up trust. In the French context, a formal meeting is not a viable substitute for a business meal – hence the comment of a sales director in our study:

> *Il arrive qu'un rendez-vous soit remis de plusieurs semaines faute d'avoir pu trouver un déjeuner de libre avant.* (It is not unknown for a meeting to be postponed for several weeks simply because of a failure to find a free lunch hour.)

In some ways then, the importance of meals derives from the fact that they contrast with the more formal office setting. Food plays an essential role in reinforcing social groups. While people may have little choice about with whom they work, they can choose with whom they eat – and the meal being considered 'private time', the French are rather particular about who sits near them outside the functional requirements of the office environment. While lunch tables tend to respect ranks, they do not always respect functions, and who eats with whom is an important indicator of the informal cliques within the organization. Exchanges of confidential information are more likely to occur at lunch times where people are more relaxed and where physical proximity tends to encourage intimacy.

Another significant social implication of the concern with food is the way it disadvantages women. Firstly, long-drawn-out meals at lunch time are fine provided one is free to compensate for the loss of time in the evening. Secondly, in the French organizational context (as outside), it is far less acceptable for a woman to be overweight than for a man. The expectation of feminity is higher in France. A female executive sees herself as needing to be slim and elegant. Furthermore, there are certain ceremonial aspects surrounding the meal which constrain the behaviour of a woman. Consider the following advice to businesswomen inviting men to lunch, from a recent etiquette guide:

> *N'hésitez pas à consulter les hommes qui vous entourent pour choisir les vins, à moins que vous ne soyez connaisseuse. Si le maître d'hôtel ne remplit pas les verres, vous proposerez à l'un des hommes de le faire.* (Don't hesitate to ask the men at your table to choose the wines, unless you happen to be an

expert. If the head waiter does not fill the glasses, suggest that one of the men does so.) (Géricot, 1994, 188–89)

Notwithstanding the fact that etiquette guides are always somewhat extreme in their advice, one can infer that, for a French businesswoman, inviting men to lunch is not a straightforward affair as it would be, say, in America. Consider a further piece of advice, relating to settling the bill:

> *Elle essaiera, pour ne pas gêner les hommes au moment de payer, de s'entendre avec le restaurateur pour que la note lui soit envoyée à son bureau.* (To avoid embarrassing the men when it comes to paying, she should agree with the restaurant owner to have the bill sent on to her office.) (Deleplanque, 1975, 185)

These are simply not issues in Anglo-Saxon countries. The point is that even in the business context, the distinction between French men and women still holds. Compared to her Anglo-Saxon counterparts, there are more potential pitfalls for a French businesswoman when conducting business. It takes considerable poise to carry off these rituals. The risk of loss of face, of being seen as pushy, or worse still, submissive, is higher in France. As Picard points out, in France more than in other western countries, *'une femme d'affaires est toujours une femme'* ('a businesswoman remains a woman') (1995, 189).

Whilst such expectations do not in themselves explain the relative absence of women from the higher reaches of French management, they draw attention to the way in which the work pattern and ceremony surrounding meals – which are deeply rooted in French culture – tend to discriminate against women.

Drinks

Another feeding ritual which characterizes French companies is *le pot* (cocktails and savoury snacks organized on the premises). This occasion typically consecrates events such as a promotion, departure or retirement. As Picard puts it:

> *Un service qui 'n'organise rien' pour le départ d'un de ses membres; un promu qui 'n'arrose pas' sa promotion . . . font généralement objet de critiques.* (A department which fails to organize anything for the departure of one of its staff; someone who fails to buy everyone drinks to celebrate a promotion . . . will be asking for criticism.) (1995, 141)

Since this is a social occasion, absences are particularly unforgivable. Bosses will generally be invited out of courtesy but their failure to take up the invitation will not go unnoticed and is likely to vex the person in whose honour the *pot* is held. The act of presence, because it is voluntary and non-work-related, is particularly important, and a brief speech on the part of the boss will prove an important mark of esteem. The boss can gain a modicum of goodwill *vis-à-vis* the personnel on these occasions but risks a far greater loss by failing to attend. As Picard points out:

> *Leur déroulement est quasi immuable; les discours qu'on y prononce se ressemblent; chacun sait d'avance ce qu'il devra dire, répondre, faire . . . elles ont souvent un certain caractère d'obligation pour ceux qui les organisent ou y participent . . . y compris parfois pour le héros de la fête.* (They all follow the same pattern. The speeches resemble each other. Everyone knows exactly what they will have to do, say, and answer . . . They are often regarded as an obligation by those who organize or take part in them . . . including the person honoured.) (1995, 141)

This rather formal event is about as close as the French get to a 'party' within the confines of the workplace. The prospect of anything as unregulated as an 'office party' – with all the informality, self-disclosure and potential for loss of face it entails – would send shivers through both French managers and employees. Once again, work and relaxation are not considered to go hand-in-hand.

Business hours

The ritual of long working days is partly a knock-on effect of the preceding ritual concerning long lunch breaks. The managers involved in our work-shadowing exercise regularly put in 11-hour days – typically starting around 8.30 a.m. and leaving after 7.30 p.m. Again this is a work pattern to which French *cadres* are accustomed from childhood since the school day often lasts from 8.30 a.m. until 5.30 p.m.

For *prima facie* evidence of this tendency to work late we need look no further than the television. In most European countries the evening news is screened at 6 p.m. or 7 p.m. whilst the French *journal télévisé* traditionally has a 8 p.m. slot – a sign that the bulk of the news-watching audience is not home before that time. Also the diaries issued to French executives have hourly slots for each day of the week which start at 7 a.m. and stretch optimistically until 9 p.m.

More systematic evidence can be found in a recent survey reported in *Le Monde* (20/3/96, 4). This showed that half of the *cadre* population worked more than 46 hours a week, with over 26 per cent of the population working between 51 and 60 hours a week. What is more, these figures probably understate the situation since the sample was heavily biased towards the public sector (69 per cent of those surveyed) and the provinces (85 per cent outside Paris). *Le Monde* (10/10/96, 1) highlights the widening gap between the hours worked by *cadres* and non-*cadres*.

The ethos of hard work is cultivated by the exacting education system. As we noted in Chapter 3, making it to a *grande école* takes remorseless effort as well as brains. And the chosen few who go all the way to state service will consider hard work as more than just a necessity; it is a duty. Dedication to the *grandeur* of the nation is a value which runs deep among servants of the state.

Since *grandes écoles* graduates dominate the higher reaches of French business, and former state officials head many of the best-known companies, the tone is firmly set. What Crozier labels 'the traditional work-obsessed culture of the French elite' (*Financial Times*, 18/1/95, 16) percolates down through French companies. As for the other company heads, those without a prestigious education, they had better work twice as hard to prove to their staff that they deserve respect. A huge *capacité de travail* (work rate) is often highlighted in articles describing French bosses. Along with brains, it is something which confirms their right to lead. It also helps to reconcile the tension between egalitarian values and hierarchy, raised in Chapter 1. Large power differences are justified by *visible* differences in effort.

The requirement to stay late is not uniform – it increases with rank (*noblesse oblige*). Thus, the hours spent are more or less proportional to organizational standing. One rung down from the PDG, for the *cadres dirigeants,* there is an unwritten obligation to be around for as long as the boss might need them – though some allowance may be made regarding their time of arrival in the morning. *Le patron* would not take kindly to the commercial or financial directors not responding to a call at 7.30 p.m.

Further down among the *cadres moyens*, leaving on time is *mal vu* (bad show) and to do so is to risk accusations of having *un esprit de fonctionnaire* (a civil service mentality) – though the criticism can be warded off by being seen to take work home. This is based on the principle that a *cadre*, unlike a civil servant or a worker, is paid to do a job, not to complete a set number of hours – a notion supported by the fact that *cadres* are not entitled to overtime pay. As one *cadre* complained, whenever he left the office at 7 p.m., his colleagues would shout out, '*Bon après-midi!*' ('Good afternoon') (*Le Monde*, 17/5/95,

28). Those who leave early cannot have important work to do, and are less likely to be promoted.

The compulsion to leave late was seen by several *cadres* in our study to have degenerated – so that they would stay behind, often to no great avail, simply *pour la forme* (for show). In one company where the working day was especially long, the *cadres* actually wished to introduce a system of clocking in (*pointage*), but none dared to make the request (*Le Monde*, 17/5/95, 28). This both confirms the inadvisability of speaking out against the boss, and the view that *disponibilité* (availability) is what the *cadres* are paid for. It is visible proof of their commitment to the firm; and complaining openly about their conditions would be considered disloyal. So most *cadres* accept it as part of their lot – just one more contributor to their much-vaunted *malaise* (see Chapter 2).

This raises the question, why do *cadres* have to stay late and why does this obligation increase with status? *Cadres* typically respond that the early evening, when the phone rings less, is the best time to deal with serious paperwork. First, the *cadre* must attend to all that thoughtfully crafted correspondence mentioned earlier in the chapter. But there are also internal reports to handle. These play a greater role than in Anglo countries, which rely more on oral presentations and discussions for disseminating information. *Cadres* will therefore spend time reading and commenting on reports which have been circulated. They will also spend time preparing such reports for others to read. These reports should of course be comprehensive, well structured, coherent, and well written. Conceptual consistency and richness is more important than practical feasibility. These things require thought.

Turning to the correlation between staying late and status, this can partly be explained by the French tradition of centralization and unwilling-ness to delegate. Assuming that senior managers have more onerous responsibilities, it is understandable that without delegation to alleviate them, they will have larger workloads. Thus, centralization of authority and decision-making automatically result in a cumulative progression of the workload through the echelons.

There is also a more subtle explanation for the *need* to work late. This has to do with the rather formal approach to management exhibited by French managers. As mentioned in the previous chapter, French executives are not particular accessible during the work day, and do not fraternize much outside the office. It is only at the end of the day (or over lunch) that they loosen up (a little). This is when information gets passed on and when many of the key discussions take place.

This has important implications. A survey of women *cadres* showed that many believed that staying late served no real purpose:

Beaucoup disent qu'il y a une propension toute masculine à traîner au bureau sans réels motifs de performance professionnelle. (Many claim that there is a particularly masculine tendency to stay around the office unnecessarily late.) (*Le Monde*, 16/6/93, 32)

Yet if our interpretation is right – and this is a key opportunity for informal exchanges, for cultivating networks, for picking up on the boss's intentions, and aligning one's own objectives – then non-participation in this process may be very damaging to women's careers. One woman *cadre* went as far as to say that this was when the real decisions were taken – so family commitments effectively barred her from playing her rightful role in the decision-making process.

As we argued earlier, the need to put in long hours is not solely responsible for the low incidence of women in the higher reaches of management; but it is indicative of a work pattern which seems more 'hostile' to the integration of women than that of most western cultures (noticeable, for instance, in the relative absence of flexitime).

The solution for many career-minded women is to switch to staff functions which tend to offer more predictable hours, even if promotion prospects are more limited.

Holidays

In most countries, particular festivals, carnivals, or fiestas may qualify as rituals, but it would be inappropriate to describe general holidays in this way. That is not the case in France where holiday habits in terms of timing, duration, destination and aspiration are deeply ingrained, not to say sacrosanct. This is particularly true of the summer holidays, aptly termed *les grandes vacances*.

Thanks to a statutory holiday entitlement of five weeks a year, a four-week break in the summer is not unusual. The French typically refer to their *mois de congé* (month off) as if holidays in smaller units were inconceivable. The French motorway system on the last weekend of July grinds to a halt as the returning *juillettistes* cross the holiday bound *aoûtiens*. The ensuing chaos is the result of an overwhelming propensity to stay in France, to head for the coast, and a widespread refusal to stagger or fragment their vacations.

This 'compulsory' duration is to some extent imposed by works' shutdowns. For instance, when the three large auto manufacturers – Peugeot, Citroën and Renault – shut down for August, there is little point in staying open for many related companies. Thus a whole host of suppliers, subcontractors and intermediaries must follow suit. There is a knock-on effect which provokes what one PDG (CEO) referred to as *'la mise en sommeil totale'* ('the hibernation') of the French economic machine. Forty per cent of French companies halt their activities for between two and four weeks in August. OECD figures show that France suffers from a 26 per cent production deficit in August, compared to the average for rest of the year. The equivalent shortfall in the UK is of 4.5 per cent, while the US boasts a surplus of 3 per cent (*L'Expansion*, 11/7/96, 55).

With the business world partly closing down from early July to late August, relations with French companies are difficult. French subsidiaries abroad will find it hard to get hold of people at head office and foreign customers will be unable to place orders with French firms. The holiday period can also prove disruptive for small French firms which are caught flat-footed and embarrassed by a sudden upswing in orders after the holidays. In spite of its penalizing effect on French industry, the ritual persists.

The main explanation for shutting down has to do with simplicity. Human resource directors in the car companies evoke two key blockages: the complexity of reconciling individual holiday requests, and the unshakable habits of the employees themselves (*L'Expansion*, 11/7/96, 56) .

These problems are revealing. First they confirm the 'sacred' nature of holidays in France. This is not something human resource managers mess around with unless they want friction.[9] But nor do they believe that they can rely on employees to resolve the matter among themselves, in their working groups. In most units, the team spirit or sense of compromise and fairness needed to come to such arrangements is lacking. Where a clash of dates occurs, the senior person will feel little obligation to make a concession – and clashes are inevitable when the perceived options limit themselves to either July or August.

From the employees' perspective, the desire to cling on to the compulsory four weeks *can* be attributed to old habits. But there is another plausible explanation based on arguments presented in the last chapter. There we argued that, relatively speaking, freedom for the French means the freedom to be left alone, rather than the freedom to do something. The same applies to holidays. Employees are willing to sacrifice the choice regarding the timing and duration of their holidays, in exchange for the security of four weeks of peace and quiet. Fixed holiday periods mean no awkward negotiations with colleagues about holiday dates, no pressure to perform heroics in order to secure the boss's signature, no last-minute refusals based on a boss's whim or an unforeseen problem – and, above all, no emergency calls from the office while on vacation. To the French, who dread dependence relationships, and who are anxious to preserve the barrier between work and private life (as noted in the previous chapter), these things matter.

For most *cadres* the summer holiday is not a chance to go somewhere exotic but a *retour aux sources* (back to the land – in a literal and spiritual sense) – typically to a *résidence secondaire* (second home) that many successful executives possess.[10] That second home may be a converted farmhouse, a modern villa, or even a small château. The French have the highest rate of second home ownership in the world – one for every nine families (*The Economist Guide*, 1990, 89) – which prompted Zeldin's quip 'a Frenchman's second home is his castle' (1980, 205).

The whole idea behind holidays is to *recharger ses batteries* (revitalize oneself) and to *faire le point* (think about things). Where British and American managers perhaps look to escape, the French look to get back in touch with reality, with themselves, with their roots. It is a time for reflection, not sensory stimulation. As Jean Gandois, head of the CNPF (employers' union), and former PDG of Péchiney, explained:

> *Je ne vais surtout pas à l'autre bout du monde. Cela, je le fais toute l'année. En été, je vais à la montagne et dans mon Limousin natal.* (I don't go to the other side of the world. I do that all year round. In summer, I go to the mountains and to my home region). (*Le Point*, 17/8/87, 50)

This is fairly typical. According to figures published in *Le Monde* (15/8/95, 7) nine out of ten French families holiday in France, mostly in non-paying accommodation; 53 per cent of holidays are spent with family, with friends or in second homes. British managers who tell colleagues they are going 'back home' – possibly to visit relatives – for their main holiday risk being laughed out of the office.

For the French a successful holiday is one which is in complete contrast to the stress and bustle of work – it is the reward for the 11 months of effort, constraint and frustration which precede it. But it is precisely this contrast which accentuates the post-holiday depression. In a month one has ample time to change one's lifestyle, and the shock to the system is all the greater on returning. Add to that the fact that everyone's holiday coincides and the result is a case of mass depression.

A measure of the concentration of the holiday period can be seen in the fact that there is an identifiable period known as *la rentrée* (the re-opening) which applies to politics, education and industry. As one *cadre* put it, towards the end of August, 'France starts back to work next week'. The degree of consensus surrounding the subject is also visible in the way *cadres* will naturally assume their peers have had a break. Throughout the month of September *cadres* ringing each other will open the conversation with 'How did the holidays go?', followed by mutual commiseration at having to be back at work, *'c'est dur la reprise'* ('it's hard to get going again'). Even circulars to other personnel may make allusion to the holiday. A note on a security issue at l'Air Liquide concluded with a PS wishing those about to leave *'Bonnes vacances'* ('A pleasant holiday') and those returning *'Bon courage'* ('Keep your spirits up').

Fortunately, there are other holidays to look forward to, notably the winter break. This is often spent skiing – in France, of course. Since the early 1980s, this too has become something of an institution. And there are 11 public holidays to fit in too. Where these fall on a Tuesday or a Thursday, individuals may use their *jours d'ancienneté* (extra days accruing through seniority) to *faire le pont* (make a four-day weekend). Again, the weekend home is likely to be the preferred destination on these short breaks.

Future trends

As in most other countries, French business rituals are losing their identity (slowly) under the influence of international business. In terms of formality, some younger *cadres* are adopting more easy-going styles. They have shown impatience with the old formal approach and are setting less store by titles and decorum. For instance, the use of first names, though still much less widespread than in Britain or the US, has become far more usual among the under-40s, especially in the newer professions such as IT and consultancy. Similarly, the *tu* form of address is steadily gaining ground at the expense of its more formal equivalent. This is particularly the case among students and teenagers and to a lesser extent among younger *cadres*. And the introduction of electronic mail in many companies means that a lot of correspondence is less formalized.

Another change is the 'Americanization' of meals. Many French executives for reasons of health and time are today putting less accent on the long heavy business lunch as a matter of routine, and will reserve it for special occasions. At other times, they will opt for a brasserie or even a snack bar. The American-style working breakfast, often in a hotel dining-room, has become popular.

According to surveys, the French are also fragmenting their holidays to a greater extent. French companies have woken up to the dangers of closing down in a global economy, when their competitors stay open. Nevertheless, the *grandes vacances* (summer holidays) retain their grip over the French nation – and anyone who disagrees should try their hand at setting up meetings in the July/August period.

Overview

Paradoxically, the foregoing rituals have as their unifying feature the fact that, by their mundane nature, they go unperceived by those who engage in them. Nor are they acknowledged by management writers. Yet their existence seems glaring to the outsider, and consideration of their deeper meaning shows that they encapsulate much of the essence of French management.

The ritualistic aspects of French management are probably more developed than in Anglo-Saxon countries which value a more explicit and direct approach. The French remain rather hierarchical and ceremonial, even if a new social informality has emerged among younger people. They continue to put value on doing things in elegant style, and on the formal courtesies and forms of address.

Of particular interest is the way the rituals reinforce the themes of hierarchy and networks, inclusion and exclusion, explored in the previous chapter. In extending a hand to shake, by the style of greeting or in electing to meet over lunch the parties reveal their relationship – and subtle breaches of etiquette convey important messages.

But perhaps the most insidious influence of these rituals is the way they discriminate against women in French business. Equal opportunity careers depend on more than diplomas, abilities and ambitions. To a greater extent than in Anglo-Saxon countries, the career prospects of French women are likely to suffer from the structure of the working day, with its long lunch break and unpredictable closure. They may also find it more difficult to reconcile the forceful and combative aspects of management with the heavy expectation of femininity. And, of course, they will find it difficult to infiltrate male-dominated networks. These features of French management are all upheld by rituals which are detrimental to women's self-confidence and sense of professional acceptance. In addition, women managers intent on making it to the top will have to contend with a very French, and rather paternalistic, notion of the role of the boss – as we shall see in the next chapter.

7 Bosses: L'entreprise c'est moi [1]

Peut-être appreciés personnellement, les patrons sont critiqués collectivement.
(People may think highly of their bosses on an individual basis, but they dislike them as a group.) (Conversation with *Directeur Général*, Accor)

JUST AS *CADRE* MEANS something more than manager, so *patron*, the subject of the present chapter, has social and cultural connotations which go beyond its literal translation as 'boss' or 'employer'. According to Priouret (1968, 14), the term *patron* gradually superseded that of *maître* (master) under the Second Empire (1852–70). It has its roots in the Latin *pater* (father), which points up the paternalistic aspect of French management. In spite of the advent of less loaded terms like *chef d'entreprise* or *employeur* or *président*, it remains the most widely used designation of the company head. The term is a catch-all that includes the chiefs of owner-managed and professionally managed companies, in the public and private sectors. It is also used to designate intermediary bosses. As one maintenance manager explained, '*Pour l'ouvrier spécialisé, c'est le contremaître son patron*' ('As far as an unskilled worker is concerned, the supervisor is his boss').

Reputation

Employers in France have traditionally suffered from a poor public image. They have been criticized for making money by exploiting others (*sur le dos des autres*). Zola's *Germinal*, published in 1885, provides a useful indication of the traditional attitude towards *le patron*. In this novel, one of the characters (Deneulin) weighs up the various ways of making money and concludes, '*l'argent que vous gagnent les autres est celui dont on engraisse le plus sûrement*' ('making money through others is the surest way of making fat profits'). The phrase endorses the popular view of profit as synonymous with profiteering. And, as Ehrmann points out, Zola's portrayal is by no means exceptional:

> For a country where literary incarnations still command wide popular appeal, it is significant that in the French novel there seems to be not a single example of an outstanding entrepreneurial pioneer; where they appear at all, they are slightly ridiculed rather than pictured as heroes. (1957, 210)

In popular circles, for those brought up on a staple diet of Marxism and Catholicism, the standard view of the *patron* was of a parasite, *un buveur de sang*. If these 'blood-suckers' happened to be successful they were labelled *aigrefins* (swindlers); if they had the misfortune to fail, they would be dubbed *incapables* (Weber, 1986, 42).

As if this handicap were not enough, the image of employers was further damaged by accusations of open collaboration with the enemy in the Second World War. The vast majority of French bosses put the survival of their companies ahead of ideological convictions and few were untarnished by their wartime activities (de Rochebrune and Hazera, 1995). Some of the disgraced employers were punished with expropriation. For instance, Louis Renault who, immediately after the June 1940 armistice, ran headlong into economic collaboration with the Germans, found his company confiscated (the same fate befell Berliet, the lorry manufacturer) in the wave of nationalizations[2] which followed the War. As Ehrmann puts it:

> The government no less than the man in the street was convinced that the employers' record during the most difficult hours of the country had been at best undistinguished, in many cases despicable. (1957, 103)

Even de Gaulle joined in the 'boss-baiting' with a sort of catch phrase *'Où étiez-vous, messieurs?'*[3] (Harris and de Sedouy, 1977, 54) with which he regularly taunted representatives of the embryonic employers' union, the Conseil National du Patronat Français (CNPF). But whatever the extent of employer collaboration, there is a strong argument for suggesting that they had actually failed their country prior to the Second World War when conservative and uncompetitive practices contributed to the weak economic base of France – one factor in the country's collapse in the face of German might.

From this all-time low at the end of the War, French employers have achieved something of a turnaround in societal esteem, especially in the last two decades. Children need no longer fear retribution when they announce that their father is a *Président-Directeur-Général* (PDG or CEO). The reversal of image is rooted in France's entry into the EEC in 1958. This prompted an important change in corporate behaviour since it opened up the French market to foreign competition, at least formally, and signalled the end of a long history of economic protectionism dating back to the fifteenth century. Ardagh drew a parallel with the effect of the Occupation – suggesting that the German menace (economic rather than military) had once again catalysed the French into action, 'This time before defeat and without bloodshed!' (1982, 37).

Further progress was made as a result of the 1968 uprisings, which emphasized the need for a change of style in corporate leadership – a point driven home by the fact that the strike had been the bitterest in the autocratic, old-style firms like Citroën. Ardagh points out that:

> May 1968 brought in a new questioning of the old assumptions about authority, and it sounded the death-knell of a certain rigidly autocratic French style of command, both in factories and offices. (1982, 96)

The rehabilitation of top management was further enhanced in the 1980s with the belated emergence of an enterprise culture in France. The process was given additional impetus from an unexpected quarter, namely the Socialist government (1981–86). It is ironic that the elevation of bosses should have been engineered by those who were initially thought to 'have it in for them', as evidenced by the *Nouvel Observateur* cover story, when the Socialists first came to power: '*Faut-il brûler les patrons?*' ('Should the bosses be burned?') (12/12/81).

In fact, the Socialist decision to varnish not tarnish was based on economic rather than ideological grounds. The entrepreneur had to be encouraged as a potential job creator and locomotive for the economy, ideas which though commonplace elsewhere were accepted only recently in France. This social change produced a subtle switch in business perspective, nicely captured by one PDG: '*Il s'agit maintenant de lutter pour et non pas contre quelque chose*' ('We're now free to fight *for* something rather than *against* something').

Throughout the 1980s, then, bosses gained in social respect, largely on the basis of their ability to create jobs, but also because of the increased legitimacy of wealth creation as an objective – for the nation, the firm and the individual.

This rehabiliation has suffered a slight setback in the 1990s, for two reasons. First, in a general sense, bosses have been personally blamed for much of the downsizing which has taken out whole layers of employees, especially distressing at the *cadre* level. In addition to this, there have been a number of corruption scandals in which high profile bosses have been implicated. The most high profile of these *affaires* concerned Bernard Tapie, the very embodiment of the successful entrepreneur and business leader throughout the 1980s – but several other pillars of the French business community have also found themselves in and out of courts and jails (the issue of corporate governance is dealt with later in the chapter).

The 'honeymoon period' seems over for French bosses and entrepreneurs. As one *cadre* observed: *'Les "chefs d'entreprise" sont redevenus des "patrons"'* ('"Captains of industry" have turned back into "bosses"'). The managerial revolution has made it possible for individual business leaders to be labelled heroes, but as a class they have lost their hard-won, and short-lived, status as role models.

Ways to the top

Three distinct avenues to corporate leadership can be identified in the research literature: inheritance, competence and intelligence. It goes without saying that these qualities are not mutually exclusive, but the terms have been selected to characterize a particular means of access to the top. And in each category below, an individual has been chosen as a representative for that group. The three individuals are introduced with a brief personal file and their careers are used to illustrate the category concerned.

Inheritance

Example: François Delachaux: PDG of a 'mini-multinational' (850 employees and 12 foreign subsidiaries), founded in 1912 by his grandfather. He is aged 47, and has an MBA from the University of Indiana.

The proportion of family-run firms in France is high, both quantitatively and qualitatively. In other words, a high number of fairly large concerns (across various sectors) are family run. The better-known ones include Bouygues (construction), Dassault (aviation), Michelin (tyres), Bich (mass consumer goods), Leclerc (retail stores), and Ricard (drinks). These companies all feature among the 84 companies which form the 'hard core' of French capitalism as identified by Bauer and Bertin-Mourot (1995a, 23).

The French seem particularly attached to the tradition of family capitalism, and there are few signs of it diminishing. Even today, power is relinquished to outsiders only as a last resort. Ferdinand Béghin, the last in the line of a sugar and paper emporium (Béghin-Say), epitomized the view, when he stated:

Je n'ai jamais trouvé dans ma famille de gens capables de m'aider! J'aurais été enchanté d'avoir des gendres à qui j'aurais pu donner des places importantes. (I have never found anyone in my family capable of helping me! I would have loved to have had sons-in-law to whom I might have entrusted important positions.) (Harris and de Sedouy, 1977, 22)

The bourgeois saw success in life in terms of augmenting the capital and reputation of their families. This spirit of 'financial affection' is not dead and continues to perpetuate values like thrift and sacrifice – the supreme duty is still seen by some as the transmission of property to their children.

Take the example of the late Francis Bouygues. He was succeeded by Martin, his youngest son, and today three of his four children work for the company. Nicolas, the eldest son, is the only one who does not. Originally, he was his father's designated successor. A graduate of l'Ecole Centrale like his father, he took charge of the group's construction activities in 1983. But father and son were too similar, and Nicolas ended up turning his back on the group in 1986. As Francis Bouygues once confessed: '*C'était ma plus belle ambition. Elle a été trahie*' ('It was my most cherished ambition, and it has been dashed') (*Le Nouvel Economiste*, 15/3/96, 48).

One is reminded of a remark by one of the Peugeot chiefs (a company notorious for harbouring family members) regarding the *raison d'être* of a business: '*Contrôler le capital, ça sert à placer les enfants*' ('Controlling the capital guarantees jobs for one's children') (*L'Expansion*, September 1978, 139).

Notwithstanding the example of Bouygues, there is now a rather more discriminating approach to nepotism, with anyone likely to jeopardize the family business sidelined early. *Le patron de droit divin* (boss by divine right – a phrase coined for Eugène Schneider, the one-time flamboyant lord of Le Creusot) is a figure of the past, even if the phrase is still used ironically. Those who are deemed a liability to the survival of the business will find their families far less indulgent than was once the case. With successive generations, inheritors multiply and the company can become a repository for family members. Aware of the dangers of such a policy, the second-generation Delachaux brothers (representatives of the family-run business) decreed:

Aucun Delachaux dans l'entreprise Delachaux. Si la maison doit servir à nourrir la famille, elle est vouée à sa perte. (No Delachaux in the Delachaux company. If the role of the firm is to feed the family, we are bound to lose out.) (Weber, 1986, 26)

So, François Delachaux's rise to power illustrates the more realistic attitude to nepotism. In order to ensure the survival of the business, the 21 second-generation Delachaux family members jointly decided to eliminate all but the single most competent family member from the company – in much the same way as the Michelin family have done. That is how third-generation François Delachaux was elected. The other family members pulled out of the company and went elsewhere to exercise their industrial talents.

Enlightened nepotism, as demonstrated here, can yield substantial benefits without incurring the traditional drawbacks. To start with, the heir-apparent is inculcated early into the ways of the company. The old adage, *Je possède, donc je sais* (I own, therefore I know), has more than a grain of truth in it. As Bauer and Bertin-Mourot put it:

> *Les hériters ont souvent été élevés dans le culte de l'entreprise familiale et n'ont vécu qu'avec (voir 'pour') celle-ci.* (The inheritors are often brought up in the cult of the family business and have always lived with (not to say 'for') the business.) (1995a, 11)

This view is confirmed by Patrick Ricard, the PDG of Pernod-Ricard and son of the founder:

> *Tout ce qu'a fait mon père, c'était avec l'objectif de me faire rentrer chez Ricard.* (My father's every action was channelled towards my joining Ricard.) (*L'Expansion*, 4/6/81, 108)

The result is very early exposure to the business. Corinne Bouygues, daughter of the late founder, and head of the advertising arm of the conglomerate's TV activities, likes to remind executives who arrive late:

> *Moi, à 7 ans, j'étais sur les chantiers à 6 heures du matin.* (When I was just 7 years old, I was already on construction sites by 6 o'clock in the morning.) (*Le Nouvel Economiste*, 15/3/96, 46)

The children are brought up with the idea that this is the family's vocation. Anticipatory socialization enables the designated successor to prepare early for the idea of leadership. The training period can be intense with no holds barred. Almost certainly, criticism will be meted out more readily and accepted more easily since both master and apprentice have the family's best interests at heart.

What is more, the argument of lack of motivation is perhaps overstated since the chosen successor must prove himself or herself[4] in relation to rival siblings, is in daily contact with shareholders and is subjected to the critical gaze of fellow-executives who may consider themselves more able. Forging one's legitimacy in such a context may require standards of conscientiousness and hard work not expected of 'normal' candidates.

Legitimacy may be further eased by acquiring educational qualifications or experience in other companies. Ideally, the heir should aim for an unimpeachable qualification. On that score, Serge Dassault's degree from Polytechnique made him an irreproachable choice for taking over his father's aeronautical company. Similarly, the grandchildren of François Michelin and Edouard Leclerc were both at Centrale together, which will facilitate their future access to power. However, not everyone is gifted enough to avail themselves of such a qualification. Marceau (1981, 118) has noted that an MBA is often used as an instrumental qualification to shake off the 'boss's son' label. This amounts to converting economic capital into more acceptable educational capital.

This was the strategy pursued by our case example, François Delachaux. His MBA was achieved without a *bone fide* first degree, thanks to America's more flexible educational system and the help of one of his father's old friends. The quest for educational legitimacy is so important in France that some parents will gladly pay out to procure a diploma for their offspring.

Legitimation through experience is perhaps easier to achieve than legitimation through qualifications, but it does not carry the same weight. It is an easier option since the family will generally have contacts which it can approach *pour placer quelqu'un de la famille* (to take on members of the family). Friendly suppliers, customers or banks should manage to put up with the offspring for a while in the knowledge that the favour might be reciprocated for one of their own. Again, economic and social capital are leveraged to provide the offspring with an accelerated track record which overshadows the advantage of heredity. A good example was the Cointreau heir who benefited from an HEC label, followed by three years with Arthur Young and a brief spell at Elizabeth Arden:

> *C'était pour moi un sine qua non d'aller faire mes classes ailleurs . . . avant d'entrer dans le groupe familiale.* (It was essential for me to get a good grounding elsewhere . . . before joining the family group.) (*L'Expansion*, 4/6/81, 113)

With the increasing professionalization of management, one would expect this trend to diminish. For instance, in retailing, a traditional hotbed of family businesses, both the Defforey brothers (Carrefour) and Antoine Guichard

(Casino) have renounced their dynastic ambitions. On the other hand, others are taking up the challenge. For example, François Pinault, founder of the conglomerate, Pinault-Printemps-Redoute, has chosen as his successor a 35-year-old HEC graduate – his son François-Henri.

The extent to which this is taken for granted was highlighted for us about ten years ago. While at Air Liquide, we asked about prospective successors to Edouard de Royère, who was then president. 'Do his sons work here?' we ventured. 'Not yet', let slip a senior manager. Ten years down the road, Jean-Marc de Royère, son of the former PDG, is now in charge of Asia, and may be a serious candidate when the current president, Alain Joly, retires in a few years time.

More striking still, is the example of Jean-Luc Lagardère, head of the Matra-Hachette high-tech and communication group. As he once put it: '*J'adore mon fils, et j'adore mon groupe. Si je pouvais joindre les deux, ce serait merveilleux*' ('I love my son and I love my business. If I could bring the two together, it would be marvellous') (*Le Nouvel Economiste*, 21/7/95, 32). The difference, in this case, is that Lagardère is not an inheritor nor a founder in the strict sense. He started off in the group Matra, back in 1963, as a salaried *directeur général*. But over time he has developed a holding group in which he is the main shareholder (9 per cent of voting rights). So much for the 'managerial revolution'!

Our aim here is not to discredit the competence, or indeed motivation, of inheritors. Being the only child of the founder does not give automatic access to power; but there will have to be a good reason for ruling him or her out as a candidate. It all seems to confirm the observation of the former head of the employers' union (CNPF), Yvon Gattaz, that the 'dynastic dream' does not seem to diminish with the size of the company. According to him there are two types of bosses in France: those who think their children are capable of succeeding them at the head of the company, and those . . .without children. (Bauer and Bertin-Mourot, 1995a, 32).

Competence

Example: Philippe Loridan: armed with only a *baccalauréat*, he found work in a forwarding agency in Morocco. He returned to France, aged 26, to start up the French subsidiary of Treifus PLC, which he turned into a resounding success employing 800 people.

Basically, there are two ways in which competence can lead to corporate leadership – either by working one's way up a single or a succession of companies over a number of years, or else by setting up a business which provides immediate access. It seems ironical that the nation which spawned the word *entrepreneur* (Jean-Baptiste Say in 1800) should have been traditionally so weak in this domain. In a scathing account of the inadequacies of French business, David Landes (1951) blamed unenterprising businessmen for holding back French growth in the nineteenth and early twentieth centuries. According to him, the bourgeois family values hampered economic growth by emphasizing social success over individual profit or industrial expansion. Innovation and success in business were held in low esteem and risk-taking was shunned for fear of bankruptcy, which amounted to absolute dishonour in the social system which prevailed.

As a result of the bourgeois influence, business creation was still frowned upon until a few years ago – at best, one would probably earn the label of *parvenu* or *nouveau riche*. So, as a road to success, it was deemed too risky for all but the most adventurous and persistent, especially without an initial capital stake. As François Pinault, founder of the conglomerate, Pinault-Printemps-Redoute, put it: '*Faute d'un grand nom, de relations, de diplômes, j'ai perdu dix ans*' ('For want of wealth, contacts, or qualifications, I lost ten years') (*Les Echos*, 10/6/96, 58).

In view of the traditional perception of business success it is hardly surprising that those most likely to take this path are those 'in a rush' to succeed – and see enterprise creation as the best short-cut – or else those whose qualifications, social standing, sex or race preclude career success by more conventional means. It is significant, for instance, that women set up 30 per cent of the new businesses created in 1994 (*Le Monde*, 5/7/95, 2).

Historically, then, France has not been a hotbed of individual, inspirational entrepreneurs. As described in the *Economist* even 'the small-companies association, based in Paris, admits that it has many fewer small and medium-sized firms than Germany: it has no *Mittelstand* worthy of the name' (2/3/96, 64). The same article later revealed that the government's proposed solution to this deficiency was to make *inheriting* companies easier![5]

Many of the companies, stunted both by hostile cultural attitudes and underdeveloped capital markets, remain small and family owned. In contrast, it is revealing that Business Objects, one of the few small companies to achieve rapid international growth, has done so by violating a number of the norms of French business. It is worth examining the company in more detail.

Business Objects was jointly founded in 1990 by two former Oracle employees, Bernard Liautaud (Centrale) and Denis Payre (Essec), then in their late 20s. The company sells software which enables end-users to access information stored on servers. Shunning the Paris Bourse which would have undervalued this high-tech company, the founders opted intead for a quotation on the stock exchange of America, the lead market. In 1994, it was the first independent French company to go public on the American stock exchange, Nasdaq.[6] Today the company has headquarters in France and the US and wholly owned subsidiaries in America, Europe and Asia. Only half of the 350 employees are based in France. Now all this might sound like a banal 'Silicon Valley'-type success story. But the point is that to emulate that model, it had to break with the French model. That meant:

1. Ambition: Having the courage to assert their ambition to be a global leader from the outset.
2. Internationalization: First, of the investment base – with recourse not to banks, but to venture capital companies, both in France and the US. Second, of the recruitment base – which demanded competitive salaries and stock options, such that the two founders were no longer the highest earners. As PDG Liautaud puts it: 'The French have some difficulty understanding that when you recruit very strong people, with different backgrounds, it pushes you up. The tendency is to see it rather as a threat.'[7]
3. Control: The reluctance to relinquish control in exchange for a bigger stake of the market typically inhibits the international development of small firms. As Liautaud explains: 'There is a fallacy in France that unless you retain 51 per cent of the company, you don't control it any more.'
4. Planning: Finance is the bottleneck in a fast-growing company. As Liautaud sees it: 'Without it you can't drive the company forward. So you always have to think ahead. Our leitmotiv is "anticipate, anticipate, anticipate" – the financial needs, the internationalization needs, the recruitment needs, the product needs.' Again this is in stark contrast to the majority of French firms – a study by 3i, a British venture capital firm, found that less than half of small French firms planned their investment in a systematic way, compared to three-quarters in Italy and Germany. (*Economist*, 2/3/96, 64)

As an alternative to founding one's company, there is the possibility of working one's way up to the top. However, trying to reach the top of an organization from a lowly starting position is a fairly remote prospect in France, unless one happens to work for a foreign subsidiary. These reputedly offer the quickest upward mobility for those without prestigious diplomas or family ties; but these companies also make explicit demands on the individual – variable remuneration, pressure for results, individual accountability and geographical mobility – which are anathema to most French managers. As one woman *cadre* explained:

Pour un Français les conditions de travail chez Xerox ou Mars – où même les cadres sont obligés de pointer – sont épouvantables. (A French person will find the work conditions at Xerox or Mars – where even executives have to clock on – quite unbearable.)

The French subsidiaries of IBM, Kodak, Nestlé, Shell, Philips or Unilever all seek continuity of leadership by appointing individuals whose careers have been with the company. But until recently, the only comparable French company was l'Oréal which systematically looks internally for its new chief executives.

The sensation caused by l'Air Liquide's appointment of Alain Joly, a 34-year veteran of the company, indicates to what extent this was a rarity. As *Le Nouvel Economiste* labelled it: '*Une révolution, dans un pays où la voie royale pour devenir patron reste le parachutage*' ('A veritable revolution, in a country where introduction from above[8] is the privileged path to leadership') (9/2/96, 48). The fact that this 'home grown product' also happened to be a graduate of l'Ecole Polytechnique was a side issue!

For those without a respectable qualification, like our example, Philippe Loridan, the only real option is expatriation. Realizing that he would not get anywhere in '*ce pays à diplômes*' ('this qualification-conscious country'), Loridan spent three years in Morocco and gained responsibilities which would have taken ten years to accumulate in France. Having made a name for himself, he returned to France and was able to find immediate employment thanks to his experience. Self-imposed exile proved a means of acquiring the experience which would have been denied him in France. This is in stark contrast to countries like the USA where geographical mobility is part and parcel of the promotion game – in France it is largely the price paid for lack of qualifications.

Intelligence

Example: Jacques Calvet: born in 1931 and a product of Sciences-Po and l'Ecole Nationale d'Administration (ENA). Successively, senior civil servant, Chairman of the Banque Nationale de Paris, and since 1984 head of the private Peugeot-Citroën car group. He managed to check the plunge of a group on the verge of bankruptcy.

A memorable article once appeared in *L'Expansion* (20/11/80). It featured the CEO of an advertising agency and was entitled, '*L'itinéraire modèle d'Yves Cannac*' ('Yves Cannac's perfect career'). The reason his was considered a model career was that he was a graduate of l'Ecole Normale (very prestigious), the *major* (laureate) of l'ENA (even better) and had spent ten years in state service to boot. What more appropriate pedigree for the head of France's number one advertising agency, l'Agence Havas?

Yves Cannac's career pattern was exceptional in content, but is by no means unusual in format. Jacques Calvet (Peugeot) boasts a similar *curriculum vitae* – after graduating from l'ENA, he took up various positions in the French administration, notably as the Directeur de Cabinet of Valéry Giscard d'Estaing when the former President was Finance Minister (1970–74). He made his transition to the business world via the public sector where he was appointed Deputy Managing Director of the Banque Nationale de Paris (BNP) in 1974. By the time he joined the Peugeot group in 1982, he had risen to Chairman of BNP.

Examining the backgrounds of most heads of large industrial concerns reveals a similar, if less distinguished, story – as does a cursory glance at the backgrounds of the new generation. The business magazine, *Challenges* (September 1994) profiles '*100 dirigeants pour demain*' ('100 bosses for tomorrow'). Of these 31 are *énarques*, 14 HEC and 12 *polytechniciens*. Only two are not the products of the higher education system – one is a software entrepreneur and the other succeeded his father, Yves Rocher, in the family cosmetic business.

It is worth noting, *en passant*, that the most highly qualified of this group is one Sébastien Cahen – whose stint at Polytechnique was followed by a doctorate in nuclear astrophysics – and is now a director of the Société Générale. Suffice to say, that French companies are not put off by qualifications.

To say that this reveals a contrast with Britain is an understatement. A similar profile of the 'new generation of business leaders' carried out by the *Sunday Times* (22/8/93) revealed that 13 of the 20 individuals had degrees, mostly from the newer universities, and that only three of the 20 went to Oxbridge.

France's largest public and private groups alike are headed by products of *la haute administration* (the higher reaches of the civil service) which also means they were the very brightest individuals of their generation.

The appointment of former state officials as heads among nationalized or recently privatized companies – such as Saint-Gobain, Elf, BNP, Alcatel-Alsthom, Rhône-Poulenc, Renault or Péchiney – is perhaps understandable. What is less obvious is their colonization of similar posts in private companies such as Accor, Peugeot, Moulinex, Eurotunnel, Axa, LVMH or even, at one time, Carrefour.[9]

The ubiquitous presence of senior state officials in the private and state sectors makes the conventional distinction between public and private industry less relevant in France since both types of company will be run in similar ways. Of course, this raises the question of competence – what exactly do companies *see* in these individuals?

First and foremost, senior civil servants are courted for their contacts (*carnet d'adresses*). In the French context, where relations with the state are more important to a company's well-being, it is desirable to be on good terms with the authorities. In what remains an interventionist economy, recruiting top flight civil servants who have graduated from Polytechnique or ENA facilitates discussions with the government. As pointed out in the *Nouvel Economiste* (9/2/96, 50):

> *Ce n'est pas un hasard si en 1983 Jacques Calvet prend le pouvoir chez Peugeot. Outre ses qualités d'animateur, l'ancien directeur de cabinet de Valéry Giscard d'Estaing peut d'un coup de téléphone obtenir les coups de pouce indispensable au constructeur, alors en danger.* (It's no coincidence that Jacques Calvet was appointed head of Peugeot in 1983. Besides his motivational skills, the former manager of Valéry Giscard d'Estaing's affairs could secure much needed help for the ailing car manufacturer, with a single phone call.)

As ex-civil servants they are accustomed to being on the receiving end of discreet pressure and are initiated in the ways of politics. They are responsible for building and maintaining the bridges between the company and the state. This does not mean they are bound to win out, but their case will not go by default of not being heard.

Moreover, the famous *carnet d'adresses*, does not just contain government contacts. A fascinating insight into the breadth of these contacts can be gleaned from a regular feature in *Capital* entitled, '*Avec qui dirige . . . X*' ('With whom does X govern'). The feature on Michel Pébereau (October 1993, 28–29) was particularly impressive. Head of France's second largest bank, the BNP, he was 'fortunate enough' to attend both l'ENA and Polytechnique (a rare double), then to spend time in state service as an *inspecteur des finance*. This gave him a particularly wide net of acquaintances – stretching from industry to politics, and from civil servants to intellectuals.[10]

Besides this capacity to open doors, and bearing in mind that they are inevitably products of l'ENA or l'Ecole Polytechnique, what else can these ex-state officials offer a company? Not much, if we are to believe a famous *bon mot* by Roger Martin, former PDG of Saint-Gobain: '*En sortant de Polytechnique, je savais tout mais rien d'autre*' ('When I left Polytechnique, I knew everything but nothing else').

There is a grain of truth in this statement in that these elite graduates lack specific expertise. However, the quip fails to do justice to the reasoning power, the depth and rigour of the study process, the addiction to hard work, and the tradition of honesty inculcated into those heading for state service. These individuals are sought after because their intellectual probity is second to none. The cachet of this scholastic achievement far outweighs a double first at Oxford or Cambridge. The compliment *'une belle mécanique intellectuelle'* ('a fine intellectual apparatus') is often employed to describe them.

The next section considers how the 'intelligence' category is bearing up in relation to 'competence' and 'inheritance'.

A new breed of manager?

There have been some important changes in France over the last ten years. Besides the privatizations, France has seen the end of price and exchange controls, the deregulation of certain industries, the internationalization of markets for labour and capital, and intensified global competition. So how have these economic changes affected the make-up and outlook of the French *patronat*?

In the 1980s, a 'new breed' of gung-ho French manager emerged. It was expected that the likes of Bernard Tapie (who has since fallen from grace) and Vincent Bolloré would open up French boardrooms for other self-starters, that this would introduce new blood into what had always been a fairly tight-knit community.

Keen to provide role models for budding entrepreneurs, the business press was quick to seize on these individuals and make national heroes out of them. As Dean Berry remarked of French business at the time: 'With business exposed, managers need heroes and they haven't had any' (*Financial Times*, 2/7/86, 18).

In their portrayals of what it took to succeed, the journals conveniently played down money, qualifications and contacts, emphasizing instead youth, imagination, courage, effort and perseverance. Their central tenet was that *'n'importe qui peut faire fortune'* ('anyone can get rich'). The new buzz words quoted by *Le Point* (28/7/86, 66) were all success-oriented: *les décideurs, les battants, s'investir, assurer* (deciders, battlers, commitment, taking responsibility) – words which had traditionally been in poor taste in 'aristocratic' France.

Beneath all the hype, however, French capitalism remained highly susceptible to a reversal of values. Oddly enough, much of the danger came from the *patrons* themselves – outwardly, they joined in the chorus of openness and mouthed the latest buzz-words, but privately they resented the invasion of

American-style values and many were simply waiting for the whole thing to blow over and for 'normal service' to be resumed.

To some extent, that is exactly what has happened. Certainly that is the verdict returned by Bauer and Bertin-Mourot (1995a) after reviewing the profiles of business leaders in France's top 200 companies over the period 1985–94. Their survey distinguishes between three categories which are not too distant from those we have used[11] – founders/inheritors (inheritence), civil servants (intelligence) and company people (competence). Some of their key findings are that:

1. The weight of founders, within the category 'founders and inheritors', has diminished: it represented 37 per cent of the population in 1985, but 26 per cent in 1994. Meanwhile the weight of inheritors has grown from 11 per cent in 1985 to 16 per cent in 1994.
2. Half of the heads of France's top companies started out in the civil service – and this trend is increasing in spite of the privatizations.
3. Of the 13 companies privatized during this period, 11 changed heads, but only one of the new heads was not a former civil servant.
4. 46 per cent of the French heads studied were the products of just two schools, l'ENA and Polytechnique (as opposed to 37 per cent in 1985). And 73 per cent are *grande école* graduates.
5. Of the top 15 industrial concerns, 12 are headed by one-time state officials, and three by inheritors or founders. Not one of the top 15 is managed by someone who has climbed up through one or several companies.
6. In 1994, founders and inheritors represented 32 per cent of the '*grands patrons*' as against 28 per cent in 1985.
7. *Autodidactes* (self-made individuals) are four times as numerous (17 per cent) as graduates from French universities (4 per cent).
8. Increases in the proportion of former state officials and inheritors have been at the expense of company people – only 21 per cent of French heads are pure products of the corporate sector, compared to 31 per cent in 1985.
9. In 1994, only 7 per cent of French bosses started out in the company they head, as opposed to 13 per cent in 1985.

Several conclusions can be drawn from this longitudinal study of French business leaders. First, French bosses are highly qualified in international terms – certainly in comparison with their British or American counterparts – and the routes to the top remain limited and well-trodden. The much-criticized British *Establishment* seems almost shapeless relative to its French equivalent (also labelled '*l'establishment*'). In France it is still possible to sketch out a 'classic' career path leading from *grande école* to civil service and on to industry. In Britain no such privileged route exists.

Drawing a comparison between France and neighbouring Germany is perhaps more meaningful in view of the similar emphasis on higher education. Bauer and Bertin-Mourot (1995b) have replicated the study in Germany. Two key differences emerge: relatively, French bosses are less familiar not just with the companies they head, but also with the world of business in general.

In Germany, 32 per cent of bosses started out in the company they head, as opposed to 7 per cent in France (1995b, 105). In Germany, the average time spent in a company before heading it is 14 years, compared to eight years in France. One might add, that over 50 per cent of French bosses are named boss within five years of joining the company, and that 36 per cent of French bosses were appointed PDG directly, as against 16 per cent in Germany (1995b, 105).

Moreover, former civil servants have, on average, entered the private sector aged 38, and their company aged 46, and been named head six years later (1995b, 89). More than half of these former state officials have joined the companies they subsequently head on one of the top three rungs. In contrast, over 70 per cent of German top bosses started out as apprentices or at lower management levels (1995b, 106).

In spite of some 23 privatizations since 1986, the influence of the state remains strong. Yet it cannot fully explain the over-representation of former state insiders in French companies. Proof that corporate success is possible in France without close state contacts comes from the group of sixteen foreign subsidiaries which feature in the top 200 French firms (Bauer and Bertin-Mourot, 1995a, 53). Not one of these is headed by a product of the state sector. The 39 successive heads over the last ten years have all been detected within the corporate sector: 58 per cent being 'home grown', and 42 per cent coming in from other companies. Another striking fact about this population is that although three-quarters of them are French, their qualifications are far 'weaker' than the norm in large French groups. Bauer and Bertin-Mourot conclude that these companies are willing to do what most French companies refuse to do, namely take responsibility for identifying, selecting and grooming their own leaders. As they see it:

> *Dans tous les secteurs de l'économie française, les grandes entreprises préfèrent sous-traiter, à d'autres acteurs, le soin de détecter leurs futurs dirigeants.* (In all sectors of the French economy, large companies prefer

to sub-contract, to other agents, the trouble of detecting their future leaders.) (1995a, 87)

On this evidence, the conventional argument that the corporate appointment of former civil servants is necessary in an interventionist economy, starts to look less convincing. A more subtle explanation can perhaps be found in the particular French understanding of the role of the leader. In French eyes a leader should be remote, reflective, all-knowing and firm – qualities which coincide well with a state service apprenticeship. This theme will be explored in more detail in the following sections.

Homogeneity?

In any country, those who run big businesses (*le grand patronat*) are very different from those who run smaller and medium-sized businesses; and those who run their own businesses are very different from salaried heads. But from our observation of all types of business, we would argue that a number of interesting and distinctive similarities can be highlighted. French bosses share something in terms of identity, activities, freedom of action and even operating style, which transcends differences of ownership or career pattern.

Identity

To start with, bosses are united under the banner of a single union, the Conseil National du Patronat Français (CNPF). It is not immediately obvious why employers, who unlike individual workers are not lacking in power, need to organize themselves. But the answers have to do with the French context. The CNPF was conceived after the Liberation as a means of facilitating contact between employers and government – and in the hope that it might help retrieve some of the employers' power and self-esteem, damaged by the Occupation. The CNPF's existence is also a testament to the weight of the French state in corporate affairs. The impact of legislation is particularly keenly felt in matters of health and safety, industrial relations and, of course, taxation. In its support for or opposition towards government, the CNPF tries to influence such legislation.

The common bond which transcends questions of ownership and background is visible at CNPF meetings which assemble both small and big bosses. Successive heads of the CNPF – sometimes referred to as *le patron des patrons*[12] – have generally been adept at hitting this unifying chord when addressing the bosses. One *habitué* of CNPF meetings we interviewed, recalled how he had seen many a skilled orator unite the various factions of employers with a few well-chosen words. According to him, all you had to do was evoke a few of their *bêtes noires* (pet hates) – union leaders, civil servants, politicians, intellectuals – to elicit Pavlovian indignation from all quarters. This points up the role of the organization in reinforcing the social identity of its members.

The collective identity of French employers extends beyond their belonging to the same union. The *patrons* are clearly perceived by the media as a discrete group sharing common political, economic and social views, rather like the *cadres* category described in Chapter 2:

> *La grogne des patrons.* (The bosses' grumble.) (*Le Monde*, 18/4/95, 9)

> *Patrons: un délit est si vite arrivé.* (Bosses: a crime is so easily committed.) (*L'Expansion*, 4/4/96, 122–23)

> *Comment naissent les patrons.* (How bosses are born.) (*Le Nouvel Economiste*, 9/2/96, 48–53)

> *Patrons: y a-t-il une vie après le pouvoir?* (Bosses: is there a life after power?) (*Le Nouvel Economiste*, 28/4/95, 58–61)

> *La cohorte des patrons devant la justice.* (Bosses troop into the dock.) (*L'Express*, 11/7/96, 36–38)

Another feature which unites the bosses, whether small or large, whether owners or salaried heads, is their possession of one or other form of capital: economic (money), educational (qualifications) or social (connections). The theme of social inequality in France is very well documented, and was touched upon in Chapter 3. It is the hobby-horse of a number of French sociologists, Alain Girard being one of the earlier contributors to the debate:

> *Tout se passe comme s'il existait une véritable transmission professionnelle de génération en génération.* (It's as if professional status could be handed down from generation to generation.) (1965, 57)

A similar argument was put forward by Bourdieu and Passeron (1966), who argued in *Les héritiers* that the French bourgeoisie had hit upon a system of 'social reproduction' whereby the various forms of capital could be passed on from one generation to the next – thanks largely to the nature of the education system.

As illustrated earlier in this chapter, social and economic capital are consolidated with educational capital, this being the most irreproachable and therefore the most precious form of capital. Inherited power is concealed beneath a veil of merited power thanks to a highly competitive and overtly objective (based on maths) public secondary and higher education system.

As Birnbaum et al. (1977) explain, this system is not guaranteed to work for a particular individual (that is where the element of merit comes in), but on a class-wide basis it does ensure the reproduction of the ruling class. That does not mean that the individuals at the top are incompetent, but simply that their accession was in part based on considerations other than pure ability – and that, in some cases, these carried more weight.

As illustrated earlier, an alternative tactic for bosses whose offspring are not bright enough to reach one of the *grandes écoles* may be to deploy social and economic capital in order to send their children to foreign universities – rather than opt for a French university with its 'second-rate' image in relation to the elitist *grandes écoles*. The value of a foreign higher degree (preferably from an American university) will go some way to offsetting the lack of a prestigious French diploma.

Whatever one's mode of access to the *patronat* (top management), the notion of predestination is strong. This view of bosses as a hereditary class is corroborated by more recent books with evocative titles such as Gaillard's *Tu Seras Président, Mon Fils* (A Chairman You Will Be, My Son) or Thélot's *Tel Père, Tel Fils* (Like Father, Like Son). It is rare in France to succeed from nothing, without any of these trump cards. Characters like F. Scott Fitzgerald's *The Great Gatsby* are nowhere to be seen in French folklore. Detoeuf, a progressive boss of the 1930s, was surely much more accurate than he would have liked to be, when he quipped: '*En France, pour réussir, un seul secret: avoir déjà réussi*' ('The secret of success in France is to have succeeded already') (in Santoni 1981, 174).

Activities

The notion that top managers all round the world partake in the same sort of activities is true to a certain extent – but there are differences of emphasis which unite bosses from a particular nation and may distinguish them from their counterparts in other countries. In the case of French bosses, the peculiarities derive primarily from the nature of the relationship with the authorities, and from a certain taste for ritual.

Whether at national level or at local level, French bosses find themselves involved with the authorities to a far greater extent than their Anglo-Saxon counterparts. In France, when there are redundancy plans to be cleared or lobbying to be done, the onus generally falls on those at the top. Partly this is by virtue of their educational background, which will stand them in good stead with like-minded civil servants. But, as discussed in the last chapter, status also enters into it. Over a good lunch, state officials will find the attentions of a PDG more flattering than those of a *directeur*. Only when the qualifications of the PDG are somehow inappropriate, will a more suitable corporate envoy be sought out.

For instance, confronted with a rather thorny issue, the head of a provincial production plant, an engineering graduate, elected to send his second-in-command, the *directeur administratif*, to meet the local *préfet* – this in the knowledge that the *préfet* would be an *énarque* and in all probability, a graduate of Sciences-Po (the favoured preparation for l'ENA). In the administrative director's own words, 'The conversation "somehow" got round to Sciences-Po and the period we were there and the dialogue was much easier after that.'

It is worth noting that lobbying in France is not generally considered an activity which can be trusted to third parties. This is not America where lobbying is an independent and respectable profession. This is France where these things happen '*entre amis*'; where threats are veiled, where promises of reciprocity are implicit, and where business dealings are couched in decorum.

At a provincial level, the heads of a production plant or a medium-sized business will be considered *personalités locales* and their presence is often solicited at official functions. Relations with the mayor and the town council will be nurtured, so that favours do not fall on deaf ears later. For instance, a hypermarket manager in our study wanted to use the municipal stadium for the corporate football team's home games. With the town council making a fuss about the additional ground maintenance, the head discreetly reminded them that the local handball team was sponsored by the company. Needless to say, access to the facilities was granted.

Another example from our study involving reciprocity was demonstrated in a communist-dominated municipality. Late one afternoon, at about 6 p.m., the communist mayor, with whom relations were strained to say the least, telephoned the head of the business. He explained that he was in a fix since he had invited a number of guests from England (neo-Marxists according to the PDG), and the factory they had intended to visit had gone on strike – so finding a substitute factory was a matter of some urgency. The PDG gave his approval and the visit went off without a hitch. Later that year, the poor results of the company's divisions meant that 50 people had to be laid off, so the PDG contacted the mayor. He outlined the situation and explained that the last thing they needed was a stirring up of public disapproval. The mayor '*qui avait la haute main sur la CGT*' ('who had control over the communist-based union, the CGT") reassured the PDG that he need not worry and stood true to his word.

At a national level, the same sort of preoccupations were evident on a larger scale. For instance, a company selling luncheon vouchers, was involved in lobbying the authorities for greater tax relief on their service where the profit margins were melting away. Of course, when secured, these concessions would benefit the entire industry, not just the company in question. But there was a rather convenient division of labour since the company's main rival happened to be a co-operative. So, if a left-wing government was in power, the head of the co-operative would 'go and see his socialist friends' – if the right were in power, it was the turn of the company's PDG *'d'aller au charbon'* ('to go to work'). In the face of this *force majeure* the two competitors collaborated to achieve the best possible deal for the industry.

In a similar vein, the head of a leading pet food company was exerting pressure on the treasury minister to place their product in a lower VAT bracket,[13] on the basis that pet food was a necessity, not a luxury. Irrespective of the outcome of this request, the pleading was designed to raise parliamentary awareness of the company's performance and shatter the illusion that *'c'est une activité facile qui rapporte gros'* ('it's an easy way of making lots of money'). The real aim was to legitimize their business so as to pre-empt 'some half-wit *senateur* from demanding that we be included in the uppermost VAT bracket'.

While French company heads may pursue an on-going dialogue with the French administration, they are less likely to engage regularly with institutional investors. In France the majority shareholder is more likely to be the government, a family or a nucleus of 'friendly' shareholders which guards against takeover. Thus French bosses probably spend less time worrying about quarterly results or in meetings with institutional investors when the firm's share price comes under pressure. On the other hand, the profusion of crossed shareholdings and interlocking directorships (where a relatively small number of directors sit on a relatively large number of boards) means more meetings with the heads of other companies.

Another feature of French corporate management is the need to comply with certain internal duties, either by law or by custom. It may be worth highlighting a few of these which distinguish the French employers from their Anglo-Saxon counterparts, at least in degree. The company head will generally attend the works' council meeting (*comité d'entreprise*). The PDG's presence will also be expected at internal ceremonies such as the occasional handing out of medals (which range from the basic *médaille du travail*, through *meilleurs ouvriers de France*, to the highly-prized *Légion d'honneur*[14]). As we saw in the previous chapter, the boss will also be expected to make speeches at the numerous *pots*, that is cocktails for special occasions such as departures and promotions. The PDG will also be called upon to attend a number of statutory assemblies with the unions or with employers' organizations. The overall impression is that French heads have more official duties foisted upon them than their Anglo-Saxon counterparts. If we add to these, the inclination towards *la réunionite* (meeting-itis), mentioned in Chapter 5, French bosses will have relatively little time left for unplanned activities, such as informal discussions, visits or tours.

Autonomy

France has a singularity in terms of company law, the *Président-Directeur-Général* (PDG). Based on the *Führerprinzip* model imposed by the Vichy regime in 1940,[15] French company law has the peculiarity of placing in the hands of one person what, in most countries, is shared out: deciding on, executing and controlling a policy. The PDG is what Britons would regard as 'chairman of the board' and 'managing director' rolled into one. The PDG's role is in even sharper contrast to that of the *primus inter pares* German *Vorstandsvorsitzender* (a chairman of the executive committee). This point was forcefully brought home by the PDG of a small firm visited, who asserted: '*Je peux tout faire sauf vendre la société*' ('I can do what I please except sell off the company').

The status of the PDG is sharply differentiated from that of the rest of top management. Traditionally, the supervisory function of boards of directors has been limited and board room absenteeism is high. As Szarka puts it, 'With little interference from the board of directors, with shareholder meetings very rarely using their power of sanctions and with take-overs rare, French chief executives are often free to do as they will' (1992, 168).[16]

By Anglo-Saxon standards, tenure is relatively secure barring political interference or sustained underperformance. To get rid of bosses, takes a spontaneous vote of no confidence from the administrative councils which elected them. But this is an extreme measure. Of course, members of the administrative council can always resign to register their disapproval, but this is also rare, not least because of the disruption to the system of interlocking directorships. As David Suddens, former CEO of the textile group DMC, observed on working in France:

> *Il y a beaucoup trop de copinages, et pas assez d'administrateurs choisis pour leur expérience et dotés d'une autonomie réele qui prennent au sérieux leurs responsabilités et posent des questions dérangeantes.* (Too many members of the administrative council, are chosen because they are 'old pals',

rather than for their experience. They have no real autonomy, do not take their responsibilities too seriously, and rarely ask disturbing questions.) (*Le Nouvel Economiste*, 2/2/96, 44)

By way of illustration, one can cite the naming, in 1994, of Jean-Marie Messier as the chosen successor to the 73-year-old Guy Dejouany as head of France's largest utilities company, Générale des Eaux.[17] By French standards, Messier had impeccable credentials: 38 years old, a graduate of both Ecole Polytechnique and l'ENA, and several years of cabinet experience with former prime minister Edouard Balladur. One of the members of the Générale des Eaux administrative council was Jacques Calvet, the head of Peugeot, and a boss renowned for speaking his mind. He disagreed publicly with the appointment of someone with no industrial experience, but stopped short of resigning. His failure to make a stand, prompted the *Financial Times* to comment: 'If the outspoken and powerful head of Peugeot is not going to carry out a resignation threat, who in France is?' (12/12/94, 10).

By Anglo-Saxon standards, the issue of corporate governance is only a recent concern for French firms, brought on largely by the spate of financial scandals in the early 1990s and the growing importance of foreign investors. In an effort to appease shareholders and to enhance their image, most large companies have introduced corporate governance mechanisms often in line with the recommendations of an influential report co-ordinated by Marc Viennot, head of Société Générale. The report called for the presence of independent administrators and management representatives on the administrative council, as well as Anglo-Saxon style audit, nomination and remuneration committees for boards. While companies have installed such measures, their impact has been very uneven – and many remain reserved about the wholesale import of Anglo-Saxon practices. In some cases, the rigour of the debate in the revamped administrative councils leaves much to be desired; in others the *real* issues don't even make it onto the agenda, as revealed by one senior executive:

> *Les choses graves peuvent effectivement se discuter en conseil. Mais celles qui sont très graves seront toujours réglées en amont, en tout petit comité.* (Serious matters can be discussed by the council. But critical matters are always sorted out elsewhere, in very small committees.) (*Le Nouvel Economiste*, 28/6/96, 56)

This observation was confirmed by a survey reported in the *Financial Times* (12/12/94, 10). It revealed that 53 percent of *administrateurs* (directors) did not have enough information to exercise proper control. Seventy per cent reckoned that an individual *administrateur* could not stop a PDG from taking 'dangerous decisions'.

Another survey, focusing on corporate governance, in *Le Nouvel Economiste* (28/6/96, 49–66) highlighted some of the prime offenders. The better-known ones included:

> Peugeot: '*Conseil écrasé par la personnalité de son président. Ni débat stratégiques, ni dialogues*' ('Board overwhelmed by the president's personality. Neither strategic debate, nor dialogue').
> LVMH: '*Ce conseil reste très hexagonal pour une multinationale, et ronronne de temps à autres*' ('This board remains very domestic for a multinational, and is sometimes complacent').
> L'Oréal: '*Malgrès la présence d'administrateurs indépendants exigeants ... le vrai pouvoir s'exerce au-dessus*' ('Despite the presence of demanding independent administrators . . . the real power is exercised above').
> Michelin: '*Ce conseil de surveillance, archidominé par la famille Michelin, se contente de donner son avis sur le montant du dividende*' ('This watchdog committee, heavily dominated by the Michelin family, does little more than express its opinion on the size of the dividend').

In spite of the rise in standards of corporate governance, then, French bosses still have a much more decision-making discretion than their Anglo-Saxon counterparts.

Behaviour and style

The authority and perceived status associated with the title of PDG affect the behaviour of both title holders and those around them. As Dyas and Thanheiser once pointed out:

> *Etre PDG* (to be a president) is referred to as belonging to a caste apart, regardless of the size of the operation being run. The respect is given almost more to the ability of a president to exercise absolute authority than to the actual power to influence. (1976, 246)

Confirmation that their observation still holds true is provided by interviews with several foreign executives working in French companies. What all of them found perplexing was the distance and deference towards the boss:

> *La hiérarchie à la française [est] dominée par un patron omniscient et*

omnipotent, lequel règne sur son conseil d'administration et sur ses cadres, et marquée par un grand formalisme dans les relations professionnelles. (The French structure is dominated by an omniscient and omnipotent boss, who rules over the administrative council and the senior managers, and where relations are marked by a considerable formality.) (*Le Nouvel Economiste*, 2/2/96, 43)

Large social distances, together with the importance of 'family capitalism', and the power invested in bosses by the law, all flow in the same direction, and perhaps explain the autocratic tendencies of French bosses. As *L'Express* once commented:

II faut voir, en particulier dans les grosses entreprises nationales, l'apparat et le phenomène de cour qui entourent les précieux PDG, avec huissier personnel, ascenseur privé et collaborateurs directs qui servent du 'Monsieur le Président' gros comme le bras a celui que des Americains appelleraient tout simplement 'Bob' ou 'Bill'. (It is difficult to imagine the pomp and circumstance which surrounds the CEO, particularly in large, national companies; what with his own 'orderly', private lift and a cortège of immediate subordinates who respectfully address him as 'Sir' when Americans would simply call him 'Bob' or 'Bill'.) (1/3/85, 33)

This reinforces a point made in Chapter 5, where we argued that authority in France is vested in the role rather than the person. French bosses do not require tremendous charisma or persuasive powers, even if they have them, because the apparels of power and authority attached to their role, guarantee acquiescence.

How this affects the behaviour of French bosses, can be seen from an interview with Jean-Louis Beffa in *Le Nouvel Economiste* (24/5/96, 68). The headline read: '*Pourquoi j'ai racheté Poliet*' and the article explained why Saint-Gobain bought a distribution company from Paribas. What is striking is the personalization of this strategic initiative. Beffa does not explain why the group bought it, but why *he* bought it! This might be understandable if he had founded the company, but this is a former nationalized conglomerate.

This example is by no means unique. In many annual reports, the PDG's opening statement will refer to what 'I' have done, not what 'we' have done. And there is considerable anecdotal evidence that French bosses systematically get involved in details which fall outside their sphere of responsibility, or indeed, competence. Peugeot's Jacques Calvet, for example, is notorious for retaining too many decisions, even to the extent of wanting the last say on the colour of the new models' door trims. Or again, a profile of Bernard Arnault, head of the luxury goods group LVMH, in *Capital* notes:

> *Ce financier adore se mêler de la pub, de la décoration des boutiques et du choix des produits nouveaux.* (This finance specialist loves to interfere with the advertising, the decoration of the stores and the choice of new products.) (March 1996, 30)

One of the behavioural correlates of smartness, can be a lack of patience and a relative inability to understand why others cannot understand. Humility is not their forte, and this may interfere with the development of listening skills. Consider the example of Alain Prestat, a polytechnicien appointed by the state to turn around Thomson Multimedia. He was criticized by his *cadres* for his *'incapacité à déléguer, à écouter, à prendre acte des critiques'* ('. . . inability to delegate, to listen, or to take account of criticism') (*Le Nouvel Economiste*, 5/4/96, 52). An example was cited:

> *Lors d'une réunion avec les administrateurs-salariés du groupe Thomson, il a envoyé promener l'un d'eux, qui se plaignait de n'avoir pas su faire fonctionner le magnétoscope acheté pour sa fille.* (During one meeting with the salaried directors of Thomson, he lost patience with one director who complained that he wasn't able to work the video recorder [a company product] bought for his daughter.) (*Le Nouvel Economiste*, 5/4/96, 52)

Prestat is a product of a system of education and career pattern which generates characteristic strengths and weaknesses. The emphasis on lightning understanding and the capacity to absorb and synthesize information, also tends to encourage what one *cadre* labelled *'l'autoritarisme et le mépris du détail rebelle'* ('authoritarianism and contempt for inconvenient details'). A joke which for years has been doing the rounds at l'ENA sums it up: 'The goal is to read a report in two minutes, and to be able to discuss it for two hours, with someone whose been working on it for two years.'

The marked difference in behaviour between leader and subordinates is not confined to the headquarters of big businesses. It also applies to smaller businesses in the provinces. The conduct of one particular boss from our sample is worth highlighting since by Anglo-Saxon standards it would appear rather unusual.

The boss in question had an obsession with picking people up on minor faults – correcting their French on a number of occasions: not *'prendre la porte'* but *'passer par la porte'*, not *'aller au coiffeur'* but *'aller chez le coiffeur'* (rather like correcting someone on 'different to' or 'equally as' in English). He also castigated a woman for chewing gum and a *cadre* for talking with a cigarette in his mouth. He was no doubt caricatural in the extremity of his behaviour, but the trait was visible among other bosses in the sample. Another boss insisted on correcting a *cadre* who used *'ennuyant'* rather than *'ennuyeux'*, and invariably drew attention to missed subjunctives. These are not, in fact, signs of disrespect for the personnel since the same boss who was such a stickler for *savoir faire* claims he would never take the liberty of sitting at a subordinate's desk – he refuses to exploit his authority.

On the positive side, for instance, the same boss made a point of complimenting one *cadre* – after checking in the dictionary – for employing an adjective never before heard by the boss. He congratulated another *cadre 'pour une lettre bien tournée'* ('for a stylishly written letter'). Perhaps such behaviour is to be expected since it is often the education of bosses which sets them apart from subordinates. Therefore to correct a grammatical mistake is a means of reaffirming one's intellectual superiority and, by the same token, one's right to lead.

A different view of leadership

The preceding discussion all points to a very different view of leadership. France has a long tradition of centralization (running back to Colbert in the seventeenth century), of hierarchical rigidity, and of individual respect for authority. French company law resembles the country's constitution in conferring considerable power on a single person. It follows that concerted corporate action, in France, is driven by the possibility of imposing a strong direction which will be followed. Relatively speaking, it has less to do with the leader's charisma, the conception of an exciting vision or the ability to stimulate buy-in.

A recurring theme throughout the chapter has been that of distance. First there is the hierarchical distance in terms of power differentials which separate the person at the helm from everyone else. This is reinforced by the interpersonal distance which characterizes relations with the leader. The model remains strongly based on the concept of an all-powerful leader. Even the emergence in the 1980s of 'alternative' leaders like Bernard Tapie did little to change the prevailing model. Before his downfall, the figure of Tapie was still typically French in that he displayed the force and posture traditionally associated with a *grand chef* (Sorge, 1993, 79). Tapie may have struck a blow for equality of access to power, but his leadership style was no more 'collegiate' than that of other PDGs.

The notion of distance, sometimes extends to the leader's knowledge of the firm. It is quite common for heads of big companies to know very little about the business of the company to which they are appointed. For example, when Serge Tchuruk (*polytechnicien*) was named head of Alcatel-Alsthom, he was concerned about knowing nothing about telecommunications. He was reassured by one of the independent administrators: '*Vous aurez l'esprit plus libre*' ('It will free up your mind') (*Le Nouvel Economiste*, 9/2/96, 50).

Now although this business inexperience applies to only a small section of the *patronat*, it is highly significant because those concerned run many of France's biggest companies. This confirms two key features of French business.

First, it is a reminder that maintaining a good relationship with the state is more likely to be a factor for French corporate heads. More importantly though, it highlights a different perception of leadership and strategy. To lack intimate knowledge of a company's activities is not considered a problem, because the strategic challenge is primarily regarded as an intellectual one. Consider Christian Blanc's comment shortly after taking over the beleaguered and highly bureaucratic Air France: '*Pour comprendre cette compagnie, ce n'est pas la* Harvard Business Review *qu'il faut lire, c'est Zinoviev*' ('Reading the *Harvard Business Review* won't help you understand this company. You'd better read Zinoviev') (*Le Nouvel Economiste*, 5/4/96, 53). What he was *really* saying, was that the keys to understanding this company were brains and astuteness – and his casual reference to the Soviet dissident philosopher was a signal that he had plenty of both.

There is a clear connection between the intellectual leader and organizational centralization. Senior executives in France believe they owe their high position to their intelligence and clarity of vision. It therefore follows that they should make all the critical decisions and that they should be told everything so that they can check on other people's decisions. One prominent PDG's instructions to his assembled directors on joining the company was: 'I want to be at all times informed of every notable event in your different sectors of activity.' Company dismissed.

The widespread view of the boss is nicely captured by Sempé's illustration (see Figure 7.1).

All this reinforces the distinctive role and expectations of a leader in France. The notion of the all-seeing, all-knowing boss is pervasive in France. This allows a certain freedom of action, but it can also be constraining. When in doubt, French bosses cannot avail themselves so easily of the advice of their subordinates. This would be seen to undermine their credibility.[18] As one *cadre* observed:

Figure 7.1: Extract from Sempé's album *Vaguement compétitif* (Denoel, 1985)

> *Il est parfois mal vu pour un PDG de consulter ses collaborateurs au sujet d'un problème dont il est censé, par sa position, connaître la solution.* (It is generally bad show for a PDG to consult his staff about a problem to which, by his position, he should know the answer.)

The expected role of the *patron*, therefore, has important repercussions; not just on the style of leadership, but also on who can aspire to be a *patron*. In particular, it helps to explain why big business, in France, is an exclusively male affair, with not a single woman featuring among the heads of the top 200 companies.

As we have seen in previous chapters, successive filters progressively reduce the number of women at each hierarchical level. It all starts with the chauvinism of the *grandes écoles* which supply industry with its business élite. The engineering schools, in particular, are founded on 'virile' values – rationality, assertiveness, camaraderie and dominance – which tend to make them less attractive to women. Once recruited into companies, women may find that the rather classical conception of management which prevails in France, the importance of networks, and the long hours expected of a *cadre*, progressively sideline all but the most tenacious.

But on top of all this, there is the prevailing image of *le patron*. First, there is the term's masculine gender. A feminine equivalent exists, but it is rather pejorative, normally referring to the proprietress of a hotel, bar or even brothel. In business, the term *la patronne*, would tend to be used ironically. Then there is the kind of self-confidence and aloofness which the *patron* is supposed to exude. These cannot be summoned up overnight. They come from a long process of socialization and the firm knowledge that one is destined to exercise power. An international study of women managers reveals that in France women have to fight 'within their own company to establish a reputation as a leader, since women are rarely spontaneously seen as leaders'. Moreover, 'women frequently have more difficulty than men getting access to information necessary to make wise career decisions' (Serdjénian, 1994, 200). This is surely true in Anglo-Saxon countries too, but it is more marked in France.

Finally there are the expectations of French employees, as described in Chapter 5. They may not know how to react to a boss who behaves differently, who is less imperious, more collaborative, whose style is more nurturing than domineering. This is not what they expect, and they may well regard it with suspicion rather than welcoming it. As one American manager lamented after a spell heading up a French firm:

> The unwary foreigner who is too generous with his time and compassion will only confuse the employees. Chances are, the French worker has not seen such behaviour in an authority figure before. (Johnson, 1996, 45)

Once again, the French business community is not especially open to anyone who is not male, *grande école* educated and French.

Is there an explanation?

One could argue that the French reputation for individualism requires strong leadership to galvanize people into collective action – as de Gaulle did both during and after the Second World War. The umbrella of his prestigious paternalism helped to provide a national focus in the period of turmoil and moral confusion after the Liberation. The French are prepared to entrust an individual with absolute authority, provided that person is remote and cannot act directly upon them.

The desire to entrust one person with absolute power is a trait identified by Crozier in his classic analysis, *Le Phénomène Bureaucratique* (1964). He started with the basic premise that the French are individualistic. Consequently they will not tolerate dependence relationships which impinge upon their freedom of action. Yet collective action requires some form of leadership. So, an omnipotent conception of authority has emerged whereby the locus of the power is sufficiently remote to preserve the independence of the individual. Crozier characterizes the French model as: 'Preferring to submit to impersonal rules and to appeal to a superior authority than to fight and compromise in its own right' (1964, 251).

Individuals are quite prepared to accept the arbitrary decision of a distant leader since it provides direction but guarantees independence. Such a perception of decision-making might seem alien to the Anglo-Saxons who believe that decisions should be taken at the point of action. But the French approach perhaps compensates for loss of detail with enhanced objectivity. As one senior civil servant explained: 'In the final analysis, the best decisions are the ones that are made when one is able to be at some distance from reality' (Crozier, 1982, 222).

This is particularly the case when radical change is required. Crozier describes France's alleged resistance to change in *La Société Bloquée* (1970). When a company wants to make sweeping changes, the task is best handled by an outsider. Insiders are considered to be hamstrung by obligations towards individuals who have helped them on the way up, and too conscious of the emotional and cultural barriers to change within the firm. Moreover, the disproportionate power invested in company heads tends to inhibit the development of internal successors, which perhaps explains the penchant for candidates from outside the corporate sector altogether. As *Le Nouvel Economiste* puts it:

> *Dès lors que beaucoup de nos grands patrons sont des monarches, leurs dauphins ont le plus grand mal à se faire une place au soleil, et les solutions internes sont rarement possibles.* (With many of our corporate leaders in the role of monarchs, their logical successors have considerable difficulty in establishing themselves as credible candidates.) (19/5/95, 58)

The final chapter tries to weigh up the merits and shortfalls of such a model, the extent to which it has served France well in the past, and its sustainability in the future.

8 Grand dessin: Grand malaise

To conclude our discussion of French management we would like to offer an evaluative summary. We will try to summarize, and to generalize the distinctive features of French management, and also to offer some kind of 'balance sheet', although this expression is too crude for the subtlety of the subject and its contextualization.

Distinctive features

French managers have an obvious advantage over their Anglo-Saxon counterparts in that they wear a legally recognized badge, that of *cadre*. Managerial status in France is not something that is handed out indiscriminately, and the word manager has no unflattering associations with, say, bar managers or floor managers, as in Britain. In France *cadre* status is generally acquired with some difficulty and it bestows social as well as a professional consideration on its incumbent.

The social standing of *cadres* probably helps to account for the quality of candidates which firms are able to attract – and a virtuous circle is established with the calibre of these recruits further enhancing the prestige of managerial careers. The only way to gain immediate *cadre* status is to graduate from one of the country's leading *grandes écoles*. This endorses the strong belief in the value of education and the use of qualifications for entry and promotion.

Firms generally deny that qualifications hold any water after initial entry; the reality is that the senior positions in French management are heavily dominated by graduates of the *grandes écoles* – even though the *grandes écoles* account for only about 5 per cent of the population in higher education. The *grandes écoles* are believed to have contributed a great deal to the growth of the French economy in the post-war period. They have ensured that people of the highest quality enter the civil service, business and government. Equally important, the products of the very top *grandes écoles* are highly mobile between these three sectors. This creates a powerful elite and old-boy network, which some find objectionable. Yet every society has such groupings; at least this one has the advantage that business, government and civil service share the same values and knowledge of each other's problems: something which facilitates cross-sector mobility and dialogue, at least among the higher echelons.

This qualitatively different relationship between industry and government was highlighted in Chapter 1. We have not since then repeatedly hammered the point home, since this is a book about management rather than industry. Yet the French difference is significant in several ways. It allows an exchange of personnel, particularly from civil service to industry, a phenomenon rare in Britain and the USA. This facilitated planning, when industry needed not only to be included in the dialogue but, especially in the earlier post-war days, to think about France as well as the balance sheet. The relationship has also facilitated some of France's particular achievements, a number of which were mentioned in Chapter 1, including achievements in aeronautics, space and telecommunications. Finally, an awareness of this feature of French life has a heuristic value: it helps us to understand what French management is like.

The last point should not be exaggerated. Privately owned industry may exhibit a distinctive identity and purpose, France is not in this sense a seamless garment. Yet the threshold between government and industry is generally lower than in, say Britain, the USA or Germany; there is not the sharp contrast in milieu and *modus operandi* that one is conditioned to expect. Indeed, the simplest answer to the question: what is industrial management in France like?, is to say it is actually quite like the civil service. It is not an accident that Henri Fayol called management '*l'administration industrielle*' (1916).

This is in marked contrast to the situation in the UK, where the isolation of the three sectors (civil service, business and government) typically continues in training, experience and career paths. What is more, the type of education imparted in the French *grandes écoles* (with its emphasis on applied science, mathematics and engineering or on commercial subjects) is broadly relevant to the subsequent careers of the French elites, especially those entering management – unlike British educational high-flyers, who have tended to be trained in the classics and other humanities subjects and therefore have a weaker grasp of the underlying needs of an industrial society. It is hardly surprising that once selected for top civil service posts, British civil servants rarely move into industry.

Of course, the reliance on the *grandes écoles* as nurseries for would-be leaders raises questions about the rather premature and irreversible nature of managerial selection and the disillusionment it produces among those cast aside. But the system has concomitant advantages – not least the fact that it pumps a high proportion of the best brains from each generation into the most productive areas of the French economy. There is a close and long-standing relationship between education and business in France. When national deficiencies have been identified it has generally been left to the education system to provide a remedy. The tradition of specialist schools is a perfect example – Polytechnique was set up in the 1790s to train engineers for the armed forces; l'ENA was founded in 1945 to turn out high-level administrators, and most recently l'Ecole Nationale de l'Exportation was created by the Socialist government (1981–86) in response to a balance of trade deficit. There was even talk, at the time of the 'American challenge' (J-J Servan-Schreiber, 1967) and France's alleged managerial lag, of setting up a business version of l'ENA. However, the idea was shelved and a co-ordinating body, the Foundation Nationale pour l'Enseignement de la Gestion des Entreprises (FNEGE), was set up instead.

Another virtue of the system is that it allows young people (mostly men) to reach positions of influence without dissipating a lot of useless energy in political gamesmanship. The *grande école* graduate is virtually guaranteed an illustrious career and can therefore concentrate on actually doing a good job without having to devote inordinate time to self-publicity. *Grande école* graduates form a very distinct elite and are very conscious of the fact, self-confident and intellectual in outlook.

If we turn to the nature of French work relations we note that they tend to be fairly structured and formalistic. French employees seem to shy away from the sort of workplace familiarity in which Anglo-Saxons indulge. The French do not appear to share the belief that openness in professional relations makes sound business sense.

From an Anglo-Saxon standpoint, the deliberate restraint and rigmarole of French office life would make it quite unbearable. However, in the French mind this lesser investment of the 'self" is considered a means of preserving personal choice and independence – which are perceived as higher order needs than the desire for enriched social contact.

The French believe that friendship obliges, provides a lever for favours, exposes the 'friend' to manipulation, and makes him or her dependent. In other words, they regard informality in the workplace as something of a Trojan horse – outwardly appealing but inherently dangerous.

It is noticeable in France that those companies which do try to impose a more informal style of work relations are often unpopular, and an excellent example of this is offered in Michael Johnson's autobiographical account, *French Resistance* (1996). There is a widespread belief that cordial relations merely serves as a means of extracting commitment from employees and of encouraging a certain freedom of expression which facilitates decision-making

– in other words, as a manipulative device which gives an illusion of freedom while actually reducing it.

In order to get round this perceived dependence and manipulation, the French have therefore concocted a system of authority relations, based on ritual, which minimizes the personality input in personal interaction.

Rituals include such things as form of address, use of first names and so forth. The rituals are a means of situating the participants and defining their respective roles, thereby leaving them in no doubt as to which one has the upper hand. These rituals serve to diffuse potential tension since they clearly identify the authority of each party – thereby reducing the need for political manoeuvring or personal involvement. As a result of the preliminary ritualistic power play (exchange of correspondence, business cards and greetings), the participants know exactly where they stand. In other words, the authority of each party stems from their position (as projected by assorted rituals) rather than from their personalities. Authority in France is vested in the role – it does not emanate from the individual.

Clearly, these rituals are more than the trivial concerns for which they are often mistaken. Beneath their apparent banality they reflect and reinforce essential traits of French management – notably its hierarchic and elitist traditions.

In terms of managerial values, the French seem torn between their respect for tradition and an infatuation with the more modern American values. On the one hand, the social and cultural norms of the pre-industrialized order seem to have had a pronounced effect on the development of business attitudes – and colour French views of money, authority, mobility and so on. On the other hand, a more American managerial ethos based on openness, pragmatism and results is beginning to have an impact on French attitudes now.

This state of tension between past and future is perhaps best illustrated by the contrasting attitudes of French corporate leaders. At one extreme there is the older style of family management, usually authoritarian, wary of expansion and innovation; and at the other there is the 1980s-plus wave of dynamic entrepreneurs, symbolized by Vincent Bolloré or François Pinault, more or less self-made men who, without any elite training, have built up small firms to achieve spectacular results.

When it comes to big business, though, the majority of heads of companies are products of the *grandes écoles* and are parachuted into firms. French companies rely to a large extent on individuals who are alien to the firm, and sometimes even to the private sector. This goes against traditions in the UK, US and especially Japan which all tend to favour established insiders.

One good reason for preferring an outsider to an insider is that when a company needs to make big changes, outsiders are freer to deliver the necessary shocks, though there is a corresponding downside that will be explored a little later.

It is customary in Britain to counterpose public and private companies. What is noticeable in the French set-up is that this traditional distinction between public and private sector is less clear-cut. Partly, this is the result of the common backgrounds of the company heads. In France, as we have seen, a large number of private companies are run by former senior civil servants. This blurring of categories probably helps to account for the relative ease with which companies such as Péchiney, Rhône-Poulenc and Saint-Gobain have made the transition from the private to nationalized sector and back again.

It might be said that French companies have confided the task of identifying and training its future leaders to the state. This demonstrates a qualitatively different relationship between state and industry from that found in Britain or the USA. Another manifestation of the positive (though perhaps overbearing) influence of the state on business is the legal obligation to spend one per cent of the payroll on training.

Coherent whole

The distinctive features alluded to so far, taken in isolation, appear contrary to received (and mostly American) wisdom regarding sound management practice. For instance, we might consider that French management is too stratified, that qualifications are accorded too much importance, that interpersonal relations are too remote, that corporate mentalities are archaic . . . All these remarks are partly justified. However, we should not forget to look at the whole picture.

To take an obvious example, it would be easy to criticize the education system for its rigidity and rather narrow focus. Yet the education system produces what it is asked to produce. It is geared to suit the exigencies of the companies, which seek help in the pre-selection of an elite of potential top executives. This allows careers to be mapped out at the recruitment stage, based on qualifications. What is expected of the education system is not that it impart particular skills, but simply that it classify students via entry and finalist examinations. Certificates guarantee a career and the most prestigious guarantee the best careers. If the companies decided to recruit and promote, not on qualifications, but on efficiency in the field, creativity and teamwork, the education system would try to develop these qualities. As it is, in France, those qualities are more or less assumed, questionably of course, to be the natural corollaries of high intellect.

What is true for the French education system also applies to the economic system, to career and salary structures, to organizational relations and to the corporate cultures of French companies. They are all attuned to one another. The jigsaw pieces may have weird configurations but they still interlock and are generally consistent with the industrial needs of the nation.

So, whatever the perceived merits or shortcomings of French management it cannot be isolated from the society that spawned it – compatibility is probably more important than adherence to an ideal in determining national success. The acid test is, does it work, and the evidence – not least France's economic performance since the war – is that on the whole it has worked so far. But . . .

Brilliance and its limitations

Against the background of these generalizations concerning linkage and fit in French society it may be helpful to point up the things that French managers do well and to indicate corresponding areas where performance may be problematic; while the phrase 'strengths and weaknesses' is too crude, too much of a blunt instrument, that is the basic intent of the present discussion, albeit one that will be qualified.

Most obviously French managers are clever. The majority of them excel in a formal educated cleverness – good at mastering complicated issues quickly; good at developing arguments and articulating them; good at sequence, inference, and logical consistency; good at a rational appraisal of proposals and documents. They are also numerate – remember the tyranny of the maths weighted *bac S* in the early stages of educational self-selection, together with the fact that many *cadres* are graduates of engineering *grandes écoles*. French managers too are distinguished by their use of language. Command of the language, as an end in itself as well as vocational pre-requisite, is more important to French managers than to their counterparts in other countries – the contrast with the USA would be particularly marked. The French these managers speak will not only be marked by a formal correctness seldom equalled in spoken English, it will also be spoken with wit, style, and elegance. French managers are not shy in meetings nor demure in dialogue. Meetings are the area in which they will demonstrate their command and cleverness, their eloquence and *élan*. Nor are their verbal qualities at the expense the ecritural. Written proposals, things drafted by French managers, are strong on precision and lucidity, on premise, inference, and the direction of argument.

All this predisposes French managers to succeed in the rational parts of the management task. The demands for analysis, rational decision-making, formal commendation, planning and drafting all play to French strengths. And this educated cleverness has another function, in that it bolsters formal authority.

It is a feature of French organizations that they rely on the formal authority of the finely graded hierarchy. And it is a criticism of French organizations that there is an *over*-reliance on the authority, a critique that is at least as old as Michel Crozier's classic study (1964) and one to which we will contribute. The strength that one must recognize is that French managers are able to make this authority legitimate and effective.

The *cadre* authority is certainly legitimated in their own eyes by their educational credentials, reinforced by regular displays of intellectual virtuosity. It is also likely, though rather more difficult to assert with confidence, that these same educational credentials give their possessors some credence with lower-level subordinates, with *la base* as it is revealingly termed (France is after all the one country in which an occupational choice survey resulted in parents giving the profession 'philosopher' as that which they would most like their children to become).

For some there are limitations to formal authority but French managers typically make the authority effective in the formal sense. The bottom line is that they will be obeyed. At best with conviction, at worst rather woodenly, but one can make the basic assumption in France that the directives of the superior will be implemented by subordinates. In this connection one of the present authors recalls an Anglo-French management seminar in London in the early 1990s where senior expatriate French managers running subsidiaries in London with British staff, complained that you could not trust British managers to implement higher-level decisions. The charge went that the (French) boss would propose directives at a meeting with subordinate, mostly British, managers; there might or might not be any critical challenge in the meeting, at the end of which the boss would re-state the proposed directive; the subordinates would then go away and quietly subvert it, variously claiming if called to account that what they did was what they thought the meeting had decided, that they fully supported the boss's decision but changed operating circumstances made it impracticable, and so on. Perfidious Albion strikes again (and it would not happen in France).

Now in this connection, we would like to make two overlapping points – the capability of French managers to have their directives accepted is distinctive, and cleverness is the force which drives the acceptance of formal authority. The directive will be coherent, it will have a certain verisimilitude, it is likely to be communicated with thrust and clarity. Furthermore, this French mix of cleverness and language prowess is a resource for disciplining subordinates. Michael Johnson (1996) writing from the vantage point of his experience as an expatriate American manager in a French organization is good at communicating this often spine-chilling technique. When the French superior prefixes his dictum with the phrase, *'je me suis sans doute mal exprimé'* ('no doubt I express myself badly') this equals 'you are an imbecile not to have got this right first time round, and you are about to be crucified!'

The downside is that this formal authority, however spine-chillingly orchestrated, is too narrow a base for getting complicated things done in situations of imperfect knowledge and limited cognition. And this downside is reinforced by education and formal qualifications, which function as a barrier between *les cadres* and *les autres*. It is more difficult for French managers to reach out to *la base* (as the lower-level employees are known) than it is for their Anglo-Saxon counterparts. There may be educational gradations in other countries but they are not so lauded as in France. Even the English in their dealings with subordinates do not pretend to intellectual superiority (dividing) but to leadership (hopefully integrating).

Thus a paradox surrounds the French manager. An elite group, well able to communicate with political and administrative elites, overlapping and interchanging with them, the whole macro-elite supported by common educational background and values. But it is also differentiated, divided, partitioned by this education, unable to communicate downwards except by the exercise of formal authority, unable to guide the behaviour of lower participants except by rules and orders.

La base has responded in kind, with an impersonal contractualism, taking refuge in rules and procedures, tight job descriptions and written instructions, a phenomenon that even pervades the management ranks in their orientation upwards. Michael Johnson again quotes a professional employee in his organization as saying:

> *Dites-moi exactement ce que vous voulez que je fasse, et je le ferai si j'ai envie.*
> (Tell me exactly what you want me to do, and if I like the sound of it, I'll do it.) (Johnson, 1997:72)

The key word in this formulation is 'exactly'. Precision defines, but it also limits, and in such cases it limits the commitment of the subordinates. In this matter then, French managers are trapped in their educational superiority, constrained to emphasize the ratiocinative elements of the management mission. As one wit once remarked regarding the strengths and weaknesses of French management:

> If it helps to be clever, they will probably do it well.
> If it doesn't, they won't.

Informal groups and team work

The reliance on formal authority together with a strain towards defensive individualism tends to work against 'teamliness' in French organizations. But it is not that the French at work are incapable of informal solidarity. There is often high work-group solidarity, typically of a protective-defensive kind. But this group solidarity has to be based on mutual solidarity and perceived identity of interest. Such groups cannot be called into life by management, created by pep talks, or be contained in an artificial way. And the French are much less given to the Anglo-Saxon style of 'We are all in the same boat, so let's pull together and make the best of it!' If this line of argument is propounded to them, they will suspect they are being made the victims of some devious manoeuvre to suit someone else's interest. Indeed the French are particularly unsusceptible to pep talks, tending to view the appeal inherent in the pep talk as intellectually shallow and designed to manipulate.

So French people in particular work groups, may have high solidarity, and people working in a particular section or department in a company are likewise inclined to see this section as a primary focus of loyalty and interest. Indeed the tensions and conflicts between the various departments of a company are likely to be more marked than in Anglo-Saxon countries.

External teams involving senior executives on the one hand and members of the political and administrative elite on the other, are often very effective. Indeed France tends to be at its best where engineering and administration meet, where companies with a high-tech capability interact with politicians and administrators to launch big projects, to remove 'road blocks' and to carry the project to a successful, not to say glorious, conclusion. But inside the company, management teams are not a natural phenomenon. A team whose members are all drawn from the same function or department, or whose members all report to the same superior, may work. But cross-function, mixed-level teams have little chance. And as for the American-style task force, where people with different bosses and from different departments come together for some management-ordained purpose, where the members pretend to like each other, develop *esprit de corps*, and unite behind a common objective – forget it – why, after all, should one surrender, identify with a group or team if it cannot do anything for you?

Motivation

We would like to suggest that motivation is also problematic in French organizations, as a result of the elitism, 'authoritism' and individualism already noted. Certainly, behaviour may be controlled by job descriptions and procedure, and by the exercise of formal authority by superiors. It may also be the case that there is some self-motivation among professional and managerial staff – though this seems to figure less in French management literature than in Anglo-Saxon. But what is conspicuous by its absence, is attempts by managers and supervisors to motivate their subordinates in a direct, face-to-face fashion, whether in one-to-one dialogue or via the medium of group pep talks. Even at manager level, this kind of motivation, taken for granted in Anglo-Saxon countries, is not on. It would be regarded as an invasion of personal privacy, of the integrity of the individual, as somehow demeaning among the *grandes écoles* intellectual elite. And so for the 'lower downs' the executive elite have no way of reaching them – French managers are not into Friday night beer busts and hamburger fests.

A postscript in the discussion of motivation concerns culture change. At least since the appearance of that famous book of the 1980s, *In Search of Excellence* (Peters and Waterman, 1982) there has been an interest in organizational culture, on the grounds that the 'right' culture should have a positive impact on corporate performance. And since not all organizations will have an appropriate, goal-supporting culture *ab initio* then it belongs to the corporate leadership to seek to effect culture change, to create by communication, symbolic act and value engineering, a culture that will be positive and functional for organizational achievement. Here again, as with 'hands-on' motivation, the culture change mission is likely to founder on the inability of the elite to reach out to *la base*, and on the suspicious and defensive individuality of the latter.

Implementation

Insofar as implementation is something that may be comprehended, prescribed, and specified, the French are likely to get it right. Or again if implementation is dependent on successful co-operation with the state, state subsidy or even facilitation, protection of the operation from distracting competition or the removal of external obstacles to achievement, then the French will do it better than anyone else.

Yet this is not the whole story. Implementation, as opposed to analysis-decision taking-policy formulation, is a messy old business. There are not any rules for it, it is not basically programmable. Implementation is opportunistic and idiosyncratic and intuitive, rather than rational and creditable. It often involves 'selling' a scheme to people who are going to have to run with it, coaxing people into giving something they instinctively distrust a try, removing obstacles, finding ways to accentuate the positive and neutralize the negative.

All this hands-on, face-to-face, grabbing their hearts and minds for the sake of getting them to do something, does not play to French strengths. It is not what French subordinates expect from their superiors, who are defined as superiors (formal authority and bureaucratic role) rather than as leaders (interpersonal affect and charisma).

Relatively speaking, then, the French elite is strategically minded and solution-driven rather than implementation-minded and problem-driven. In his most recent book, Crozier attributes this bias to the education system and the leadership selection process:

> *L'absurdité française, c'est de croire que la formation des ingénieurs comme machines à trouver des solutions est la bonne formule pour recruter des dirigeants qui auront surtout comme tâche de déterminer quels sont véritablement les problèms.* (The French folly is to believe that engineers trained to churn out solutions evolve naturally into leaders capable of diagnosing the real problems.) (Crozier, 1996, 100)

The national elite

As has been suggested at several points, France is distinguished by having a semi-integrated national elite that spans industry – commerce – administrations – politics. What serves to integrate this elite is the fact that:

* its members are overwhelmingly *grande école* educated;
* there is mobility between elite sectors, especially from the civil service into industry and commerce;
* these elites are centred on Paris;
* they know each other, or at least are in a position where it is usually acceptable to 'access' each other on the basis of common elite membership or shared educational antecedents.

For the most part we have been concerned at various points in this book to indicate the advantages of this state of affairs, especially in terms of a state-industry collaboration, rare in other countries, that has served to get things done, on occasion, to get some very impressive things done. But again our purpose now is to raise the question: are there corresponding disadvantages?

First the national elite suffers from the same limiting exclusivity as does the executive elite. It is neither popular nor populist. It cannot communicate downwards, it cannot motivate across social categories. This means that the national elite cannot organize support outside its own body, cannot orchestrate a more broadly based popular support for its policies and initiatives. This in turn means that the elite is turned back in upon itself, is an organ of self-approval. This is arguably unhealthy.

Second, besides this limited capacity to reach downwards, to listen, involve and motivate, French executives may also face a distinctive problem in engaging with the environment. It can be argued that the French elite lacks what Ashby (1956) called 'requisite variety', meaning the internal variety needed to cope with environmental variety. In a competitive environment of increasing complexity, different perspectives are needed to spot and respond appropriately to diverse opportunities and threats. This diversity of background and outlook is clearly not a French strength. The managerial elite is drawn from a restricted social pool; those selected respect the same logical processes, share the same values, generate similar insights and suffer from similar blindspots. So the uniformity of the French elite probably impedes the ability to 'see' alternatives as well as the ability to mobilize co-operation.

Third, while the national elite is quasi-integrated the component parts are not equal. The senior partner is government-administration, not commerce-industry. And since this is perceived by the various elite members, an odd situation has arisen where he who would aspire to high office in Elite B (industry) aims to get there via Elite A (the civil service). In turn, this has odd effects on educational itineraries whereby graduates from the commercial *grandes écoles*, the so-called sup-de-cos (*écoles superieurs de commerce*), represent over half of the candidates trying to get into l'ENA, the prestigious civil service school. They do this knowing that the way to be the top in industry is via *pantouflage* at a later stage. So that many top posts in industry and commerce come to be occupied by people whose experience is neither industrial nor commercial.

Fourth, there is arguably a problem of objectivity. Whenever members of an elite run into a problem, face difficulties, need support, they 'call each other up' and the matter typically is resolved with dispatch. Fine, a neat system that works much of the time. But supposing agreement is not reached? In this case because of the quasi-unitary, club-like nature of the elite, disagreement is somehow more personal, more disruptive. The elite lacks a mechanism for *objectifying* disagreement, a service admirably provided in 'another country' by American corporate lawyers.

Finally the club-like nature of the elite also seems to undermine accountability. Anyone who fails, whose organization turns in a disappointing performance, is likely to be protected by 'the club'. If they are moved from the site of underperformance it will be to another top job,[1] e.g. Haberer. Any underperformance will be attributed to circumstance, to situations over which the individual has no control. The external discipline of either market-place or political sanction is lacking.

Change?

A theme of this book is the stability of *les cadres*. The origins, character and style of management in France seems to be persistent over time. Portraits of French management, from the 1960s to the 1990s, seem remarkably consistent. Yet at the end of the first chapter we raised the spectre of changes in the world of French business – growing internationalization, privatization, liberalization, and a certain kind of 'business ethics' style accountability whereby corporate wrongdoers might be proceeded against. These developments, against the background of persistently high unemployment rates and incipient unemployment among *cadres,* may impact upon the stability of French management. In short, business may change management.

The aim here is that having briefly re-run this argument another dimension may be added to it. One of the forces for change in the French business world indicated above, internationalization, is externally driven. It is the product of developments beyond the borders of the French state – increase in the volume of world trade, the development of global markets in many industries and therefore of global competition. So the French international initiative is in a sense a response. This same globalization, of course, exposes France to stronger external influence. Even in the early 1990s it is arguable that world events – the fall of European communism, German re-unification, the Gulf War – impacted on France more strongly than such events would have done a decade earlier.

There is also a purely European strand to these developments in terms of the politics of the European Union (EU). The Single European Act of 1986, the moves to the Single European Market of 1992–93, the EU plans for monetary union, and more distant aspirations to heightened political integration are all narrowing France's room for manoeuvre, are all gentle pressures for conformity to wider European order. And some of this, for example, Single Market provisions for cross-border competitive tendering by public authority, episodes of industry deregulation, may affect this very French national elite alliance between government and industry. That is to say, it may be more difficult for the French state to succour chosen industries, such as airlines, control the capital base and share distribution of big corporations, and appoint their CEOs (from the state sector).

So that while the character of French management still appears rather stable, it may be the case that it is changed in the middle term by changes in business and in France's exposure to European and wider international forces. But there is of course a counter-argument, particularly with regard to these EU developments.

Not for nothing was French for centuries the language of diplomacy. Has not France always known how to *soigner les relations* with other states? France has had a pre-eminent role in the EU since its inception. The French state has also had more experience in matters of industrial policy and corporate intervention than most of the EU member states. It has also shone in the administration of large projects, in for example, nuclear power, tele-communications, and aviation, and on occasion these projects have been cross-border as with Airbus or the Channel Tunnel, so that France may be better equipped than most states to maintain its individuality within a more EU-driven, homogenized Europe.

We should not underestimate the possibilities of choice within an evolving system, nor the French genius for exploiting them.

References & Bibliography

Chapter 1

Ackermann, K. F. (September, 1988) *Europe Ahead: the changing role of human resource management in German companies.* Paper at International Comparisons in Human Resource Management Conference, Cranfield School of Management, England. Excerpts adapted by the authors.

Albert, Michel (1991) *Capitalisme Contre Capitalisme.* Paris: Editions du Seuil.

Babeau, A. (1994) 'Qui possède les entreprise francaises?' *Le Monde*, 11/10/94, IV.

Gordon, Colin (1996) *The Business Culture in France.* Oxford: Butterworth-Heinemann

Hofstede, Geert (1980) *Cultures Consequences.* Beverly Hills, Sage.

Morin, F. (1988) 'A qui appartient le capital des 200 premières entreprises privées?' *Science et Vie: Economie*, 41 (juillet-aôut), 45–64

Morin, F. (1994) 'Les trois pôles du pouvoir économique' *Le Monde,* 8/5/94, V.

Szarka, Joseph (September, 1996) *French Business in the Mitterand Years: the Continuity of Change.* Paper at 'The Mitterand Era in Perspective' ASMCF Annual Conference, Royal Holloway, University of London.

Thurow, Lester (1992) *Head to Head.* New York: William Morrow.

Chapter 2

Ardagh, J. (1982) *France in the 1980s: The Definitive Book.* Harmondsworth: Penguin.

Benguigui, G., Griset, A., Jacob, A. and Monjardet, D. (1975) *Recherche sur la Fonction d'Encadrement.* Two-volume report by the Groupe de Sociologie du Travail. Paris: CNRS.

Blazot, J. (1983) *Cadres sur Table.* Nancy: Presses de Berger-Levrault.

Boltanski, L. (1982) *Les Cadres: la formation d'un groupe social.* Paris: Editions de Minuit. Translation: Goldhammer, A. (1987) *The Making of a Class.* Cambridge: Cambridge University Press.

Doublet, J. and Passelecq, O. (1973) *Les Cadres.* Paris: Presses Universitaires de France.

Euriat, M., and Thélot, C. (1995) 'Le recrutement social de l'élite scolaire en France', *Revue Française de Sociologie*, Vol. 36 (3), 403–38.

L'Expansion (25/1/96) 'Sondage: Cadres, vous êtes décidément formidables', Deschamps, P., Beau, N., and Gibier, H., 36–45.

L'Expansion (2/2/96) 'Etrangers en terre française', Vidalie, A., 42–45.

L'Expansion (7/3/96) 'Sondage: Les Français prudents sauf les cadres', 73.

Grunberg, G. and Mouriaux, R. (1979) *L'Univers Politique et Syndical des Cadres.* Paris: Presses de la Fondation Nationale des Sciences Politiques.

Horovitz, J. (1980) *Top Management Control in Europe*. London: Macmillan.

Lawrence, P. (1980) *Managers and Management in West Germany*. London: Croom Helm.

Maurice, M., Sellier, F. and Silvestre, J.-J. (1977) *Production de la hiérarchie dans l'entreprise: recherche d'un effet social Allemagne-France*. Laboratoire d'Economie et de Sociologie du Travail, Aix en Provence. Translation: Goldhammer, A. (1986) *The Social Foundations of Industrial Power: A Comparison of France and West Germany*. Massachusetts: MIT Press.

Le Monde (23/6/87) 'La fin du congrès de la CFE-CGC', Noblecourt, M., 44.

Le Monde (3/293) 'Nos amis les cadres', Boucher, H., 29.

Le Monde (10/1/94) 'Le spleen des cadres', Normand, J.-M., 16.

Le Monde (10/2/94) 'Des consommateurs à états d'âme', Vaysse, F., 17.

Le Monde – Initiatives (12/4/95) 'La banalisation des cadres', Lebaube, A., 1.

Le Monde (23/4/95) 'Les cadres, une catégorie choyée par les candidats', Noble, M., 7.

Le Monde – Initiatives (17/5/95) 'Cadres au double langage', Aizicovici, F., 28.

Le Monde – Initiatives (11/6/96) 'Les cadres s'adaptent à l'incertitude', Leroy, C., 1.

National Economic Development Office (1987) *The making of managers: a report on management education, training and development in the USA, West Germany, France, Japan and the UK*. London: NEDO.

Reynaud, J.-D. and Grafmeyer, Y. (eds) (1982) *Français, qui êtes-vous? des essais et des chiffres*. Paris: Documentation Française.

Zeldin, T. (1983) *The French*. London: Collins.

Chapter 3

Ardagh, J. (1987) *France Today*. London: Penguin.

Boltanski, L. (1982) *Les Cadres: la formation d'un groupe social*. Paris: Editions de Minuit. Translation: Goldhammer, A. (1987) *The Making of a Class*. Cambridge: Cambridge University Press.

Bourdieu, P. and Passeron, J.-C. (1970) *La Reproduction*. Paris: Editions de Minuit.

Capital (June 1994) 'Quelle école de commerce choisir?' Benichou, P., 116–29.

L'Etudiant (March 1996) 'Le Guide des Etudes Supérieures 1996'. Complete issue, *hors-série*.

Euriat, M., and Thélot, C. (1995) 'Le recrutement social de l'élite scolaire en France', *Revue Française de Sociologie*, XXXVI, 403–38.

L'Expansion (4/4/96) 'Ecole par école, le palmarès des salaires', Gibier, H., 78–92.

L'Express (23/5/96) 'Ce que vaut votre université', Baumier, A and Léotard, M.-L., 36–47.

Le Figaro – Economie (17/6/96) 'Les écoles de commerce s'ouvrent aux littéraires', Cohen, E., 28.

Financial Times (18/4/90) 'Tradition still rules the roost', de Jonquières, G., 13.

Frémy, D., and Frémy, M. (1996) *Quid: tout pour tous*. Paris: Robert Laffont.

Le Monde (18/4/95) 'La grogne des patrons', Faudjas, A., 9.

Le Monde (6/7/95) 'Les nouvelles frontières du monde étudiant', Delberghe, M., 9.

Le Monde (18/7/95) 'Baccalauréat 1996', Gurrey, B., 8.

Le Monde (28/3/96) 'Réussite au baccalauréat', Gurrey, B., 9.

Le Point (23/3/96) 'Débat: François Bayrou – François de Closets', Dufay, F., 96–97.

Szarka, J. (1192) *Business in France*. London: Pitman.

Vincent, C. (1981) 'La Fin des Illusions'. In Santoni, G. (ed.), *Société et Culture de la France Contemporaine*. Albany: State University of New York Press.

Whitley, R., Thomas, A., and Marceau, J. (1984) *Masters of Business: The making of a new elite?* London: Tavistock Publications.

Chapter 4

01 Informatique (24/5/96) 'Un destin tracé de manager', Boudard, F., 67.

Boltanski, L. (1982) *Les Cadres: La formation d'un groupe social*. Paris: Editions de Minuit. Translation: Goldhammer, A. (1987) *The Making of a Class*. Cambridge: Cambridge University Press.

Capital (June 1993) 'Graphologie: Avez-vous l'écriture de l'emploi?' Henno, J., 120–24.

Capital (May 1995) 'Les entreprises qui paient le mieux', Henno, J. , 126–35.

Capital (June 1996) 'Le guide pratique du premier emploi', Henno, J. , 126–39.

Challenges (November 1995) 'Rebondir à mi-parcours', Dufour, J.-F. , 50–60.

Coale, D. J. (1994) 'International barriers to progress', *Journal of Management Development*, 13 (2), 55–58.

Derr, C. B. (1987) 'Managing High Potentials in Europe: Some cross-cultural findings', *European Management Journal*, 5 (2), 72–80.

Derr, C. B., and Laurent, A. (1987) *Internal and External Careers: A theoretical and cross-cultural perspective*, Insead Working Paper, No. 87/24.

L'Essentiel du Management (November 1996) 'Le Guide des Salaires', Péretié, M.-M., 145.

Evans, P. A. L. (1986) *Apple Computer*, INSEAD-CEDEP Case.

L'Expansion (7/12/95) 'La France contre ses élites', Moatti, G., 95–108.

L'Expansion (25/1/96) 'Sondage: Cadres, vous êtes décidément formidables', Deschamps, P., Beau, N., and Gibier, H., 36–45.

L'Expansion (4/4/96) 'Zoom sur le marché de l'emploi 1996', Deschamps, P.-M., and Gibier, H., 62–65.

L'Expansion (4/4/96) 'Promos 95', Gibier, H., 74–75.

Janis, I. L. (1971) *Victims of Groupthink*. Boston, MA: Houghton Mifflin.

Johnson, M. (1996) *French Resistance*. London: Cassell.

Maisonrouge, J. (1985) *Manager International*, Paris: Editions Robert Laffont.

MOCI. Moniteur du Commerce International (21/12/95) 'Salaire des cadres: Le retour du marketing', Collet, V., 83–84.

Le Monde – Initiatives (15/3/95) 'Comportement et passion', Betbeder, M.-C., 2.

Le Monde – Emploi (20/11/96) 'L'élaboration d'un référentiel des qualifications suscite inquiétudes et scepticisme', Baverel, P., 2.

Le Monde – Emploi (20/11/96) 'Le rapport de Michel de Virville intéresse les syndicats qui en redoutent l'application', Leroy, C., 3.

Le Nouvel Economiste (21/3/96) 'Palmes académiques', Beaufils, V., 3.

Le Nouvel Economiste (21/3/96) 'Où, combien et sur quels critères ils vont recruter', Game, F., 66–67.

Orleman, P. (1992) *The global corporation: Managing across cultures*. Masters Thesis, University of Pennsylvania.

Le Point (5/10/87) 'La fin du règne des autodidactes', Jeambar, D., 54.

Le Point (28/9/96) 'Crise: Les 8 recettes pour réussir sa carrière', Golliau, C., 78–88.

Rebondir (November 1996) 'Spécial Cadres', Hors série no. 15.

Szarka, J. (1192) *Business in France*. London: Pitman.

Tixier, M. (1987) 'Cultures nationales et recrutement', *La Revue Française de Gestion*, September-October, 59–68.

Thulliez, G. J. (1989) 'The view from France: French CEOs look ahead', *The McKinsey Quarterly, Autumn*, 2–45.

Chapter 5

Amado, G., Faucheux, C., and Laurent., A. (1991) 'Organizational change and cultural realities: Franco-American contrasts', *International Studies of Management and Organization*, Vol. 21, No. 3, 62–95.

Barsoux, J. -L. (1993) *Funny Business: humour, management and business culture*. London: Cassell.

Beer, W. R. (1982) *Strategies for Change: The future of French society*. Massachusetts: MIT Press. Translation of: Crozier, M. (1979) *On ne change pas la société par décret*. Paris: Grasset.

Blanchard, K. (1983) *One Minute Manager*. London: Willow Books.

Closets, F. de (1982) *Toujours plus!* Paris: Grasset.

Crozier, M. (1964) *The Bureaucratic Phenomenon*. Chicago: University of Chicago Press.

L'Expansion (25/1/96) 'Cadres, vous êtes décidément formidables', Deschamps, P., Beau, N., and Gibier, H., 36–45.

Exportation (October 1990), 'Comment travailler à l'anglaise', Combal-Weiss, R., 32–38.

Graves, D. (ed.) (1973) *Management Research: A Cross-cultural Perspective*. Amsterdam: Elsevier Scientific.

Gruère, J.-P. and Morel, P. (1991) *Cadres Français et Communications Interculturelles*. Paris: Eyrolles.

Iribarne, P. d' (1989) *La Logique de l'Honneur*. Paris: Seuil.

Johnson, M. (1996) *French Resistance*. London: Cassell.

Kotter, J. P. (1982) *The General Managers*. New York: The Free Press.

Laborit, H. (1992) *L'Esprit du Grenier*, Paris: Les Editions de l'Homme.

Laurent, A. (1981) 'Matrix organizations and Latin cultures', *International Studies of Management and Organization*, 10 (4), 101–14.

Laurent, A. (1983) 'The cultural diversity of western conception of management', *International Studies of Management and Organization,* 13(1-2), 75–96.

Laurent, A. (1986) 'The cross-cultural puzzle of global human resource management', *Human Resource Management*, Vol. 25, No. 1, 133–48.

Lawrence, P. and Spybey, T. (1986) *Management and Society in Sweden*, London: Routledge & Kegan Paul.

Mole, J. (1991) *When in Rome* . . . New York: AMACOM.

Le Nouvel Economiste, (12/5/80) 'Cadres: La course aux pouvoirs', Antoni, M.-L., 42–47.

Le Nouvel Economiste. (2/02/96) 'Managers étrangers en terre française', Vidalie, A, 42–45.

Reynaud, J.-D. and Grafmeyer, Y. (eds) (1981) *Français, qui êtes-vous?* Paris: Documentation Française.

Santoni, G. (ed.) (1981) *Société et culture de la France contemporaine*. New York: State University of New York Press.

Sorge, A. 'Management in France' in *Management in Western Europe*, Hickson, D.J. (ed), 65–87, New York: de Gruyter, 1993).

Stevens, O. J., cited in Hofstede, G. (1991) *Cultures and Organizations*, London: McGraw-Hill, 140–42.

Wall Street Journal, (31/7/90) 'GE's Culture turns sour at French unit', Nelson, M. and Browning, E.S., 4.

Chapter 6

Blanchard, K. (1983) *One Minute Manager*. London: Willow Books.

Boltanski, L. (1982) *Les Cadres: la formation d'un group social*. Paris: Editions de Minuit. Translation: Goldhammer, A. (1987) *The Making of a Class*. Cambridge: Cambridge University Press.

Capital (October 1993) 'Quel vin avec quel fromage?' Romillat, S. 176–77.

Capital (August 1994) 'Toutes les méthodes pour 'apprendre' le vin', Bagot. L., 56–57.

Daninos, Pierre (1954) *Les Carnets du Major Thompson*. Paris: Hachette.

Deleplanque, M. (1975) *Le Guide du Savoir-vivre*, Paris: UNIDE.

The Economist Guide: France (1990) London: Hutchinson Business.

L'Expansion (10/7/95) 'A la table des présidents', Scott, P., 122–23.

L'Expansion, (4/4/96) 'Patrons, un délit est si vite arrivé . . .', Gibier, H., 122–23.

L'Expansion, (11/7/96) 'Dossier: L'économie en vacances', Moatti, G., Mas, I. and Collomp, F., 54–66.

L'Express (1/3/85) 'Les dix blocages de la société française', Fallot, E. 21-33.

Financial Times (18/1/95) 'Daily grind of 7 to 9', Jack, A., Rich, M., and Terazono, E., 16.

Géricot, C. (1994) *Le Savoir-vivre aujourd'hui*. Paris: Payot & Rivages.

Johnson, M. (1996) *French Resistance*. London: Cassell.

Le Bras, F. (1995) *La Bible du Nouveau Savoir-Vivre*. Paris: Editions Marabout.

Le Monde – Initiatives (6/1/93) 'Parcours d'initiation', Azicovici, F., 27.

Le Monde – Initiatives (16/6/93) 'Les jeunes diplômées entre la famille et le travail', Lebaube, A., 32.

Le Monde (3/2/95) 'Les forcenés du dictionnaire', Cressard, A. 31.

Le Monde – Initiatives (17/5/95) 'Cadres au double langage', Azicovici, F., 28.

Le Monde (15/8/95) 'Vacances' Betbeder, M.-C., 7.

Le Monde (20/3/96) 'Enquête sur les cadres', Baverel, P., 4.

Le Monde (10/10/96) 'Les cadres travaillent trop', Lemaître, F., 1.

Le Nouvel Economiste (7/4/95) 'Faut-il vous appeler Loulou, M. le président?' Berthon, M. and Thérin, F., 87–89.

Le Nouvel Economiste (2/2/96) 'Etrangers en terre française', Vidalie, A., 42–45.

Picard, D. (1995) *Les Rituels du Savoir-vivre*. Paris: Seuil.

Le Point (17/8/87) 'Comment les patrons prennent congés', Coignard, S., 50-51.

Schneider, S., and Barsoux, J.-L. (1997) *Management Across Cultures*, London: Prentice-Hall.

Weinshall, T. D. (1979) *Managerial Communication: Concepts, approaches and techniques*. London: Academic Press.

Zeldin, T. (1983) *The French*. London: Collins.

Chapter 7

Ardagh, J. (1982) *France in the 1980s*. Harmondsworth: Penguin.

Bauer, M., and Bertin-Mourot, B. (1995a) *L'accès au sommet des grandes entreprises françaises: 1985–1994*, Paris: CNRS.

Bauer, M., and Bertin-Mourot, B. (1995b) 'Le recrutement des élites économiques en France et en Allemagne', in Suleiman, E. and Mendras, H. (eds) *Le recrutement des élites en Europe*. Paris: Editions La Découverte.

Birnbaum, P., Baruco, C., Bellaiche, M. and Marie, A. *La Classe Dirigeante Française*. Paris: Seuil.

Bourdieu, P. and Passeron, J.-C. (1966) *Les Héritiers*. Paris: Editions de Minuit.

Capital (October 1993) 'Avec qui dirige . . . Michel Pébereau', Genet, P., 28–29.

Capital (March 1996) 'Vuitton, l'entreprise la plus rentable de France', Bialobos, C. 26–30.

Challenges (September 1994) 'Cent dirigeants pour demain', anon., 56–73.

Crozier, M. (1964) *The Bureaucratic Phenomenon*. Chicago: University of Chicago Press.

Crozier, M. (1970) *La Société Bloquée*. Paris: Seuil.

Crozier, M. (1979) *On ne Change pas la Société par Décret*. Paris: Grasset. Translation: Beer, W. R. (1982) *Strategies for Change: The future of French society*. Massachusetts: MIT Press.

Dyas, G. P. and Thanheiser, H. T. (1976) *The Emerging European Enterprise: Strategy and structure in French and German industry*. London: Macmillan.

Les Echos (10/6/96) Arnault et Pinault, deux réussites hors normes, Lamm, P., 58–59.

The Economist (2/3/96) 'Petits patrons', anon., 64.

Ehrmann, H. W. (1957) *Organized Business in France*. New Jersey: Princeton University Press.

L'Expansion (September 1978) 'Le triomphe des Peugeots', Jannic, H., 130–41.

L'Expansion (4/6/81) 'Les fils à papa', Beaufils, V., 104–13.

L'Expansion (4/4/96) 'Patrons: un délit est si vite arrivé', Gibier, H., 122–23.

L'Express (1/385) 'Les dix blocages de la société française', Fallot, E. and Brossolette, S., 21–33.

L'Express (11/7/96) 'La cohorte des patrons devant la justice', Abescat, B., 36–38.

Financial Times (2/7/86) 'Europe warms to business punditry', Lorenz, C., 18.

Financial Times (12/12/94) 'France puts her 'affaires' in order', Buchan, D., 10.

Financial Times (18/8/95) Management: Monarchs, not gurus, Jack, A., 9.

Gaillard, J.-M. (1987) *Tu Sera Président Mon Fils: Anatomie des grandes écoles et malformation des élites*. Paris: Ramsay.

Girard, A. (1965) *La Réussite Sociale en France*. Paris: Presses Universitaires de France.

Gruère, J.-P. and Morel, P. (1991) *Cadres français et communications interculturelles*, Paris: Eyrolles.

Harris, A. and de Sedouy, A. (1977) *Les patrons*. Paris: Seuil.

Johnson, M. (1996) *French Resistance*. London: Cassell.

Landes, D. S. (1951) 'French Business and the Businessman: a social and cultural analysis', in Earle, E. E. (ed.), *Modern France*. New York: Russell and Russell.

Marceau, J. (1981) 'Access to elite careers in French business', in Howorth, J. and

Cerny, P. (eds) *Elites in France: Origins, reproduction and power*. London: Frances Pinter.

Le Monde (18/4/95) 'La grogne des patrons, Faujas, A., 9.

Le Monde – Initiatives (5/7/95) 'Battantes et plafond de verre', Menanteau, J., 2.

Le Nouvel Economiste (28/4/95) 'Patrons: y a-t-il une vie après le pouvoir?' Golliau, C., 58–61.

Le Nouvel Economiste (19/5/95) 'Les cinquante managers les plus recherchés', Michel, D., 56–63.

Le Nouvel Economiste (21/7/95) 'Les Héritiers: Lagardère', Nouzille, V., 31–39.

Le Nouvel Economiste (2/2/96) 'Managers étrangers en terre française', Vidalie, A., 42–45.

Le Nouvel Economiste (9/2/96) 'Comment naissent les patrons', Golliau, C., 48–53.

Le Nouvel Economiste (15/3/96) 'Les Bouygues', Bouaziz, F., 42–49.

Le Nouvel Economiste (5/4/96) 'Après l'effet Zorro', Beaufils, V., 48–55.

Le Nouvel Economiste (24/5/96) 'Jean-Louis Beffa: Pourquoi j'ai racheté Poliet', Beaufils, V., 68–69.

Le Nouvel Economiste (28/6/96) 'L'Enquête: Gouvernement d'entreprise', Beaufils, V., 49–66.

Le Nouvel Economiste (15/11/96) 'Partir, c'est mourir...un peu', Lecasble, V., 30–35.

Le Nouvel Observateur (28/9/95) 'Ce que gagnent vraiment les grands patrons', Routier, A., 64–76.

Le Point (25/11/95) *Les Patrons Français sous l'Occupation: ombres et lumières*, Bentégeat, H., 102–05.

Priouret, R. (1968) *La France et le Mnagement*. Paris: Denoël.

de Rochebrune, R., and Hazera, C. (1995) *Les patrons sous l'occupation*, Editions Odile Jacob.

Santoni, G. (ed.) (1981) *Société et Culture de la France Contemporaine*. New York: State University of New York Press.

Serdjénian, E. (1994) 'Women managers in France', in *Competitive Frontiers: women managers in a global economy*. Adler, N. J. and Izraeli, D. N. (eds) Cambridge, Mass.: Basil Blackwell. 190–205.

Sorge, A. (1993) 'Management in France' in *Management in Western Europe*, Hickson, D.J. (ed), 65–87, New York: de Gruyter.

The Sunday Times (22/8/93) 'The gold-collar workers', Lynn, M. and Olins, R., 3:3.

Szarka, J. (1992) *Business in France*, London: Pitman.

Thélot, C. (1982) *Tel père, tel fils*. Paris: Dunod.

Weber, H. (1986) *Le Parti des Patrons: le CNPF* (1946–86). Paris: Seuil.

Chapter 8

Ashby, R. W. (1956) *Introduction to Cybernetics*. London: Chapman & Hall.

Crozier, M. (1964) *The Bureaucratic Phenomenon*. Chicago: University of Chicago Press.

Crozier, M. (1996) *La Crise de l'intelligence*. Paris: Inter-Edition.

Fayol, H. (1916) *L'administration generale et industrielle*. 2nd edn. Paris. Also (1949) *General and Industrial Management*. London: Pitman.

Johnson, M. (1996) *French Resistance*. London: Cassell.

Peters, T. J. and Waterman, R. H. (1982) *In Search of Excellence*. New York: Harper & Row.

Servan-Schreiber, J.- J. (1967) *Le défi américain*. Paris: Denoël. 8–18.

Notes

Chapter 2

1   Higher qualifications are generally designated by the number of years the course lasts after the *baccalauréat,* e.g. *bac*+2 for DUT, BTS, DEUG and DEUST, *bac*+4 for a *maîtrise* or some business school diplomas and *bac*+5 for engineering schools and DESS.

2   *Le Nouvel Economiste* (21/3/96, 49) reported that 87 per cent of engineering graduates were cadres within two years of graduating.

3   Decades even, since it is often a nominal, end-of-career gesture to reward *bons et loyaux services.*

4   The term *employé* only includes office workers, not *cadres.* Sixty years ago a *cadre* would have been *un employé supérieur* but they have managed to discard that association and distinguish themselves from the rest of the office personnel.

5   INSEE – Institut National des Statistiques et des Etudes Economiques.

6   AGIRC – Association Générale des Institutions de Retraite des Cadres.

7   APEC – Association Pour l'Emploi des Cadres, a placement service for unemployed *cadres.*

Chapter 3

1   His wider point is that, for all its merits, the French education system is in danger of extinguishing the intrinsic desire to learn. As he puts it: *'Le problème est qu'à l'école on commence par étudier les choses avant de les avoir fait aimer . . . Transformer un poème en problème, c'est tuer l'amour de la poésie'* ('The problem is that in French schools children start to study things before they have learnt to appreciate them . . . When poetry is presented as a problem to resolve, what love can remain for poetry?') (*Le Point,* 23/3/96, 97).

2   In the French system, it is common to repeat a year (*redoubler*). But in a system where success depends on being in the right place at the right time, repeating a year spells disaster. It is interesting to note that the children of cadres *supérieurs* and teachers have about a 15 per cent chance of repeating a year by the age of 15, while the children of workers and administrative staff have a 47 per cent chance of doing so (Euriat and Thélot, 1995, 418).

3   L'ENA was founded in 1945, to renew France's high administration which had been compromised in the collaboration.

4   It is worth pointing out the contrasting situation of the universities which have to carry out substantial reductions at the end of the first and second years to compensate for the impossibility of selection at entry. At some universities, less than 50 per cent of those admitted will actually graduate (*L'Express,* 23/5/96, 42).

5 The STT *bac* is aimed at those who want to start working quickly, perhaps after a two-year DUT or BTS course. It typically leads to technical or commercial positions in sales, market research or purchasing.

6 The high pressure experienced during this training period once prompted *The Guardian* to dub preparatory schooling, 'the cram de la crème' (Ardagh, 1982, 511). In preparatory schools everyone is under pressure, whereas in the *grandes écoles* it concerns mainly those competing for the top places.

7 *L'Expansion,* 7/3/85, 81.

8 A league table in *L'Expansion* (4/4/96, 92) shows that top two business schools, HEC and ESSEC, accept one candidate in eight or nine, while the less prestigious ESC of Lille or Grenoble take on one in 20.

9 Further evidence of the widespread demand for help in negotiating France's educational labyrinth.

10 The *grands corps* are all organized by the state to administer France. On the civil service side, they include the diplomatic *corps* and the prefectural *corps*. On the engineering side, they include the telecom *corps,* the civil aviation *corps,* and armament *corps*.

11 The size and quality of a *grande école*'s alumni boy network features increasingly in the promotional literature, since such connections are critical in an uncertain job market.

12 ESCAE – Ecole(s) Supérieure(s) de Commerce et d'Administration des Entreprises, often referred to as the Sup-de-Co.

13 Only 50 or so commercial schools recruit from the *classes preparatoires* that feed the *grandes écoles*.

14 The *taxe d'apprentissage* is a levy on companies (0.5 per cent of the payroll) which they may donate to any pre-entry training establishment. Responsibility for prospection and collection of the funds is left to the students themselves who act on behalf of their institute.

15 According to a survey in *Capital* (June 1994, 116–29) only two universities feature among the top 40 schools targeted by employers: they are Paris Dauphine (which comes in 9th) and Paris Sorbonne (17th).

16 Interview with François Michelin, 'Le plus discret des grands patrons', broadcast by *France Inter* in its series 'La Rue des Entrepreneurs', 8/7/93.

17 The importance and relevance of qualifications was neatly summed up in the epigram, 'With one you can do nothing, without one you can get nowhere' (*L'Expansion,* July/August 1977, 66).

18 Although the top commercial schools have opened up their entrance exam to students without a maths background, it has made little difference to intakes. In 1995, HEC admitted 12 students with a literary *bac,* ESCP 4 and ESC Lyon only one (*Le Figaro,* 17/6/96, 28).

19 The total numbers in the *grandes écoles* are less than 5 per cent of all those in higher education, but their influence is large out of all proportion.

20 The pattern of socially biased recruitment was set by the engineering schools in the eighteenth century using Latin as a social filter. The discipline has since changed, but the mechanism lingers on even in the business schools.

21 The top four *grandes écoles* are: l'ENA for access to administrative and political power; Polytechnique (X) for access to industrial and administrative power;

l'Ecole Normale for access to intellectual or administrative power; and HEC for access to economic and commercial power (Euriat and Thélot, 1995, 414).

Chapter 4

1 Careful readers will note that the text of the job ad overlooks the fact that the candidate may be a woman. Adjectives referring to the prospective candidate are strictly masculine: *rataché* not *rataché(e)*, and *âgé* not *âgé(e)*. This oversight is not uncommon and constitutes a psychological barrier for women, which may even be compounded, in the text, by an explicit call for *'un homme de terrain'* ('man of action').

2 Laurence Wylie maintains that this linguistic bias is instilled very early on in childhood. Looking at the table of contents of a French geography textbook, he notes that the chapters tend to have nouns as titles (the soil, the vegetation, the climate and so on). In contrast to this, an American social studies book typically uses participles, indicating some kind of action, for its headings: growing rice, mining coal, and so forth (in Santoni, 1981, 30).

3 In their pay scales many French companies initially award points depending on the type of institution attended. But this factor stops counting after two or three years.

4 'X' is a reference to the emblematic crossed cannons of Polytechnique.

5 More recently, Gérard Moatti wrote in *L'Expansion* (7/12/95, 98): *'La France, c'est un système où le rang obtenu à un concours passé à 20 ans offre un passeport direct pour n'importe quel poste managérial pourvu qu'il soit élevé.'* (In France, one's ranking in an exam taken at the age of 20 offers a direct passport to any managerial position, provided it is senior.')

6 'Gadzarts' is a contraction of *'gars des arts et métiers'* ('alumni of l'Ecole des Arts et Métiers').

7 For example, there are 10,000 Centrale graduates in the working population, but the alumni placement service signals that only 100 or so are out of work. The unemployment rate is therefore 1 per cent, compared to 12.6 per cent for the general working population (*L'Expansion, 2/2/96, 62*).

8 The only two French groups which clearly escape these negative connotations are LVMH and l'Oréal whose image of luxury and prestige shakes off the mass market aspect and allows them to attract the very best graduates.

9 The fact that French companies tend to identify their high flyers from a much narrower population may explain the relative absence of assessment centres in French companies. There is less need for a system to appraise and identify high potentials, since it is possible to track them informally.

10 Association pour l'emploi des cadres, *Cadroscope 1995*.

11 A civil service career is still prestigious but increasingly it is regarded as a short-cut to senior positions in the private or nationalized sectors, rather than an end in itself.

12 The *grands corps* are the most prestigious parts of the French civil service, like the Treasury or the Foreign Office in Britain.

13 Moreover, given France's tradition of state entrepreneurship, French civil servants are perhaps less tainted by bureaucratic values.

14 Companies have to draw up a training plan to be submitted to and discussed

with the *comité d'entreprise* (works council). If a company falls short of the statutory requirement, the balance is forfeited to the Treasury.

15 CEREQ: Centre d'étude et de recherche sur les qualifications.

Chapter 5

1 A striking example of this distinction between the individual and the function was provided by the French writer and philosopher Michel de Montaigne: '*Montaigne et le maire de Bordeaux sont deux*' ('Montaigne and the mayor of Bordeaux are separate'), he stated – which provided convenient justification for his leaving Bordeaux at the time of the plague (in Santoni, 1981, 61).

2 In any case, French employees tend to interpret MBWA as mistrust and surveillance, not supportiveness. So why would managers even want to engage in it?

3 As Gruère and Morel (1991, 59) once put it, '*Négocier constitue une faute contre la logique et l'esprit cartésien*' (The practice of negotiation offends logic and the Cartesian ethos). In other words, faith in resaonsing renders negotiation superfluous.

4 Interview with François Michelin, 'Le plus discret des grands patrons' in the radio series 'La Rue des Entrepreneurs', *France Inter*, broadcast 8/7/93.

5 The same 'opportunity to inequality' perhaps also characterizes US society. The difference, in France, is that inequality sticks. As we saw in Chapters 3 and 4, those who are left behind at 18 will not get a second chance.

6 An everyday example of this 'negative solidarity' can be seen on French roads. Under normal circumstances, French road users show little consideration for the rights of other road users. Yet when faced with the common threat to their freedom represented by police speed traps, one witnesses sudden co-operation. Drivers who spot speed traps on the other side of the road will warn drivers coming in the opposite direction by flashing their lights (*appels de phare*).

Chapter 6

1 Kissing is occasionally seen in organizations – primarily between women, but sometimes mixed sex and more rarely involving *cadres*.

2 We observed one case where a *directeur* refused to acknowledge a lowly subordinate who had the affrontery to extend his hand unsolicited – a cardinal sin.

3 This comment has a ring of truth about it insofar as French education in general, and the élite *grandes écoles* in particular, are notorious for promoting individual effort (symbolized by the dreaded final year rankings) over joint effort – an approach not particularly conducive to developing friendship ties.

4 This may be a learning point for foreign callers who, in their myopic attempt to play down status distinctions such as titles by eliminating 'unnecessary' formalities, succeed only in making themselves comfortable, whilst their French colleagues become uneasy or even irritated.

5 The fact that formality is the rule may be inferred from the surprised reaction of an experienced *cadre* on entering a new company: 'I was kind of surprised, because in business you don't see people slapping each other on the back very often and calling each other by their first names, at least not for long.' (Boltanski, 1987, 301, English trans.).

6   This does not imply that he also used the *tu* form with them – *vous* and the first name are perfectly compatible – they denote affinity whilst preserving distance. The permutations are numerous.

7   Or again, consider French television's oldest surviving game show, created in 1965. It is not a game of chance, nor a game which offers big prizes. It is not based on esoteric knowledge but on *'culture générale'*. It is called 'Des Chiffres et des Lettres' and demands mastery of language and maths – contestants have to make up the longest word from nine randomly drawn letters, then add, multiply, subtract or divide six randomly drawn numbers to obtain a given figure (*Le Monde*, 3/2/95, 31).

8   In France, restaurants play a similar role to saunas in Finland, as focal points for informal business discussion. Both are ambivalent public/private places. Both serve to diminish hostility whilst fostering intimacy by increased physical proximity. In both settings, inhibitions are lowered: in the one case by absence of clothes and in the other by the consumption of alcohol.

9   In some of the traditional manufacturing companies, the choice of the precise date for the start of the four-week shutdown is an issue for management-union negotiations on the same scale as the big social debates.

10   The high proportion of second homes is the result of a relatively late shift from an agricultural to an industrial society. Many families have rural properties which belonged to their families just two or three generations ago – and they cherish these roots. What is more, the fragmented nature of farm properties means that there is an abundance of small properties which are vacant and affordable.

Chapter 7

1   A reworking of the proclamation of Louis XIV, the great centralizing monarch, '*L'état c'est moi*' ('I am the state').

2   Also included were Air France, the coal mines, electricity and gas, and the larger insurance companies and clearing banks. Much of this was done in an anti-capitalist spirit with de Gaulle's backing.

3   Analogous to, on the German side, the evocative title of Heinrich Boll's novel, *Wo warst Du, Adam?*

4   There are two frequently cited women among the heads who have inherited. They are Annette Roux, the PDG of Bénéteau pleasure crafts (and the only woman on the CNPF's executive council), and Francine Gomez, who inherited and rebuilt Waterman pens, before selling the company on to Gillette.

5   A more promising initiative has been the subsequent creation by the French bourse of the Nouveau Marché, designed to attract small, fast-growing firms.

6   Rated second only to the New York stock exchange, but ahead of London and Tokyo, Nasdaq is the stock exchange which counts the most for high growth sectors such as IT, biotechnology and telecom.

7   Personal communication.

8   The term *'parachutage'* is close but not synonymous with the term 'pantouflage' mentioned in Chapter 4. The latter refers to transfers from state to private sector, usually at managerial level. The former refers to introduction at very senior level, either with the backing of the state or that of the patron.

9 The retail sector is normally renowned in France for not conforming to the elitist 'French model'.

10 It is difficult not to read something into the fact that on Pébereau's office wall there hangs a picture of his idol, France's foremost centralizer, Colbert.

11 The key difference is that Bauer and Bertin-Mourot group founders with inheritors not with career managers.

12 François Michelin, the head of Michelin tyres, who broke off relations with the CNPF back in the late 1960s, maintains that this is a misnomer. The real *patron des patrons*, he says, is the customer.

13 France had three basic VAT rates (33 per cent, 20.6 per cent and 5.5 per cent).

14 Where the PDG is himself the recipient of the Légion d'honneur it may be pinned on him by the Minister for Industry. At Accor, those not privy to attend the ceremony in person, were cordially invited to watch it live on closed-circuit TV.

15 The Germans imposed this highly centralized model in order to speed up the rate of production in the factories. When the Liberation came, Germany progressively established a more democratic approach while France retained the existing model.

16 A good example of this is the way several ageing PDGs have been able to bully their boards into extending their mandates. Numerous companies are headed by bosses over the legal retiring age, some of them in their seventies. (*Le Nouvel Economiste*, 15/11/96, 30–35).

17 The PDG's selection of his own successor, not only highlights the PDG's power, but also the dynastic feel of appointments even in public companies. The board did not dare to repudiate Dejouany's strong desire to annoint Messier as his dauphin for fear of provoking a boardroom row that the group could ill afford.

18 A parallel can be drawn with the teacher-student relationship. French MBA students at Insead are often less comfortable with an interactive teaching style, than their Anglo-Saxon counterparts. It is not that they are afraid to speak up, but rather that they expect the professor to have the answers. Asking students for their opinions suggests that the professor does not know.

Chapter 8

1 For example, Jean-Yves Haberer's spectacular failure at Crédit Lyonnais led to his dismissal as executive chairman. Yet he was given an honourable way out, the chairmanship of Crédit National, formerly France's long-term credit bank, which is not even state-owned or state-subsidized (*The Banker,* 'Tragedy turned farce,' de Quillacq, L., June 1994, 25–29).

General index

Index of authors cited